Children, Teachers and Learning Series

General Editor: Cedric Cullingford

Assessment versus Evaluation

IU4

Titles in the *Children, Teachers and Learning* series:

Assessment versus Evaluation

Edited by Cedric Cullingford

CASSELL

Cassell
Wellington House
125 Strand
London WC2R 0BB

PO Box 605
Herndon
VA 20172

© Cedric Cullingford and the contributors 1997

First published 1997

British Library Cataloguing-in-Publication Data
A catalogue record for this book is available from the British Library.

ISBN 0-304-336211 (hb)
      0-304-336203 (pb)

Typeset by Action Typesetting Limited, Gloucester
Printed and bound in Great Britain by Biddles Ltd, Guildford
& King's Lynn

Contents

Contents

CHAPTER 1
Introduction

CEDRIC CULLINGFORD

The price of everything and the value of nothing. Oscar Wilde.
Lady Windermere's Fan

This is not the only time that this quotation appears in this
book. It strikes a chord that reverberates in every chapter.
For in every case and in every aspect of assessment, there
are negative and positive effects: assessment has sharp
edges. Assessment of some kind or another is a necessary
tool. It is a starting point to manufacture something good,
to improve and refine good practice or a work of art. Used
in a different way it is destructive. It destroys what it ostensibly seeks to improve.

At one level it would be possible merely to juxtapose one
theme – the negative tendency of simple-minded testing –
against another – the formative and constructive processes
of diagnosis. It sometimes feels as if we were in a battle
between the two, an attempt to turn swords into ploughs. A
book of analysis and discussion would then be more about
the pathology of human nature, exploring the reasons for
the negative tendencies that so dominate people's lives. But
if the destructive side of assessment were so obvious we
would not be witnessing so much damage inflicted on so
many people at so much expense. If the destructive side of
assessment could be so easily detached from the constructive
we would not have so much investment in certain practices,
whatever the dogma that protects them. Assessment is, after
all, an essential act, and part of the creative process. Some
form of criticism, some manifestation of judgement, is
necessary so that there is an empirical base upon which to
act. But criticism is a way of thought; as a sign of ultimate
inadequacy it is merely the pathological end of judgement.
Those who cannot create can criticize. This is itself useful,

ut the distinction should be made clear. It is like the many full-time academics who concentrate on the limitations of research methodology, on the complexities of validity and reliability. What they say is often valuable, but they can no longer carry out research. The act of criticism can become an end in itself, and the erudite destruction of other people's research or ideas a type of melancholy pleasure where the habit of spleen feeds on itself without awareness of the effects.

The chapters in this book deal with a range of issues that surround this central subject. There are differences in tone, contradictions between the positive and negative aspects of assessment. This is a necessary reflection of being part of a system, having to adapt to this system, and looking carefully both personally and empirically at that system. For the problems of assessment and evaluation are complex and embedded in particular cultures. The chapters in this book acknowledge the complexity and the underlying tensions between the positive and the negative, between the analysis of the motivations that provoke assessment, including power and dogma – and the practical means of responding to them.

Educational organizations have become more and more dominated by the processes of assessment and evaluation in various guises such as teacher appraisal, accountability and the financial management of schools, SATs, school league tables and OFSTED. These processes are consuming an extraordinary amount of time and other resources and attracting a great deal of critical attention. What appears to be missing from this spate of critical attention is serious theoretical and empirical work designed to deconstruct these processes and to indicate the very significant areas of distinction as well as similarity between the processes we call 'assessment' and the family that we call 'evaluation'.[1]

There are clear overlaps between the two sets of processes, in the sense that both aim to examine surface evidence that will give insight into underlying processes or states of affairs. In the case of assessment the focus is narrow; the area of analysis of underlying processes is restricted, and does not need to be defined in terms of other relevant areas. One thinks for example of the assessment of mathematical achievement where the surface features are test or exam results, and the deeper processes and features are the underlying cognitive/mathematical abilities into which the tests give insight. The evaluation of the mathematical achievements in a class would entail the assessment procedures but would also have to be extended to include some account of the effects of teaching methods, the expectations of teacher and pupils, and the resources available. The process of evaluation is generally far more deep-seated and is directed at the structural features of situations. One of the problems with the OFSTED reports and with the OFSTED guide is that they blur this distinction between assessment and evaluation. They are ostensibly aimed at evaluation, but, since the model against which everything is being checked seems to be treated as a given, then each report consists effectively of a series of assessments of discrete areas of activity within the school. Thus the checklists against which teachers are to be judged are as likely to contain political points – the 'correct' method of teaching reading – as more neutral ones. It is therefore not altogether a surprise to find attempts to measure the immeasurable, and to hear the Chief Inspector make remarks such as 'Last year there was a 13 per cent drop in spirituality'. 'Spirituality' was, indeed, an item on a checklist.

There is an increasing interpenetration of the state and the education system via the processes of assessment in the face of international competition and the need for different types of skill. The danger of this is that epistemological distinctions between critical and successful evaluation and assessment are not made. The consequence is to improve circumstances only superficially. In the outcome-based assessment systems, for example, there is a danger of oversimplified procedures leading to tight control and accountability but no significant gains in organizational or individual performance. There is a need to make evaluation and assessment procedures cost-effective (and therefore, as simple as possible) but not at the expense of the insight.

Because of the deep structure/surface structure relationship evaluation and assessment are inherently problematic.
They present in fact the same sorts of methodological problems as are present in social research. There are some
important questions to ask about these processes:

- What hidden assumptions underpin current practice?
- What is the theoretical credibility of each practice?
- How can we import scientific insight into areas that are
  inherently unstable and subjective?
- What underlying questions are implicated in the
  various practices under review?
- What are the effects of assessment?

But we are living in a time of OFSTED, of accountability,
where competition is the *sine qua non* of life. Such questions
seem either inappropriate or far-fetched. The Office for
'Standards' in Education is a theme of our time, an almost
emblematic example of the application of the machinery of
control. When it is pointed out that 'assessment can influence and even control teaching'[2] it is said as if this were
something new or unexpected. Assessment possibly always
creates the conditions and limitations of knowledge. If what
is easily assessed is what is most important all types of unac-
knowledged influences can come to bear, influences so
subtle that we find it difficult to discern them. They seem so
rational, and so precise.

This book seeks, in various ways, to look at the processes
and the results of assessment and evaluation. The chapters
represent something of the complexity. There might be the
sound of a familiar chord of scepticism and concern, but
there is no simple polemical theme. They vary, justifiably, in
tone and approach. They reveal the necessary tensions
between what is possible and what is not. They show what
can be done as well as what is being done. Each chapter
stands in its own right but the idea of the book as a whole is
to lead to different levels of evaluating the result of what is
going on. We therefore explore both practical uses of assessment and the questions which underlie it, in terms of the

curriculum, of the effectiveness of schools, of profiling, of teacher appraisal, of examining, and of self-assessment. Each chapter raises practical as well as theoretical issues. But in some the theoretical questions that are raised give even more reason to look at practice. The TGAT report is a monument of our time, but what does it stand for? Nothing could express more clearly the distinction between the intention and the reality, the hope and the manipulation of assessment. The chapters all raise, in different ways, both the theoretical issues and the practical outcomes of the 'family' of endeavours that are thrown together under the terms of assessment and evaluation (and, of course testing and judgement and opinion and many other terms).

Attempts to define exact distinctions sometimes replace true understandings. Thus we see the slippery terms which surround the evaluation of 'true reality'.[3] There are so many to choose from. This is reasonable enough given the all-pervasive nature of assessment. It is when a particular concept is applied rigidly that the problem begins. This application can be either the result of a system or of a dogma. Earlier we used the term 'postmodernism' as if that could most easily describe the present era. When one considers, for example, Foucault's definitions of postmodernism as the fragmentation of structures and attitudes, then it seems we are living, by the same definition, in an old-fashioned world of modernist centralism, of control and unified practice, at least as presented by the educational system in Great Britain today. The system tries to define itself, to create what is assessable and then make it the target of assessment. As for dogma, that lies in the belief that surrounds particular discourse. It is sometimes possible to impose inappropriate assumptions on to the very systems that are supposed to work. The idea of 'market forces' for example is not automatically appropriate to all circumstances. Does one need to create a larger market, or be entrepreneurial when it comes to disability or child abuse?

It is probably best here to make an analogy, for so many teachers will be able to find examples of their own of incidents of absurdity. The analogy rests on the idea of 'performance indicators'.[4] Railways might seem both a long way from schools and an easy target, but an anecdote serves to highlight the point. Someone travelling to a meeting by train discovers that he is held up for half an hour by engineering works. After the day's work the assumption that the same thing could happen on the way back is reasonable. Nevertheless, having made suitable arrangements for his return, he arrives twenty minutes before the train is due to leave, only to discover that the train has left half an hour early. It was the last train. Eventually he tracks down the explanation: in order to meet the performance indicator of arriving on time the train had to leave that much earlier. Over the loss of revenue, let alone the blighted passengers, we will be silent.

It all depends on where the judgement lies and where the control lies. If one form of assessment prevails at the expense of others then there are many unforeseen consequences. The analogy used here, as in so many stories of the privatization of British Rail, might seem too absurd even if true; but the gentle questioning that these chapters undertake at least raises the question whether, in the experience of teachers, such absurdities are so far-fetched. For they are not absurd to those whose careers are dependent on performance indicators of a certain type. Examples of assessment, charters, contracts and many other such inventions, abound. But they all have unexpected effects and consequences. We need at least to question the principles that underlie such dogma. Is the result, in the end, beneficial? Is the emphasis on improvement or assessment? These are questions worth asking.

Words which are attracted to the magnets 'assessment' and 'evaluation' abound. The problem is that each tries to manipulate the definitions according to their control. This is why it is timely to question and analyse what is taking place. As Lewis Carroll wrote, through the unexpected mouth of Humpty Dumpty, 'When I use a word, it means exactly what I want it to mean, neither more nor less. The question is which is to be master – that's all'.

Many issues discussed in this book are about power and

control. There may be different vocabularies and different outcomes but we need to speculate on the possibility that the machinery of assessment is itself in control.

Notes and references

1. With acknowledgements to valuable conversations with Lewis Owen. See also Chapter 12.
2. Torrance, H. 'Introduction'. In Gray, J. and Wilcox, B. (eds) *Good School, Bad School: Evaluating Performance and Encouraging Improvement* (Buckingham: Open University Press, 1995), x.
3. Kant, I. *Kritik der Reinen Vernunft* (Riga, 1781).
4. Ranson, S. and Stewart, J. *Management for the Public Domain: Enabling the Learning Society* (London: Macmillan, 1994).

CHAPTER 2

Assessment and the Curriculum

DAVID BRADY

Introduction

If there is one aspect of education more than any other
which has shown steady growth during the past 150 years it
is assessment. Formal, public assessment is now a multi-
million pound industry. Assessment is concerned with
measuring pupil and student performance during or following a programme of study. It applies to individual pupils
and students although the results may later be aggregated.
It uses performance in set tests or tasks as its indicators and
is consequently concerned with both knowledge and skills,
primarily as outcomes. It attempts to measure these, sometimes in terms of pass/fail, but more often in terms of a fine
grading, with the resulting generation of quantitative data
which can be put to a variety of uses, not all of them justified. According to some writers, a major flaw in the National
Curriculum assessment system is its use of the same assessment information for several purposes.[1] This focused,
quantitative, individualized aspect of assessment distinguishes it from evaluation which is concerned with broader
aspects of the curriculum. Indeed while assessment may be
used in a variety of ways, one use is as an effective aid to
curriculum evaluation.

That there is an intimate connection between assessment
and the curriculum is immediately apparent from a glance
at the National Curriculum of GNVQ programmes; the
history of curriculum change is very much one of extending
and elaborating assessment procedures. Gipps and Stobart[2]
cite the introduction of the GCSE as an example of a
curriculum change linked through emphasis on positive
achievement with a change in assessment. One reason why
so much effort and money is devoted to assessment is that as

educational provision expands and becomes more costly so it is only reasonable to check that money is being spent wisely; we need to find out what students and pupils have actually learnt. This in turn raises issues of teacher accountability.

Few would want to quarrel with this. However, once having started along such a road, numerous pitfalls await us in the form of problems concerning the amount, type and frequency of assessment and, more importantly, the presentation and use of the results. Failure to deal adequately with these problems can have extremely damaging effects on the curriculum; there may well be distortion of curricular aims, processes and products. As Harlen notes 'there is an unavoidable backwash on the curriculum from the content and procedures of assessment'.[3]

There is a cyclical relationship here in that, while it may be intended that assessment should serve the curriculum, there is a grave danger that assessment may come to dominate the curriculum. For example, the National Curriculum has been seen as a mechanism for testing performance of pupils and teachers as much as a curriculum framework.

The emphasis on assessment at all levels of education fits wells with the current obsession with performance indicators which are assumed to relate to the elusive concept of quality. However it is easier to generate figures (whether marks or other performance indicators) than it is to make clear what they signify or how they should be used. We should once again remember Wilde's dictum in *Lady Windermere's Fan* – a cynic is one who knows 'the price of everything and the value of nothing'.

If we are in an idealistic mood we might suggest abandoning assessment altogether.[4] After all, is not education, and therefore the curriculum, concerned with experiences and encounters with value systems, with the world around us, with other people's ideas? At first sight assessment may appear to distort the curriculum. Newman[5] played a part in reforming college and university life so that studies in Oxford were taken more seriously and yet he warned against the tendency towards too much emphasis on formal assessment. He preferred 'residence and tutorial superintendence' to 'professors and examinations'.

In the real world there are, of course, some powerful arguments in favour of assessment as part of the curriculum process. We shall encounter some of these later when we consider the historical aspects of assessment but we can also note practical issues such as teachers' needing some indication of pupil progress in order to facilitate further pupil development and to enhance motivation. According to Satterly[6] the main effects of assessment are motivational. Further education teachers who have been required to teach non-assessed subjects (on courses where most work is assessed) will bear witness to the problems (attendance, behaviour, lack of learning) if there is no assessment.

At a deeper level there may be objections to assessment on moral grounds in that some would wish to question the assessor's or the teacher's right to pass judgement on another human being. Such a feeling often underlies some of the debates concerning the effectiveness of different forms of assessment. Perhaps this feeling should guide us, at least to the extent of reminding us of our serious responsibilities in devising and operating assessment procedures. On the other hand there are some serious moral arguments in favour of assessment and these must not be disregarded when concern is expressed about the extent or form of assessment. To fulfil teachers' responsibilities to their pupils, to parents, to potential employers surely requires measures of accountability. If we allow that the curriculum should have structure and purpose then we are obliged to give serious consideration to how we are going to use assessment.

The purposes of assessment

We have already noted the considerable sums spent on assessment and we can also note that many recent curriculum developments (e.g. BTEC, GCSE, GNVQ) require classroom teachers to spend much time and effort on the formal assessment of their pupils and students. It is therefore important that we clarify the purposes to which assessment can be put. Recognizing that there is a plurality of purposes reminds us that this is a complex and sensitive area. There may be debate about the legitimacy of some of the purposes of assessment; there will certainly be dispute about the relative importance of different purposes of assessment for different forms and stages of education. Assessment may perform contradictory functions.

Thus we need to ask questions about assessment, particularly about its intended purpose and about how it is used in practice. While it may be legitimate to conduct assessment of pupils to satisfy a stated purpose, there is always a danger that the same assessment could be put to some other, and unjustified, use. (Aggregation and league tables are examples.) We need assessment procedures which achieve maximum validity and reliability but they will be of no value if they are misused.

What then are the main functions of assessment? One obvious purpose, which applies to any form of vocational education whatever the level, is to ensure that minimum standards required for occupational practice have been achieved. Hence we have the idea of qualifying examinations for entry into trades and professions. One aspect of reform in the last century was the introduction of legislation to regulate entry into the professions. Assessment can therefore be seen as a vital part of what would now be regarded as 'consumer protection'. However restriction of entry into an occupation through the use of assessment can be seen not so much as protecting the interests of the public at large but as protecting the interests of the profession. Educational achievement, as measured by various assessment procedures, is related to social position and so professions tend to be self-perpetuating. This 'entry gate' function of assessment requires a considerable degree of central (national and increasingly international) control of assessment and therefore of the curriculum. There is a consequent danger that preparation for such occupations may involve a rather restricted curriculum.

In the classroom teachers and pupils need to measure the

learning that has taken place in order to plan further teaching and learning. Also, in addition to measuring learning, we may also attempt the more difficult task of measuring effort (as is done in many schools). Such measuring of effort could remain as a private communication between the assessor (the teacher) and the learner (and possibly parents). Hence the results of assessment may be used for reward. This brings in the motivational aspects of assessment. It can be argued that knowledge of what has been achieved by oneself as a learner can act as a spur to further learning. Finding out that pupils have learnt something can also motivate teachers. Of course, information about what other pupils have learnt can also be motivating through the effects of competition, although some might see this as morally undesirable.

Any learners, children or adults, may self-assess; at a very basic level this may involve covering up words in a vocabulary list and seeing how many they can remember. Finding out what has been learnt is important to the learner as well as the teacher, the administrator and the politician. Here we can consider the 'private' and 'public' aspects of assessment. As will be discussed later there is a reasonable case to be made for some public assessment but there is certainly a case, as has been recognized by most teachers for a long time, for private assessment in which the results of an assessment procedure are communicated only to the learner (in the case of children, sometimes the parents) and no comparisons are made with other learners. Are we now in danger of pushing too much assessment into the public realm with the danger of highlighting some data and disregarding other data?

Another important aspect of assessment is selection, either for a particular job or for further study.[7] As both jobs and places in further and higher education are limited, such selection again brings in the idea of competition. The relationship between assessment procedures and the further study or work is often tenuous. An employer demanding four GCSEs grade C or above is probably using a crude selection device based on a vague feeling concerning general educational attainment. The advent of competence-based vocational education can be seen as an attempt to remedy this, although it certainly brings problems of its own.[8] Basically the problem is that assessment, which looks back in time to see what learning has been achieved, is also used to predict suitability for a particular future programme of study or for a particular occupation.

Finally in our consideration of the purposes of assessment we note that some assessments (usually but not always examinations) as well as being used as indicators of achievement or potential are usually made only once (e.g. 11-plus, Common Entrance, classified honours degree). Thus they 'label people for life' with serious educational, social and personal consequences. It may not be assessment or the basic form of assessment which is at fault, but rather the use made of the assessment. The restricted focus of the curriculum is also a problem. Other forms of assessment, e.g. A levels, are not used in quite the same way. It may not be a sensible thing to do but people can go on adding to their total of A levels if they so wish or they may retake A levels in order to improve their grades. Related to this is the question of aggregation (e.g. School Certificate compared with separately recorded O levels). If asked, most people would probably not favour aggregation of separate assessments into a single mark or award, but in practice there is often a tendency to revert to such aggregation. Extending the range and type of assessments may increase the danger of attempting to add unlike factors. This stems partly from a desire to use assessment to label children in a convenient but misleading way.[9]

Eisner[10] reminds us that assessment, like evaluation, is not one, but several things. Such consideration of its uses highlights some of the moral dilemmas associated with assessment. Underlying some of the debates concerning the effectiveness of various forms of assessment is perhaps a reluctance to pass judgements on others.

Historical aspects

Written and oral examinations go back a long way. However, in the middle of the nineteenth century there was in the UK quite a sudden introduction or reintroduction of examinations for various purposes. In 1850 the College of Preceptors set external examinations for grammar and private schools. More significantly the India Act of 1853 opened appointments in the Indian Civil Service to competitive examination. There was limited competition for entry to the Home Civil Service from 1855 and open competition from 1870.[11] Such use of assessment can be seen as a social reform. No longer would somewhat desirable posts be accessible through corrupt means such as nepotism but instead the 'best person for the job' would be appointed. Putting it so strongly is a reminder of the great claims and expectations of educational assessment.

The introduction of Science and Art Department examinations in 1854 provided a considerable boost for the work of the Mechanics' Institutes. Such national assessment, and therefore curriculum, provided a common target and successful students achieved geographical and social mobility. Employers had some measure of the abilities of applicants for posts and as industrial competition increased in the second half of the nineteenth century this proved a factor in providing the technical personnel required.[12]

During the nineteenth century the government started to make grants to support schools and this resulted in central control of the curriculum (most notably in the Revised Code of 1862) as government sought accountability. For more able pupils in the very limited secondary education provided at the time, the introduction of common examinations such as the Oxford and Cambridge 'locals' provided motivation.[13] This brief glance at some historical aspects reminds us that the general tendency has been for the range and scope of assessments to expand and for the numbers of young people affected by assessments to increase considerably.

The effects of assessment

There is an obvious effect on the curriculum in that syllabi and examinations set by national bodies may be seen as restricting the curriculum by limiting teachers' and students' opportunities to explore issues of interest. On the other hand, such a system could be regarded as protecting students from the whims of individual teachers.

Internal assessment, which is usually a feature of continuous assessment (see pp. 228–54), may be regarded as making teacher–student relationships more difficult because the teacher is combining the role of teacher with that of assessor. This applies more to schools and further education than it does to higher education. The move towards greater involvement of teachers in the assessment of pupils and students can be seen as enhancing the professional role of teachers but it has also had the effect of greatly increasing their workloads.[14] It has also resulted in a shift from what could be called informal to formal assessment. Informal assessment is when a teacher assesses pupil performance (perhaps through some simple exercise or test) and the result is communicated only to the learner; it is used to remedy some immediate problem or to provide encouragement. Formal assessment is that which counts in some official way.

The time spent on assessment can have a serious effect on the curriculum. One advantage of an end-of-year examination is that, despite the tensions as the examination approaches, the rest of the year can be devoted to learning. Newer curricula tend to involve considerable amounts of continuous assessment and this may prove time-consuming and disruptive. BTEC phase tests are a possible example.

Although assessment schemes may appear to ensure that all pupils or students encounter a common curriculum in a given subject, in practice this may not be so. Under an end-of-year examination system there may well be 'question spotting', resulting in incomplete coverage of the curriculum; this problem is compounded by giving candidates a choice of question as is the case in many written examinations. Use of assignment or project work may not provide an answer here because pupils or students, by concentrating on a particular topic, may not deal with all the curriculum content. This is not to argue against project work, it is simply to highlight a potential problem with regard to coverage of the curriculum. In turn this assumes that curriculum content as well as process is important. Some forms of assessment are better suited to one aspect and others are better suited to other aspects.

Recognition of the problems associated with traditional written examinations led to the development of alternative forms of assessment. However these too can have a restricting influence on the curriculum. Short answer and multiple choice tests may have value in testing recall and possibly reasoning ability but they are of little use in assessing pupils' ability to organize ideas and to express themselves. A further drawback, particularly with multiple choice tests, is that some time may have to be spent in practising the interpretation of somewhat complex rubrics.

Values, assessment and the curriculum

It has already been noted that most assessment procedures in our education system involve an element of competition. This is less acute in pass/fail situations than when fine grading of some sort is attempted. Nevertheless it can be said that competition rather than diagnosis tends to dominate thinking about the curriculum and children may pick up this message from an early age. While the motivational effects of assessment cannot be denied they have to be balanced against the possible harm to social relationships; it may be that only those who have begun by doing reasonably well in assessments are motivated; those who do less well may soon be demotivated and so come to regard the curriculum as inappropriate for them. We have to balance the necessity of assessment against the danger that assessment can have unhealthy competitive effects, particularly if there is too much of it or it is introduced too early. If nothing else this consideration should warn us against using 'once for all' assessment. The effects of 'failing' the 11-plus are well documented.

Owing to the widespread and perhaps necessary use of assessment in selection procedures there is a tendency to relate the importance of topics within the curriculum to how easily they can be assessed. Thus the curriculum becomes distorted because what is assessed is taken as an indication of what is important and there is a temptation to assess only what is easy to assess. 'Too many recent developments are deeply rooted in Taylorist principles, notably the implicit proposition that human skill and knowledge are ultimately reducible into elementary units'.[15]

In the past the assessment of many technical subjects tended to be based on theoretical tests because these were easier to set than practical tests. With the introduction of NVQs the pendulum may have swung too much the other way, with the knowledge underpinning any skill being neglected. Butterfield[16] goes so far as to say 'In the case of NVQs the curriculum is obliterated altogether'. Thus whatever curriculum planners may say officially, the curriculum message that comes from assessment procedures is that knowledge is more important than practical skill.

The question of what can and should be assessed is a difficult one. Another aspect concerns what in Bloomian terms is the affective domain. To what extent should personal qualities be measured and recorded. Teachers' reports, references and to some extent records of achievement involve this and raise serious problems about the validity of the measures and raise the potential problem of conflicting value systems. Attempts to make assessment more meaningful and useful may result in assessment becoming more extensive and pervasive.

A major curriculum issue relating to assessment is the question of cultural bias. Firstly, there is the question of whether particular forms of assessment favour one gender or one ethnic group over another. Thus some have attributed the superiority of girls in most GCSE subjects (compared with O levels) to the introduction of some assessment of course work in GCSE compared with O levels which were very largely examination-based. It has been argued that much, possibly all, assessment is culture-biased and therefore discriminates against certain ethnic or social groups; there are also linguistic problems in assessment.

This bias may be reflected in the content of the curriculum or in the nature of the assessment; it may apply to assessment both in schools and in further education.[17] Curriculum content and the related assessment procedures can be seen as reflecting the social interests of a dominant group and neglecting the interests of other groups. However, if challenged, many examination boards and assessors would claim that they try to be as fair as possible (perhaps by providing a variety of questions and exercises) while doing justice to the essential nature of the subject. Too ready an acceptance of relativist arguments here could lead to absurd situations with assessments for different groups varying in type and in content. This would make a nonsense of the use of assessment for predicting suitability for a particular occupation. There is a further problem here which is that of identifying groups or sub-groups who may feel disadvantaged by particular assessment procedures. A dilemma here is that one can hardly make claims on an individual basis that there has been culture bias if one did not know something in a test. Perhaps the real issue here is to ensure that the curriculum, at every level, is comprehensive and full enough to reflect the needs of a multicultural society.

Patterns of assessment

There are probably as many different patterns of assessment as there are courses. We often find traditional 'terminal examinations' contrasted with 'continuous assessment'. However, many courses draw to some extent on both. It is important to distinguish between features (of the type of assessment) which are logically connected and features which are usually found together. For example, final examinations are often associated with external marking but they could be teacher marked, as they usually are in higher education. It is essential that assessment procedures are made as fair as they can be. Writing about the National Curriculum Black[18] says 'confidence in the fairness and compatibility of pupils' results across various teachers,

various schools and the country as a whole has t̤
lished'.

Other alternatives in assessment, which should not
sarily be seen as totally opposed, include short answe ̗
essay questions, assignment or unseen tests, group or individual assessment. The starting point should be to ask what
information about pupil achievement or progress we
require. Each type of assessment has its strengths and weaknesses. Recognition of the drawbacks of one form of
assessment should not lead us too readily and uncritically to
embrace some other approach. We should recognize also
that there are variations and modifications of each type of
assessment (e.g. open book rather than traditional examinations). There are many sub-divisions within each type of
assessment and when discussing assessment we have to be
clear just what type of assessment we are considering.

Several strong arguments against terminal examinations
can be produced.[19] These include the stress factor, the
emphasis on memory and the 'sampling' of knowledge.
However, there are points in favour of such a system. These
include greater degree of objectivity than with other forms
of assessment (e.g. definitely student's own work). They may
still have greater credibility with the public than other forms
of assessment.

> Any attempt to abolish or replace public examinations is likely to
> be constrained by the degree to which any alternative procedure
> has as much competence, in providing some degree of control
> over what is to be taught and, most important, in regulating and
> legitimating the process of occupational selection and rejection.[20]

Examinations lend themselves to external marking or
moderation more readily than some other forms of assessment. As the range and scope of assessments have increased
so has the tendency to increase the amount of official,
recorded assessment. Consequently pupils and students
have fewer opportunities to 'try things out' and risk getting
them wrong before there is some official assessment which
'counts'.

Terminal examinations represent a form of summative

assessment and there are occasions when an overall picture of what a learner has achieved is what is required, although there may be other ways of obtaining this synoptic view. If we seek a unity in the curriculum, and see it as more than the sum of its parts, then summative assessment is needed in some form. However this is only one function of assessment. Frequently we are concerned with current progress and achievement, and so we also need formative assessment. This often takes the form of assignment work which can be realistic and relevant and can test skills other than memorizing material and rapid writing. Prompt feedback from the marker can help pupils to improve and can give the teacher early warning about students who are having problems. While terminal examinations bring one form of pressure, such continuous assessment brings other forms. There is the danger of a 'halo' effect where the teacher subconsciously marks the learner's work according to previous perceptions or performance; it may also affect the learner's self-image and consequently the quality of work. If a class teacher is the main marker of a student's work, this may put undue pressure on the teacher–student relationship.

A curriculum problem is that assignment and project work involve sampling and therefore the intentions of curriculum planners may not be totally realized – the learners may have concentrated on just some topics in the curriculum. There are also technical problems to be considered such as plagiarism and other forms of cheating; in addition there is a large 'grey area' concerning the amount of help which learners should receive (e.g. from teachers, peers, parents). There is a danger of a conflict between a desire to encourage parental interest and mutual student co-operation and the use of project work as part of official assessment. A combination of assessment methods will prove to be more effective than relying on a single or limited range of assessment strategies.

It is important when considering assessment procedures at any level that the curriculum be seen as a whole. A variety of assessment procedures is needed but it is important at secondary and further levels of education that not all subjects are assessed in the same way and that 'over-assessment' is avoided.

Profiling can be seen as a development of continuous assessment in which a detailed account is given of a student's performance across the range of topics or competencies or on one topic but through a range of assessment methods. It is claimed that this detailed picture is much more useful to a potential employer and to the student than a single degree class. Sometimes very detailed profile forms are prepared; these often place considerable emphasis on 'affective' competencies. (Assessing these can be difficult.) These more detailed profiles may do away with grading altogether and replace grades with brief (or not so brief) reports about the student in each area designated on the profiling form. As Hitchcock[21] notes, this can be very time-consuming and there is a danger of the previously noted 'halo effect' and of subjectivity and social control. This perhaps illustrates the danger of expecting too much from any one approach to assessment.

Conclusion

Assessment is a difficult and contentious issue which touches the curriculum at all levels of education and in all aspects. The processes of assessment and the uses to which it is put have social and political implications which cannot be ignored. We need assessment practices which are (and are widely acknowledged to be) valid, reliable, fair to individuals and which serve the needs of society. The continuing debates outlined here show that this is an area of education which certainly requires further research and analysis.

For the present we have to accept that assessment procedures are not perfect and, at best, represent a compromise. Indeed the two main requirements appear to be the use of a combination of assessment procedures while avoiding 'over-assessment', and taking great care concerning the use which is made of assessment results. If we hold a broad view of the curriculum, that it involves content and processes, knowledge and skills, and has an affective aspect, then assessment procedures must reflect this. Assessment should serve the curriculum not dominate it.

Notes and references

1. Harlen, W., Gipps, C., Broadfoot, P. and Nuttall, D. Assessment and the improvement of education *Curriculum Journal* **3** (3), 1992, 215–30.
2. Gipps, C. and Stobart, G. *Assessment: A Teacher's Guide to the Issues* (London: Hodder and Stoughton, 1993).
3. Harlen et al. op. cit. p. 218.
4. Holt, J. *The Underachieving School* (London: Pitman, 1969).
5. Newman, J.H. *The Idea of a University* (San Francisco: Rinehart Press, 1960 edn, first published 1852), 122–4.
6. Satterly, D. *Assessment in Schools* (Oxford: Blackwell, 1981), 7.
7. Jencks, C. *Inequality* (London: Routledge and Kegan Paul, 1973), 135.
8. Hyland, T. *Competence, Education and NVQs* (London: Cassell, 1995).
9. Gipps, C.V. National Curriculum assessment: a research agenda *British Educational Research Journal* 18 (3), 1992, 277–86.
10. Eisner, E.W. Reshaping assessment in education: some criteria in search of practice *Journal of Curriculum Studies* 25 (3), 1993, 219–33.
11. Roach, J. *Public Examinations in England, 1850–1900* (Cambridge: Cambridge University Press, 1971), 191, 210.
12. Roderick, G.W. and Stephens, M.D. *Education and Industry in the Nineteenth Century* (London: Longman, 1978), 60.
13. Matthews, J.C. *Examinations: A Commentary* (London: George Allen & Unwin, 1985), 9.
14. Butterfield, S. *Educational Objectives and National Assessment* (Buckingham: Open University Press, 1995), 34.
15. Smith, D. Assessment, technology and the quality revolution Chapter 3 in Bell, C. and Harris, D. (eds) *Assessment and Evaluation: World Yearbook of Education* (London: Kogan Page, 1990), 47.
16. Butterfield, S. op. cit. 89.
17. Target, F. Cultural and linguistic factors in assessment Chapter 6 in *Assessment Issues in Further Education* (Coombe Lodge Report: FEDA, 1995).
    Powell, J.C. *Selection for University in Scotland* (London: University of London Press, 1977).
    Ingenkamp, K. 1977 *Educational Assessment* (London: NFER, 1977).

18. Black, P. Assessment policy and public confidence: comments on the BERA Policy Task Group's article 'Assessment and the improvement of education' *Curriculum Journal* 4 (3), 1993, 421–27.
19. See for example, Matthews, J.C. op. cit., p. 29.
20. Broadfoot, P. Alternatives to public examinations In Nuttall, D. (ed.) *Assessing Educational Achievement* (Lewes: Falmer, 1986), 58.
21. Hitchcock, G. *Profiles and Profiling: A Practical Introduction* (London: Longman, 1990) (2nd edn).

CHAPTER 3
Whatever Happened to TGAT?
PAUL BLACK

To tell a story about one's disappointments is to risk indulgent self-pity. Given this risk, what justifies the telling? One of my hopes is that the disappointments illuminate the inherent difficulties in framing public policies that aim for radical changes in education. A most important lesson is that policy advice calling for radical change has to be scrupulously cautious and realistic. Of course, I also want to claim that no better policy has even been proposed, let alone implemented.

I shall tell the story in a personal rather than a historically logical sequence. I shall first describe events leading up to the publication of the TGAT reports. Then I shall sketch how the recommendations came to be adopted as government policy. This will be followed by an account of the way they were implemented in part, and then gradually abandoned. In a final section I shall revisit the original context and re-assess the underlying principles.

Producing the TGAT reports

In mid-1987, the Secretary of State for Education, Kenneth Baker, was formulating the Education Reform Bill and planning its implementation. I was invited to a personal discussion with the permanent secretary at the DES with two senior staff. I thought I was being considered for the proposed working party on the science curriculum, but the discussion also explored assessment matters. It was a great surprise when I was invited to chair the group on Assessment and Testing, and I saw it at first as a poisoned chalice.

I came to accept the task partly because I realized that some form of national curriculum and assessment was envisaged in the 1987 election manifestos of all the three main parties – this was not an exclusively Conservative exercise. In addition, my experiences of testing (as an examiner and board member of the Joint Matriculation Board) in the Assessment of Performance Unit's science monitoring, and with the Inner London Education Authority's graded assessments scheme, made me optimistic that valid and helpful national assessment was possible. Another essential feature was that the importance of teachers' own assessments was recognized in the first consultation preceding the formulation of the 1988 Act[1], and was later confirmed by Baker.[2]

A further comfort came as negotiations about the terms of reference and membership of the group unfolded. In particular, I was able to suggest alternatives to some proposed names, to enquire fully when names strange to me were proposed, and to make suggestions of my own – with alternatives when names were blocked.

The group comprised four who had both technical expertise and institutional experience with public examinations, a researcher with expertise in the interface of vocational training and economic performance, a chief education officer, two headteachers (one secondary, one primary), the chief personnel officer of a large engineering company, and a former HMI with long experience of the primary sector. In addition, civil servants and a representative of HMI took part in all of the meetings.

The group faced a deadline of Christmas 1987. Kenneth Baker imposed this urgency because he wanted the recommendations of the two groups already at work, on the science and the mathematics curriculum respectively, to be ready by mid-1988. These groups could not approach closure until the assessment and testing framework had been settled.

The group held its first meeting on 11 September, and before Christmas it met over two week-ends and in four more one-day meetings. During this period there were also seven one-day meetings with invited groups, e.g. some CEOs, a set of selected school heads, and teachers from European schools. There were also meetings between myself and the chairs of the mathematics and the science working parties, and meetings of a sub-group looking at the primary phase.

I obtained Baker's agreement to report in two stages so that we could defer some issues until after Christmas. I talked with him on only two occasions. These discussions left me bemused. Either I was not communicating, or he wished to leave us free. Such steer as there was is documented in his letter expanding the terms of reference.[3] Even there, I was able to comment on drafts beforehand. Whilst problems arose which needed private discussions with the DES staff and with the Senior Chief Inspector, there was little private pressure. There were veiled warnings of political struggles to come from other quarters.

The Task Group settled into productive discussions with remarkable speed. Essential ingredients were the spur of urgency, the strongly shared sense of a difficult but important task, and the integrity of all of the members in their approach to it. The evolution of the report, as it can be read from the minutes and working papers, was a remarkably smooth one. A working paper for the second meeting set one priority:

> A scheme will only start to work when teachers begin to make it their own. If they do this with some enthusiasm because it provides a framework for them to deploy professional skills and to pursue their professional development, then all will be well.

However, the group's commitment to enhancing teachers' roles in assessment was tempered with realism. A private report by HMI described current practice:

> a plethora of assessment, implemented in a generally unco-ordinated way and ineffective in providing for pupils, teachers and parents and the outside world a clear and full picture of pupils' progress, attainment or potential.

The group did not take seriously the proposition that a set of external tests, set independently at each age, could on their own raise standards. Better formative assessment would be the key, and there was no point in providing assessments at 7, 11 and 14 unless they supported learning through links to formative practice. Therefore these assessments had to be related to clear criteria. Also, given evidence that pupils' attainments at any one age covered a range corresponding to several years of normal progression, it seemed clear that the best framework would be a single scheme of criteria, spanning across the age ranges and setting out guidance for progression in learning.

It was also clear that economically feasible external tests could not serve the purpose on their own – the constraints would render them invalid in relationship to many important aims of learning, and their reliability was bound to be limited. However, we were also agreed that test instruments and procedures, fashioned and tested by experts, could be powerful instruments for helping raise the quality of teachers' assessments. So we came to recommend that teachers' assessments should be combined with the results of external tests, with uniformity of standards secured through peer review in group moderation. Here, we drew on the experience of moderation procedures built up in GCE and CSE schemes over many years.[3]

Thus the four principles on which a system should be based – criterion referencing, progression, formative and moderated – were distilled. Working from these, we hoped to avoid our nightmare – narrowly based external tests which would give misleading results whilst constraining teaching.

There remained three problems. One was publication of test results; we were clear that this should not be recommended for age seven, but felt that the public's right to information was clear at the other ages. All were concerned about unfair use of league tables, and we struggled to find ways to frame reporting that would not mislead.

The second problem was the primary school curriculum, where we foresaw terrible difficulties. Following discussions, I wrote a joint letter to Baker, with the chairs of the mathematics and science groups, on 23 November. We emphasized the problem:

> For this age [*age* 7] a primary class teacher could not be expected to handle attainment targets and assessments in the large number of profile elements which would be implied by the content of all nine foundation subjects.

To meet the difficulty we proposed some combination of the first elements of the nine subjects into a smaller number of profile components (as later explained in sections 119 to 124 of our first report), and argued for a co-ordinating group: 'We cannot foresee how the separate subject working groups can properly develop their contributions in the primary phase through a set of separate offerings'. The reply was that this would be looked into after our first report had been published.

Partly to serve the same strategy, we also recommended that the external tests at age seven should be extended 'tasks', rather like well-designed pieces of teaching which engaged children and gave them the opportunity to show performance in a range of appropriate targets. The general term Standard Assessment Tasks was coined to emphasize that classroom validity should characterize the external test exercises at all ages.

The third problem was about timing. Here we stated (section 199)

> We recommend that the new assessment should be phased in over a period adequate for the preparation and trial of new assessment methods, for teacher preparation, and for pupils to benefit from extensive experience of the new curriculum. We estimate that this period needs to be at least five years from the promulgation of the relevant attainment targets.

It was also emphasized that

> The times we have given are minimum times. ... The phasing should pay regard to the undue stress on teachers, on their schools and the consequent harm to pupils which will arise if too many novel requirements are initiated over a short period of time.

This was a prophetic statement.

At the last two meetings members produced draft sections for revision. DES participants were not asked to draft, but at the last stage, I finally re-structured and revised and then a DES officer turned it all into clear and consistent prose. The main task was completed on Christmas Eve.[4]

The developing response

FIRST REACTIONS

Shortly after New Year's Day 1988, three of the group met Baker, with his fellow ministers and staff, to explain the report. The event lasted over two hours. At the close he said that he would publish immediately. When asked 'What about your colleagues, Minister?' he responded that he would look after that. A few days later, I was the chief presenter at the press conference. No minister was present. The published report bears no statement from the Minister or the DES.

Margaret Thatcher complained that she only saw this complicated document on the eve of its publication. She later wrote in her memoirs[5] that

> Ken Baker warmly welcomed the report. Whether he had read it properly I do not know: if he had it says much for his stamina. Certainly I had no opportunity to do so before agreeing to its publication ... that it was then welcomed by the Labour party, the National Union of Teachers and the *Times Educational Supplement* was enough to confirm for me that its approach was suspect.

Her immediate response was in a 'private' note to Baker which was leaked and so became public. I was told that a civil servant would inquire into this 'leak', but heard no more.

The Prime Minister's concern, that it was the left wing and the educational establishment who welcomed the report, was ill-informed. Of the many public lectures that I gave over the next six months, the only really hostile reception was at the hands of academics at a meeting of the British Educational Research Association. Conversely, *The Times* expressed the following views in an editorial on 14 January:

> In other words, Professor Black's elegant and sensitive system meets every criterion the Government could have wished. Mr.

Baker, quite contrary to the teaching unions' assertion that he is embarrassed and discomfited, has let it be known that he is positively delighted ... Could it be that [*the unions*] believed, as they often proclaimed and Mr Baker as often denied, that the government really intended to impose simple, menacing pass–fail tests of the 11-plus variety? In which case, can we now look forward to a period of quiet contemplation, followed perhaps by general recantation?

Many commentators were suspicious – was it a Trojan Horse of the right, or a subversion by the educational establishment? The Task Group had not consciously engaged in either manoeuvre: they were focused on constructing the optimum system.

THE TASK GROUP'S SECOND PHASE

The Task Group met again in February and March and submitted the second report on 25 March.[6] This bore the less than prepossessing title of *Three Supplementary Reports*. The first of these was a response to the feedback on the first report. Nothing new was added here, but the original explanations were expanded in order to meet confusions and misunderstandings. There was particular emphasis on the proposals for moderation.

The second report summarized the outcome of inquiries carried out to establish whether the ten-level criterion referenced system would be at least feasible, if not positively helpful, over a wide range of school subjects. We consulted professional associations of teachers in English, history, geography, art, music, CDT and home economics. They foresaw positive advantages rather than serious problems.

A more difficult task was discussed in the third report entitled *A System of Support*. Here we set out a system, with costing, to meet all the administrative requirements, based on collaboration between GCSE groups and LEAs, and including the substantial programme of teacher training that we saw to be essential.

At the end of January, Baker rejected the November request to set up a group to oversee the formulation of the primary curriculum. Instead, he invited us to meet in a liaison group between TGAT and the mathematics and science groups. A few meetings were held, but this group's power was limited; the new chairman of the mathematics group did not support the work, and TGAT itself was disbanded at the end of March. A report was produced and handed on to the new National Curriculum Council, who effectively shelved the problem.[7]

THE POLICY DECISION

The fate of the TGAT recommendations was announced by Baker in Parliament on 7 June. He published the second report on the same day. His statement could have been read as an endorsement of almost all of the proposals. It accepted the ten-point scale, and by implication the principle of criterion referencing and of grouping of attainment targets 'to make assessment and reporting manageable'. On the formative principle, he stated:

> (e) the results of tests and other assessments should be used both *formatively* to help better teaching and to inform decisions about next steps for a pupil, and *summatively* at ages 7, 11, 14 and 16 to inform parents about their child's progress. [emphasis in original]

On the balance between external tests and teachers' assessments, there were two separate statements as follows

> (d) assessment should be by a combination of national external tests and assessment by teachers ...
> (g) in order to safeguard standards, assessments made by teachers should be compared with the results of the national tests and with the judgements of other teachers.

These were in line with TGAT recommendations numbers 13 and 14 and implied, in the last phrase of (g), use of group moderation. They stopped short of recommendation 17, which was that 'the final reports on individual pupils to their parents should be the responsibility of the teachers, supported by standardized assessment tasks and group moderation'.

Baker found the proposals about the system for managing

31

the implementation of the new scheme 'complicated and costly'. New proposals were to be worked out by the newly established councils – SEAC and the NCC.

The abandonment of TGAT

From mid-1998, the evolution of policy and practice lay between the new School Examinations and Assessment Council and ministers. It is significant that only one member of TGAT, the researcher with expertise in the interface of vocational training and economic performance, was appointed to the new Council.

It is not possible to do justice here to the chequered history of that evolution. It would also be superfluous, as it has been documented very fully by Richard Daugherty,[8] who, as a member of SEAC throughout the period, had access to the papers and the arguments. It is only necessary here to refer briefly to what I regard as the milestone events.

FROM TASKS TO TESTS

The first casualty was the TGAT vision of Standard Assessment Tasks. The trials in 1990 of the first attempts at such tasks attracted considerable and mainly adverse publicity. One burden on the design was that a result should be produced in each of the 32 attainment targets which comprised the three core subjects – a requirement which the TGAT members would never have contemplated. The media inevitably emphasized the heavy burden on teachers. The design was then changed to separate out the assessments of the three core subjects, but the burdens were still extensive.

In 1991 however there was a new minister. He looked at these tasks, and at the first trial tasks for Key Stage 3 in the core subjects, and declared them to be 'elaborate nonsense'. A new design was imposed on SEAC for the 1992 tests. The language of tasks disappeared – Clarke required 'written terminal examinations' and 'short written tests'. The emphasis was on manageability and reliability and the purpose clearly summative. Later evaluation of the Key Stage 3 trials showed that teachers had found them acceptable;[9] a questionnaire about possible alternatives for the science tasks revealed that teachers did not prefer the features which were imposed for the 1992 tests.

Given the steady narrowing of the tests from then on, the boycott of all testing in 1993 can hardly be regarded as a protest against the TGAT model. However, whilst teachers' representatives complained that the tests were now too narrow, some critics were blaming the complexity of the original design.

ASSESSMENT BY TEACHERS

The second casualty was teacher assessment. Daugherty reports[8] that in its first three years teacher assessment appeared as a separate item on SEAC's agenda on only one occasion, and only then because they had to respond to a DES request for advice on the subject. The second appearance came over two years later in November 1992, then in the context of a need to decide how it would be audited. The inconsistency between this neglect and the rhetoric which had supported the TGAT approach is staggering. It could be that it was assumed that teachers knew how to do this without help. Perhaps it was the sheer overload of a system for which the priority of setting up the SATs pushed all else off the agenda. A third possibility is that much of the 'acceptance' of TGAT was a pretence, to be slowly abandoned as a different political agenda was implemented.

SEAC first published material to guide teachers' assessments in 1990.[10] This was long on generalizations and short on any practicalities. Some useful examples of 'pupils' work assessed' subsequently appeared as guides to the interpretation of the curriculum criteria.[11,12] A guide for primary teachers produced jointly, and on their own initiative, by the subject teacher associations for English, mathematics and science, was far more useful – it showed what might have been achieved if serious programmes of development and trial had been established.[13]

When teachers, whose assessment practices were known

to be weak, had to work with both formative and summative roles in a new curriculum, there was sure to be confusion. Ample evidence that help was needed soon emerged.[14–18] Nevertheless, it also emerged that despite all the problems, positive improvements in teachers' assessment practices did slowly develop.[19, 20]

Decisions about the function of teachers' assessments in relation to the SAT results were changed year by year. The outstanding decision was that SATs should give the main result for each individual pupil; the TGAT proposals for group moderation were dismissed at the outset. Any lingering concern with moderation became a concern to audit teachers' marking of the SATs and teachers' assessment of those targets in the curriculum which could not be measured with written tests. More recently, the marking has become external and all auditing has been abandoned. Teachers' assessments are simply to be reported to parents alongside SAT results.

The distrust of teachers, and the belief that external measures and the rigours of the competitive market are the best way to raise the standards of learning, seem to have been the driving forces. Consider Baker in 1989:

> The balance – characteristic of most GCSE courses – between coursework and an externally set and marked terminal examination has worked well. I accept the Council's judgement that assessment by means of coursework is one of the examination's strengths. (letter from Kenneth Baker to SEAC, July 1989, quoted in Daugherty[8])

In his 1991 speech to the Centre for Policy Studies, John Major reached a different conclusion.

> It is clear that there is now far too much coursework, project work and teacher assessment in GCSE. The remedy surely lies in getting GCSE back to being an externally assessed exam which is predominantly written. I am attracted to the idea that for most subjects a maximum of 20 per cent of the marks should be obtainable from coursework. (quoted in Daugherty[8] p. 137)

John Major's speech led to reduction of the coursework component of GCSE. There is no public explanation of how this policy decision came to be made; it was not preceded by any public consultation.

DROWNING IN CRITERIA

The TGAT group envisaged that assessments were to be designed to report on a small number (about four) of profile components. It was explicitly stated[4] that:

> 57. ... We assume that there will be more attainment targets to be met at any reporting age than can reasonably be assessed on a single occasion for national assessment purposes.

The group were never advised that this assumption was not legitimate, and indeed developed the point thus:

> 61. ... If reliable results were to be required about every single attainment target, an excessive amount of assessment would be needed in order to disentangle the effects of context from more fundamental individual differences in the sequence of achieving targets. But profile components based on the <u>aggregation</u> of target achievements <u>can</u> be reported with acceptable degrees of confidence. [emphasis in original]

It was subsequently ruled by SEAC that pupils' results would have to be reported against every separate attainment target. The Secretary of State had by then promulgated Orders with 17 targets in science and 14 in mathematics, yet the absurd impracticality of the requirements was not appreciated until test agencies and the GCSE boards were faced with meeting it. The resolution was that the 1989 Orders for Science and Mathematics had to be revised in 1991, to be framed in four attainment targets. Thus attainment targets came to serve the purpose TGAT planned for profile components. It is clear that because of this expensive confusion teachers suffered from disruption because the 1989 Order was replaced just as they had ended the onerous task of re-organizing their teaching to meet its demands.

Lying behind this administrative failure were more intractable issues about criterion referencing. In the original versions of the national curriculum orders, each level in each attainment target was specified with several statements.

35

SEAC tried to demand that every statement be separately assessed for success or failure, and made up rules so that the aggregation of these data could be used to decide attainment of a level. This demand could not be met in short tests. There were far too many statements of attainment, so it had to be abandoned. These problems are aspects of the more general difficulty which besets any attempt to specify goals for learning by criterion statements. This could have been foreseen.

THE TEN-LEVEL SCHEME

In early 1993, I was invited by the Centre for Policy Studies to be one of a panel of four speakers at a half-day meeting to discuss national assessment. Only when I was on the platform did it become clear that this was an occasion for mounting an attack on the ten-level system. The opinion of several of my colleagues who were in the audience was that the CPS speakers had not made their case, mainly because they had misunderstood the arguments which were the basis of the system and knew nothing about the research evidence that supported these arguments.

Shortly after this, Sir Ron Dearing treated the ten-level scale as one of the outstanding problems. I was involved, at his request, in lengthy debate on this issue. As far as I could understand it, the opposing position was that, since a test at age 16 on a GCSE syllabus worked well, why not replicate this with three separate syllabuses and tests at 7, 11 and 14? Dr John Marks even quoted the Common Entrance examination as a successful examination for the younger ages. The critics appeared to have nothing to say about the TGAT arguments on the importance of progression, on assessment as a guide to learning, and on continuity between key stages. I believe we won that debate, witness the following quotations from the final Dearing report[21]:

> 7.37 The conclusion I draw from this discussion is that the scale can be revised so that it provides a better and more manageable framework for teaching and learning. It can offer a statement of progression which can help teachers to plan the curriculum and match work to pupils of different abilities.

7.60 ... We should devote our energies to an improved version of the ten-level scale as described in paragraphs 7.21–7.37 above.

However this conclusion appears to have been reversed within six months,[22] without further open debate, in a statement very close to the position that the opponents had adopted:

> We have concluded that it is the programmes of study which should guide the planning, teaching and day-to-day assessment of pupils' work. The essential function of the level descriptions is to assist in the making of summary judgements about pupils' achievements as a basis of reporting at the end of a key stage.

This statement, with the decision not to use the new level descriptions scheme for GCSE, virtually put an end to the ten-level system, which was by then the final vestige of the TGAT proposals.

GCSE

The Task Group's recommendations about alignment of their new system to what was then the quite new GCSE system were very limited and seen as interim and holding measures. It was clear that 'it would not be helpful to specify equivalencies between the two systems whilst they operate in different ways'. Here, the assessment debate was overshadowed by the debate about the extent to which the curriculum at Key Stage 4 should be prescribed. As the TGAT model for the first three key stages was abandoned, the potential problems of marrying two different systems began to disappear. Indeed, the 1988 model for GCSE has been moved further away from the TGAT model by the attack on coursework assessment.

Reflections

THE IDEOLOGICAL AND POLITICAL BACKGROUND

The above history might be understood as a struggle for power between competing ideologies. In this perspective, the TGAT report was an aberrant obstacle in the path of a right-wing bulldozer.

Conservative policy on education has long been influenced by a belief that left-wing conspiracies seek to undermine it. Take, for example, the following account of Keith Joseph's view by Knight[23]:

> Here Joseph shared a view common to all conservative educationists: that education had seen an unholy alliance of socialists, bureaucrats, planners and Directors of Education acting against the true interests and wishes of the nation's children and parents by their imposition on the schools of an ideology (equality of condition) based on utopian dreams of universal co-operation and brotherhood

In a more up to date and comprehensive account Lawton[24] also, sees that 'Tories really do seem to believe in the existence of left-wing, "education establishment" conspiracies'.

Given this perspective, one can understand why research evidence is rejected and features hardly at all in the educational writing of the New Right – those responsible for this evidence are part of the conspiracy, so their evidence is not to be trusted. Marsland and Seaton[25] under the exciting title *The Empire Strikes Back* developed the theme of a left wing conspiracy:

> This wretched tale shows how the National Curriculum was subverted and undermined by the very Education Empire whose ideas it was meant to eradicate. Ministers were duped ...

> Their aim was to sabotage the government policies of 'back to basics' in schools ... Their strategy was simple: infiltration, then subversion.

However, this picture only raises a further question – why construct and then adhere to a conspiracy theory in the first place? Lawton[26] points to an important clue:

> The dominant feature of the Tory Mind that has emerged from this study is, unsurprisingly, an exaggerated concern for tradition and past models of education and society. But what did surprise me when reading so many speeches and autobiographies was the Tory *fear* of the future and of the non-traditional. I was even more surprised by the kind of fear which took the form of an almost paranoid belief in conspiracies among the 'educational establishment'.

BAKER VS. THATCHER

Margaret Thatcher's dismay about the TGAT report could have been predicted. She did not trust Baker. He had fought for over a year for a ten-subject curriculum against her view, supported by the head of her policy unit, Brian Griffiths, that all that was needed was the three core subjects and simple tests. Taylor's article[27] describes how Baker won this battle, but to Thatcher's dismay rather than by changing her judgement. In particular, she was opposed to the setting up of the TGAT. Three comments (as quoted by Taylor) by an anonymous civil servant illuminate the picture. The first is about the orientation of policy: 'Baker was not prepared to let things be hijacked by the ideological right'. The second is about reactions to the TGAT report: 'Needless to say, Brian Griffiths thought it [*the TGAT report*] was abominable'. The third is about the aftermath: 'TGAT was not wanted ... the "right-wing" camp, if you like, were trying to recover ground and as soon as they saw the chinks opening up, they went in'.

Baker's victory turned out to be a Pyrrhic one. His successor, John McGregor, made little change, but after McGregor, Kenneth Clarke began to 'recover ground'. Consider the following quotation from the Westminster Lecture by Clarke[28]:

> The British pedagogue's hostility to written examinations of any kind can be taken to ludicrous extremes. The British left believe that pencil and paper examinations impose stress on pupils and demotivates them. ... This remarkable national obsession lies behind the more vehement opposition to the recent introduction of 7-year-old testing. They were made a little too complicated and we have said we will simplify them ... The complications themselves were largely designed in the first place in an attempt to pacify opponents who feared above all else 'paper and pencil' tests ... This opposition to testing and examinations is largely based on a folk memory in the left about the old debate on the 11-plus and grammar schools.

Here, the conspiracy view is showing, and arguments given by TGAT for its proposals were ignored. John Major's speeches have shown clear signs of the same beliefs, and both Major and Clarke have included in their speeches attacks on child-centred education and on John Dewey – attacks clearly deriving from a Centre for Policy Studies publication.[29]

Brian Griffiths replaced the dismissed chairman of SEAC. It is clear that the changes to the memberships of the national councils for curriculum and for assessment made by Clarke gave each of these a new bias. Eric Bolton, who as Senior Chief Inspector had worked with Baker, drew attention, in a speech in 1992, to the new and overwhelming influence of the right wing pressure groups, notably the centre for Policy Studies.[30] Sir Malcolm Thornton, the Conservative chairman of the House of Commons Select Committee on Education, commenting on events since the departure of John McGregor, said[31]:

> From that point on, I believe that both the wider debate and the ears of Ministers have been disproportionately influenced by extremists – extremists whose pronouncements become even wilder and further from the reality of the world of education which I recognise, in which I work in and for which I care deeply. And who are they to foist upon the children of this country ideas which will only serve to take them backwards? What hard evidence do they have to support their assertions?

It could be argued that, in the above scenario, the TGAT policy was merely a creature of a prince: when that prince lost his power at court, his creature was doomed. It would have had to be a very strange policy to have commanded the prince's patronage and yet to have survived his downfall.

A FLAWED BLUEPRINT?

However, even on this view, one might ask whether the creature itself was so ill-formed that it contributed to that downfall. It is important to look critically at the TGAT design and ask whether the flaws were such that it could never have been put into practice.

It would not be possible here to deal with all the critical commentaries that have been made on the TGAT proposals.

I shall discuss only a few main issues, but I shall approach them in a very specific way by spelling out the work I believe should and could have been done if the proposals had been taken seriously. Such work would have revealed many needs, and would have shown that the proposals required more explanation and implied a need for far more development than the report indicated, or indeed than the group actually envisaged. Therein lay its main weakness.

I shall say little here about the thorny issue of reporting of school performances in league tables.[32] The TGAT proposed that assessment results be reported in a context of interpretation so that they would not mislead those they were meant to inform. With hindsight, it was naïve to imagine that the government, with its commitment to a market where choice would be guided by tests, would support a complex approach. On the other hand, no convincing alternative has been produced. It is naïve to think that publication of results can be resisted, and equally naïve to propose that the public should agree that the interpretation is so complex that they can't be allowed to see the raw scores.

The issues of criterion referencing have raised many problems. It seems simple to say that assessments results should be meaningful in indicating what pupils can or cannot do. However, most significant outcomes of education are complex: they cannot be represented by a short list of explicit criteria. Even when it appears that this has been done in the abstract, it usually turns out that test items for any one criterion can be set in many different ways and that pupils will succeed on some and not on others. The attempt to define every aim in multiple atomized forms also leads to invalid test items and to problems about how to aggregate the large and uneven collections of results that any one pupil attains. This is a well known trap in this field[33] – but that did not stop SEAC falling into it.

A more robust approach is to define broader domains of performance, represented by more holistic and complex items. The numbers of such domains have to be determined with reference to the important learning aims in each subject, and their meaning and boundaries have to be explored by iteration between definitions in principle, by attempts to construct relevant test items, and by evaluation of pupils' responses to those items. APU science developed its domains by such a process.[34] However, that work also showed that it might then take a large number of items to reliably assess any one domain. The outcomes will be more ambiguous and vague than the ideal envisaged, and there will be no escaping the need for professional judgement in setting up and operating such an array of domains. The change that the Dearing revision has made to the levels statements can be seen as a move in this direction, but an amateur one because of the impossibly short time allowed for the formulation and the absence of any developmental testing.[35] Given this, it was almost inevitable also that SCAA would move, as it appears to have done, to a testing strategy in which total subject marks over each level will simply be added to give total scores on which success will be judged. The attempt at criterion referencing has been abandoned.

Linked to this is the issue of the ten-level system. Many objections to this – for example that it assumes a linear or a hierarchical model of learning – are based on misunderstandings. The only assumptions are that, over the years from 5 to 16, the subjects are not taught in a completely random order at completely random levels of sophistication, that when a pupil fails to achieve an aim it is not permissible to abandon that aim altogether, and that when a pupil succeeds teachers decide in some non-arbitrary way what that pupil should learn next. The particular model of progression that is adopted can be very different between different curriculum areas and between different domains in the same area. The opponents of the ten-level model who argued a case before Dearing wanted a separate syllabus and test for each key stage, i.e. a four-level model. They agreed that there would have to be a structure in each set of test results and that there would have to be some relationship between the structures of each key stage and the next. It was hard to see why they were not on the way to re-inventing the ten-level system. Of course, such a sequence would have to be very flexible – one level every two years seemed to allow this.

One objection is the age-independent nature of the scale. Given the substantial evidence that there is a very wide overlap between spreads in the attainments of pupils at different ages,[36,37] it is hard to see how several age-dependent scales could be justified. Of course, the teaching approaches to be used with a 7-year-old overcoming a particular difficulty and a 14-year-old facing the same obstacle might be very different. If however the criteria were to be different, that would imply that the low-attaining older pupil is to follow a curriculum with different aims from the high-attaining younger one. I have not seen this argued through.

A very different but equally fundamental objection has been that it is not possible for the same assessments to serve the several different purposes of assessment, and this has led some to argue that the formative and summative purposes should have been uncoupled and served by different instruments and procedures.[38, 39] It should first be clear that those who say this both agree on the outstanding importance of teachers' formative assessment as an agent to raise standards, and agree that a great deal of effort is needed to improve current practice in such assessment. There is ample evidence that good teacher assessment can raise standards and that there is much room for improvement in present practice.[40] Some also agree that teachers' assessments must have both a formative role and a summative one, if only because teachers have to sum up any pupil's work to report annually to parents and to guide a new teacher when the pupil transfers between years. There are problems in holding both these roles: they do not necessarily require the collection of different assessment evidence, but they may require the same evidence to be selected and interpreted in different ways according to the purpose.[41] All of this emphasizes the need for more exploration of practice in this area and for extensive training. A weakness of the TGAT report was that it did not discuss this difficult interface between the formative and the summative roles of teachers in assessment.

If quite separate external tests were to be used to serve school accountability and pupil certification, then such tests would dominate teaching and devalue teachers' assessments.[39,42] They would also be invalid because affordable external tests cannot reflect many important learning aims. Their reliability would also be limited.[43, 44] The test/re-test reliability of SATs and GCSE examinations has not been researched. Adequate internal homogeneity of such tests can be obtained, and can then be quoted as evidence of reliability, but this is often attained by omitting aberrant items thus reducing the validity. In the common GCSE approach, each question may span more than one domain: the collection of a pupil's responses may then give an adequately reliable measure over the subject as a whole, but no meaningful measure of any one component part. There cannot be any profile, and domain referencing is reduced to a single domain – the subject, and there is no formative value. These are dire consequences.

Why then bother with external tests at all? There are many countries and states where these are seen to be unnecessary except for leaving examinations. The State of Queensland abandoned all external testing in 1982, but it has taken over twelve years to build up a system based on teachers' assessments, with moderation based on groups of schools in each locality working together.[45, 46] It is significant that the development has also been integrally linked with substantial responsibility of the same groups for local curriculum development.

However, public confidence in most countries won't countenance such a radical delegation of responsibility. Good external tests can set a good standard if rigorously developed and trialled. Banks of such items could help teachers' assessment practices in both roles. This has been recognized in France, where national external tests have been imposed at three ages – with one important difference[47]: they are to be taken at the beginning of a school year, so that the teacher is not responsible for what his or her new pupils achieve, but is responsible for acting on the information in meeting their needs.

Whilst affordable external tests cannot give reliable results for individual pupils, they could do so over a class as a whole. They can also reinforce good teaching practices. A great deal of progress has been made in this area in the growth of so-called 'performance assessments' and 'portfolio assessment' in the USA,[48] although this work has also confirmed that reliable generalization about individuals cannot be made from the performance results on a small number of complex tasks.[49-51] They also reveal that reliability of teachers' assessments can be attained, but requires a great deal of work. This is why TGAT wanted SATs to help set each school's overall average and distribution, but to leave assignment of individual pupils to the school (as is done in Sweden[52]). Also, contrary to what many critics affirm, TGAT did not intend that SATs should rule over the teacher assessment for a school; they were to be one important piece of evidence to help a group moderation to reconcile local with national standards.[53]

The TGAT case was a closely argued one and the design was a carefully articulated structure. Critics have generally focused on a single aspect, without looking at the need to repair the whole design if that aspect were to be changed. As soon as SEAC and the government decided that group moderation was unacceptable, and that SATs would have to be designed to give a result on their own for each individual pupil, teacher assessment was down-graded and the SATs were given a task that they cannot possibly perform. Thus the design was virtually destroyed at the outset before anything had been tried.

Daugherty regards the TGAT model as unworkable, but he recognizes that it is the only coherent model that has been proposed and he does not propose an alternative. It is evident, for example, that neither the pre-Dearing amputations, nor the Dearing cosmetic re-designs, have tackled the basic problems. His diagnosis of the immediate causes of the débâcle rings true. The many changes made since 1988 have not been informed by any overall strategy, and have been rapidly contrived rather than carefully argued, let alone researched.[54]

There have been two other fatal weaknesses. One was the separation of the development of curriculum and assessment. Assessment development, when (as it ought to be) is as close to pedagogy as the formative function requires, has to go hand in hand with curriculum formulation and renewal. The Queensland development is a telling example here. The development of the APU monitoring tells a similar story. The national curriculum subjects have never been developed in this way – it would have taken too long.

The other even more fatal weakness was the pace of change. Even if designers had known exactly how to implement a new scheme, it should have been allowed many more years in implementation. Teachers cannot possibly, in two or three years, grasp and incorporate into the complexities of classroom practice the radically new departures of the TGAT plans whilst dealing also with a quite new curriculum. Yet if teachers cannot make the new practices their own, then nothing of value will happen. All serious studies of educational change show that reform cannot be achieved by diktat, and cannot be achieved quickly.[55, 56]

But in fact the TGAT designers did not know exactly what to do. They knew of (had indeed been involved in) examples of all the components of the new practices that they were recommending. They did not have time to think through all of the evidence that pertained to their case, and they failed to consider realistically the full implications of imposing these practices, in a newly articulated whole, on all teachers. If they had done so, then perhaps they should then have had the courage to adopt the position that at least ten years of careful development work was essential to develop the proposals into a workable system. If they had stated this as their main proposition, it is certain that they would have been dismissed and their report might never have been published.

The position still needs stating today, and still has little chance of being taken seriously. An outstanding obstacle is that the public generally, and policy makers in particular, have a very imperfect understanding of the functions and limitations of assessment and testing, and of their interactions with effective learning.

Notes and references

1. DES *The National Curriculum 5–16: A Consultation Document* (London: DES and the Welsh Office, 1987).
2. See Appendix B in DES *Task Group on Assessment and Testing: A Report* (London: DES and the Welsh Office, 1988a).
3. Wood, R. *Assessment and Testing: A Survey of Research* (Cambridge: Cambridge University Press, 1991).
4. DES *Task Group on Assessment and Testing: A Report* (London: DES and the Welsh Office, 1988a).
5. Thatcher, M. *The Downing Street Years* (London: Harper Collins, 1993), 594–5.
6. DES *Task Group on Assessment and Testing: Three Supplementary Reports* (London: DES and the Welsh Office, 1988b).
7. See Chapter 2 in Galton, M. *Crisis in the Primary Classroom* (London: Fulton, 1995).
8. Daugherty, R. *National Curriculum Assessment: A Review of Policy 1987–1994* (London: Falmer, 1995).
9. Swain, J.R.L. Standard Assessment Tasks in science at Key Stage 3: the 1991 pilot *British Journal of Curriculum and Assessment*, 2, 1991, 19–30.
10. SEAC *A Guide to Teacher Assessment; Packs A, B and C* (London: SEAC, 1990).
11. SEAC *Pupils' Work Assessed: English, Mathematics and Science* (London: SEAC, 1992).
12. SEAC *Pupils' Work Assessed: Science: Four Pupils' Folders* (London: SEAC, 1993).
13. ASE *Teacher Assessment: Making it Work for the Primary School* (Hatfield: ASE, 1990).
14. SEAC *National Curriculum Assessment: A Report on Teacher Assessment by the NFER/BGC Consortium* (London: SEAC, 1991).
15. Harlen, W. and Qualter, A. 1991 Issues in SAT development and the practice of teacher assessment *Cambridge Journal of Education* 21 (2), 1991, 141–52.
16. Bennett, S.N., Wragg, E.C., Carre, C.G. and Carter, D.G.S. A longitudinal study of primary teachers' perceived competence in, and concerns about, National Curriculum implementation *Research Papers in Education* 7 (1), 1992, 53–78.
17. McCallum, B., McAlister, S., Brown, M. and Gipps, G. Teacher assessment at Key Stage One *Research Papers in Education*, 8, 1993, 305–27.
18. SEAC *Teacher Assessment in Mathematics and Science at Key Stage 3: A Report by the NFER and Brunel University* (London: SEAC, 1992).
19. Brown, M., Gipps, C. and McCallum, B. Private communication.

Unpublished results of primary schools project (1996).

20. Fairbrother, R.W., Black, P.J. and Gill, P. (eds) *Teachers Assessing Pupils: Lessons from Science Classrooms* (Hatfield UK: ASE, 1995).

21. Dearing, R. *The National Curriculum and its Assessment: Final Report* (London: SCAA, 1993).

22. SCAA *Science in the National Curriculum: Draft Proposals* (London: HMSO for SCAA, 1994).

23. Knight, C. *The Making of Tory Education Policy in Post-War Britain 1950–1986* (London: Falmer, 1990).

24. Lawton, D. *The Tory Mind on Education 1979–94* (London: Falmer, 1994), 145.

25. Marsland, D. and Seaton, N. *The Empire Strikes Back: The Creative Subversion of the National Curriculum* (York: Campaign for Real Education, 1993).

26. Lawton, D. 1994 op. cit., 144.

27. Taylor, T. Movers and shakers: high politics and the origins of the National Curriculum *Curriculum Journal* 6 (2), 1995, 161–84.

28. Clarke, K. *Education in a Classless Society* The Westminster Lecture, given to the Tory Reform Group, June 1991.

29. O'Hear, A. *Father of Child-centredness: John Dewey and the Ideology of Modern Education* (London: Centre for Policy Studies, 1991).

30. *Times Educational Supplement* Visions of Chaos: Report of a speech by Professor Eric Bolton to the Council of Local Education Authorities, p. 10 No. 3970, 31 July 1992.

31. Chitty, C. and Simon, B. (eds) 1993 *Education Answers Back: Critical Responses to Government Policy* (London: Lawrence and Wishart, 1993), 45–60.

32. See Chapter 5 in Daugherty, R. 1995 op. cit.

33. Popham, W.J. *Educational Evaluation* (3rd end) (Boston: Allyn and Bacon, 1993).

34. Johnson, S. *National Assessment: The APU Science Approach* (London: HMSO, 1988).

35. See Chapter 5 in Gipps, C.V. *Beyond Testing: Towards a Theory of Educational Assessment* (London: Falmer, 1994).

36. Hart, K. (ed.) *Children's Understanding of Mathematics 11–16* (London: John Murray, 1981).

37. Chapter 8, Black, P., Brown, P., Simon, S. and Blondel, E. Progression in Learning. Issues and Evidence in Mathematics and Science, and Chapter 10, Lee, P., Dickinson, A. and Ashby, R. 'There were no facts in those days'. Children's ideas about historical explanation in Hughes, M. (ed.) *Teaching and Learning in Changing Times* (Oxford: Blackwell).

38. Harlen, W., Gipps, C., Broadfoot, P. and Nuttall, D. Assessment

and the improvement of education *Curriculum Journal* 3 (3), 1992, 215–30.

39. Black, P.J. 1993 Assessment policy and public confidence: comments on the BERA Policy Task Group's article 'Assessment and the improvement of education' *Curriculum Journal*, 4 (3), 1993, 421–27.

40. Black, P.J. Formative and summative assessment by teachers *Studies in Science Education* 21, 1993, 49–97.

41. William, D. and Black, P.J. Meanings and consequences: a basis for distinguishing formative and summative functions of assessment (Submitted for publication, 1996).

42. For evidence of effects of SATs on science teaching see ASE Key Stage 3 Monitoring Group: Report on the Monitoring of Key Stage 3: *Education in Science* November 1992, 18–19.

43. Black, P.J. Examinations and the teaching of science *Bulletin of the Institute of Physics and the Physical Society* 1963, 202–203.

44. Black, P.J. 1990 APU science: the past and the future *School Science Review* 72 (258), 1990, 13–28.

45. Butler, J. and Bartlett, V.L. School-based criterion-referenced assessment and curriculum design: some comments on the Queensland scheme *Studies in Educational Evaluation* 15, 1989, 91–107.

46. Butler, J. Teachers judging standards in senior science subjects: fifteen years of the Queensland experiment *Studies in Science Education* (1995) Vol. 26 pp. 135–57.

47. See Chapter 4 in Black, P. and Atkin, M. 1996 *Changing the Subject: Case Studies of Innovations in Science, Mathematics and Technology Education* (London: Routledge for OECD, 1996).

48. See Chapter 6 in Gipps 1994 op. cit.

49. Gao, X., Shavelson, R.J. and Baxter, G.P. Generalizability of large-scale performance assessments in science: promises and problems *Applied Measurement in Education* 7 (4), 1994, 323–42.

50. Ruiz-Primo, M.A., Baxter, G.P. and Shavelson, R.J. On the stability of performance assessments *Journal of Educational Measurement* 30 (1), 1993, 41–53.

51. Shavelson, R.J., Baxter, G.P. and Gao, X. 1993 Sampling variability of performance assessments *Journal of Educational Measurement* 30 (3), 1993, 215–32.

52. See Chapter 10 in Black, P.J. (ed.) *Physics Examinations for University Entrance: An International Study* Produced under the auspices of the International Commission for Physics Education. UNESCO Science and Technology Education Document series No. 45 (Paris: UNESCO, 1993).

53. See paragraph 11 in DES 1988b op. cit.

54. See Chapter 8 in Daugherty, R. 1995 op. cit.
55. Fullan, M.G. with Stiegelbauer, S. *The New Meaning of Educational Change* (London: Cassell, 1991).
56. Black and Atkin 1996 op. cit.

CHAPTER 4

Teacher Appraisal: The Connection between Teaching Quality and Legislation

BOB BUTROYD

How do we judge our own teachers?

> I certainly wouldn't choose anybody from my prep school where all the teachers seemed drunk or mad.
> ... at Malvern there were two teachers who were wonderful ... George Sayer ... He was a wonderful man. I can see him now, sweeping into the room, always slightly late and saying 'Do it Boy! Do it!' It was an invitation to engage.
> I didn't get particularly good 'A' levels. (Jeremy Paxman, Journalist, Author and Broadcaster).[1]

> There were two teachers ... It was just a normal mixed 11–18 Secondary, all glass and blue concrete.
> He had an unforgettable style. He'd use this deliberately affected voice just to wind people up and a sort of friendly, matey manner about him ... he was your friend, not just your teacher ... he and other staff in his department gave me a crash course so that I got my Highers in a year.
> The other teacher was in a very different mode ... I was studying Steinbeck and Hardy and had become fairly keen on them, but she introduced me to Voltaire and Chekhov and Dostoevsky. (Pat Nevin, Professional Footballer, Scotland and Tranmere Rovers.)[2]

> John Brian Gledhill was my best teacher. He taught me at La Page Street Secondary Modern for Boys in Bradford ... he'd been a PE instructor in the Army ... I was the second smallest kid in the class and had failed the 11-plus ... I didn't believe I'd be any good at anything. But Mr. Gledhill always told us we could do anything we wanted. We only had to believe.
> He was a dab hand with the cane. If somebody had done something and he couldn't find out who, he'd flog the whole class. But I didn't hold it against him. (Robert Swindells. Children's author and winner of the Carnegie Award for Children's Literature.)[3]

51

On this evidence it is doubtful if more than one of these would have done well in an OFSTED inspection, and yet all were highly thought of by at least one of their pupils. Recently the British Government has been so preoccupied with the question of teacher quality that it has launched four initiatives in order to judge teachers and what they do. It has demanded that schools appraise their teachers, challenged school governors to financially reward those who are considered to be 'excellent', set up an agency to publish judgements on all state schools in England and Wales, and made available a wealth of information to help parents make their own judgements.

How have we arrived at this situation? What are we trying to judge? What sort of answers are we getting? Is this the best way to judge teachers? It is important to ask these questions, because if we don't there is a danger that at the end of all the appraisal, inspection and publication of performance indicators we will be none the wiser about how well our children are being educated.

Over the years the search for a simple yardstick that can be used to measure teachers, and can be understood by all, has not been helped by the tendency to look for 'hard', external forms of assessment, and then when they don't work to retreat behind 'soft' approaches, often internal to the school. The pattern is familiar: once the 'hard' assessment associated with objectivity, competence, outcomes and market forces is applied to the classroom teacher doubts arise as to its validity, and 'softer' perspectives associated with subjectivity and an ill-defined professional judgement are called into play. Both these approaches have obscured the reality of the classroom experience. The former fails to assess the reality and the latter is cloaked in mystery and is vulnerable to charges of élitism.

How have we arrived at this situation?

There is nothing new in the search for clear criteria by which to judge teachers. By the mid-nineteenth century concepts such as dominance, authority, respect and ideological reliability were commonly used to measure teacher performance. The Newcastle Commission of 1861 reported the popularly held view that the

> success, or teachers in working class schools, was seen to be related to 'the role of maintaining exact order and ready and active attention as the first necessity and after that as much kindness to the children as is compatible with a habit of entire obedience'.[4]

The Revised Code of 1862, by measuring immediate pupil outcomes, radically changed the nature of teacher evaluation. This extract from a Science and Art Department Report of 1871 illustrates the preoccupation with what was considered to be the product of education. 'If a teacher produces nothing, he gets no pay ... The object of the State is to have results; the machinery for producing them is immaterial'.[5] Teacher quality was subjected to 'hard' assessment through the testing of pupils by visiting inspectors. Teachers' pay was directly related to the outcomes of these tests. However, by the end of the nineteenth century, this method of teacher evaluation was heavily contested. The problem was that these simple yardsticks concealed the truth of the classroom experience.

Doubts about the validity of assessing teachers through pupil tests led many leading educational figures, including Sir George Kekewich, Secretary to the Board of Education, to consider the teacher's perspective.

> Imagine the feelings of the unfortunate teacher when he looked over the inspector's shoulder and saw failures being recorded wholesale, and knew that his annual salary was being reduced by two and eightpence to each failure.[6]

The end of the nineteenth century was also a time of a preoccupation with the nature of universal secondary education.[7] This debate, allied to the rise to prominence of newly formed political and industrial organizations, including the National Union of Teachers, further revealed the inadequacies of a construct of teacher evaluation which depended solely upon pupil outcomes. Beatrice Webb, in discussing the virtues and difficulties associated with the extension of secondary schooling to working-class children, once again raised the issue of ideological reliability, but this time it was to be evidenced by a teacher's 'high standard of culture'.

> Now the best education atmosphere, it was thought, could be maintained only by keeping up a high standard of culture. It could not, as a rule, be given by teachers, however industrious and sharp witted, who came from working class or lower middle class homes ... and who had concentrated their energies from an early age upon the acquisition of the technique of instructing large classes of undisciplined children ... The accent, the manner, the expression ... and the clothes of the elementary school teacher were compared adversely with the more attractive personal characteristics resulting from well to do homes and the ordinary public school and university education.[8]

This model of teacher evaluation perhaps says more about the values of the assessor than the achievements of the teachers, a theme to which I will return.

After the General Strike teachers were allowed more freedom and a period of professionalism developed which encouraged the subjective construction of 'professional ethics'.[9] Grace felt that

> such professionalism was now about relative autonomy; it was about particular expertise; it was about white collar status and security and it was about the teacher being at a distance from the political and the economic and the agency of the state. Such a version of professionalism suited the aspirations of many teachers in the popular system and it suited those who saw in such professionalism an effective non statutory control over the teaching force.[10]

According to Ball 'professionalism' rests on two claims: status and autonomy. He argues that autonomy was 'licensed' between 1926 and the late 1970s when governments and teachers were assumed to share a similar view of the value of state schooling. As a result of this teachers were allowed to determine certain aspects of the curriculum, develop teaching methods and negotiate conditions of service. This continued whilst the teachers complied with the main condition of the licence: that they would remain non-political and non-controversial 'professionals'. It is at this point that the ambivalence of teacher professionalism begins to cloud the classroom situation. Teacher professionalism is used to define very different perceptions of the legitimate role of the teacher. A teacher's professional view can be alternatively interpreted as: 'subversive of the best that man[*sic*] has said',[11] reflective of the reality of the situation,[12] or irrelevant to the needs of the economy,[13] depending upon how the assessor perceives the professionalism of the teacher.

The history of teacher assessment up to the mid-twentieth century is one of movement between the hard assessment of payment by results, to be assessed by outside inspectors, and the softer internal assessment characterized by the notion of professional judgement. One measures those things which are not necessarily the result of good teaching, and the other draws a veil over those processes for which teachers are responsible. This failure to articulate these processes, and, indeed on occasions to mask them, is being repeated in the second half of this century. The move from a soft, professional judgement model of assessment to a harder, technical perspective is failing to advance an understanding of the role and performance of teachers. As a result assessors are turning to professional judgement in order to cover the deficiencies of the present systems of assessment. Most people do not know what teachers are trying to achieve, and how they are doing it. Much of the mystique associated with teaching lies with a failure to define the professionalism claimed by teachers.

What are we trying to judge?

This depends upon how the assessor defines the object of inquiry. Schön[14] outlines two models which underpin the idea of the professional teacher. Firstly, he describes the development of a technical rationalist view of the teacher through the first 60 years of the twentieth century. This period saw the advancement of learning theories. These theories were to be taught to student teachers in the universities and applied in the schools. Teachers, as practitioners of 'scientific' theories of learning, were endowed with status, an important claim to professionalism.[15] Secondly, Schön describes a reflective practitioner model which further enhanced the status of the classroom practitioner, at the expense of the centralized curriculum developer.[14]

When teachers are called to account for their performance they often invoke professional judgement as justification. Professional judgement arises from the teachers' claim to professionalism; the argument often is that teaching is a profession, and that as a professional relies upon advanced learning it is only those who have access to this learning who are in a position to make judgements regarding education. Often the criteria used in such judgements are left undefined. Norris[16] makes reference to the 'contingent and complex' nature of professional judgement, whilst Gardner says that the values upon which professional judgement is based 'may or may not be explicitly identified' and that there is often only 'an assumed association with a commonly shared value system'.[17] It is in part the failure to articulate this 'shared value system' which has led to claims that teachers are unaccountable.

As we shall see, recent legislation has attempted to marginalize the role of professional judgement in teacher assessment. Concern for teaching methods and the curriculum has led to greater regulation of the teacher and, consequently, classroom performance. This has happened partly through a revised notion of teacher professionalism.

This revision began in the mid 1970s when Britain's relative economic performance was a central concern of the UK government. The speech made by the then Prime Minister, James Callaghan, at Ruskin College, Oxford, in 1976 marks the beginning of the intense political interest in Education, particularly over the control of the curriculum. Callaghan, in broadening the debate about the nature and purposes of education not only gave impetus to the attack upon the professional status of the teacher, but also placed at the centre of the debate a view that education should be directed towards the needs of an underachieving economy. It was this that gave impetus to the technical models of teacher evaluation; a development described by Grace as a return to basics. Ball provides evidence to suggest that since the early 1980s teachers have been blamed for Britain's economic decline.[18] They have been accused of both hanging on to old curricula and methods, and succumbing to 'progressive methods'.

The 1988 Education Reform Act represents a move from a period of relative teacher autonomy to a period of public accountability which has intensified the search for accurate measures of classroom performance. The Act attempted to regulate teachers and to offer harder methods of assessing them. It did this, in part, through prescribed external procedures for assessing pupil achievement and a ten-level National Curriculum.[19] In addition, Local Management of Schools and Formula Funding introduced market forces into education.

Elliott suggests that market forces encourage a 'technical' view of the teacher, a view which, as we shall see later, negates the idea of professionalism. Alongside this technical view he describes the reflective practitioner, and provides rationalist models. However, it is difficult to find this rationalist view represented in the current literature. The rationalist model is being replaced by what could be termed the ideologically reliable model of the 1850s, a model described by Lawlor and O'Hear.[20] This view emphasizes the transmission of attitudes as well as 'objective knowledge'.

Norris expresses doubts about the current aims of evaluative enquiry in education because of the limits that contractual control places upon the wider debate about policy.[21] These external constraints reflect the values of the contracting agency and create a form of education which is restricted to a measurement of predetermined social utility. Willms considers that monitoring school teachers and their performance cannot be objective because decisions have to be made about the time, place and topic of the monitoring.[22] The picture of teacher evaluation is further confused by the absence of an uncontested model of teacher effectiveness and a lack of consensus on the goals of schooling.

Vold and Nomisham make reference to the criteria used for evaluation.[23] Their examples range from 'appears enthusiastic', 'has sense of humour', 'believes in God' through to 'competence in varied types of instructional technology'.[24] They recognize the drawbacks attached to identifying criteria which attempt to be neutral. The same criteria cannot be applied to all teachers in all situations, and the isolation of bits of teacher behaviour is not only difficult, they claim, but also undesirable because:

> observing only the technical skills tends to ignore the emotional ramifications of teaching, and the ingenuity that effective teachers have to invent dynamic patterns which create learning and excite students.[25]

Finally, Vold and Nomisham warn against drawing conclusions about student achievement from the assessment of teacher attributes. Elliott develops this point more fully in his critique of the social market perspective on education.[26]

In the social market system performance indicators are meant to represent a value-free production process. In order to judge a school and teacher's performance selected data representing pupil performance is taken out of context and simplified. Elliott contends that in this way the data itself becomes meaningless. He argues that education is an enabling process. It should be evaluated through the extent to which the educational process enables the pupils to access the resources they need to develop their potential. He concedes that this form of evaluation is dependent upon values, but claims that it is bogus to suggest that performance indicators are not. Performance indicators are biased because they only measure certain things, and these reflect what their authors view to be important. In addition, a technical difficulty associated with performance indicators is the possibility that teachers will not see the urgency of the collection of accurate information, if the items are perceived as being selected by outside interests.[27]

Elliott argues for a different kind of indicator, and makes reference to an OECD project in Italy where quality indicators were used to measure the success of educational practice. This approach emphasizes education as an enabling rather than a causal process. Quality indicators measure a teacher's performance against a number of educational values. He argues that these values need to be constantly reviewed and defined. As examples of quality criteria Elliott offers Stenhouse's procedural principles:

> discussion rather than instruction should be the core activity in the classroom;
> teachers should protect divergence in discussion;
> teachers should avoid using their authority position to promote their own views by adopting a role of procedural neutrality.[28]

Evidence of these indicators would be ethnographic and qualitative in nature, provided through collaborative action research, an approach that lies within the reflective practitioner model and is very different to the technical view. It is the technical view of those who wish to see education involved in a social market which has led to the development of competency-based approaches to teacher education in the UK.[29] This market approach has encouraged attempts to define the basic skills of teaching. The Council for the Accreditation of Teacher Education lists five competency areas.[30] Beardon *et al.* identify seven groups of competence and advocate certification at NVQ level 4.[31] This would lead to level 5 for further professional qualifications. They stress that

> For accurate communication of the outcomes of competence and attainment, a precision in the use of language in such statements needs to be established, approaching that of a science. The overall model stands or falls on how effectively we can state competence and attainment.[32]

This view of competence in classroom performance provides a 'technical' perspective, one where it is easy to argue that measurement of teacher performance can be objective and value free.

Kyriacou criticizes this perspective of competence.[33] Whilst he too produces a list of seven 'key teaching skills' he contends that:

There cannot be, nor could there ever be a definitive list of classroom teaching competences or a definitive set of classroom rating scales. Nevertheless, the degree of overlap between the different lists and observation schedules in current use does suggest a fair degree of consensus has emerged.[34]

Despite agreement on the essential areas of classroom performance there is a difficulty when it comes to the calibration of competence in the manner suggested by Beardon.[35] Kyriacou describes classroom expertise as 'complex and problematic' and is concerned with competence-based approaches to teacher education, in that 'a narrow conception of classroom expertise in terms of competences can in effect de-skill and undermine professionalism'.[36]

Both the reflective practitioner and the technical views of teacher evaluation have regard for the intellectual and moral development of children. However, the former links the development of individuals to the context and specifics of the learning situation, and draws upon the creative nature of the educational process, whilst the technical perspective isolates the educational process from its surroundings, as competence once achieved is understood to be appropriate to any number of contexts and changed circumstances. These traditions owe much to the philosophy of naturalism, an approach to education which, in England and Wales, has often been associated with the education of 'low achievers', and those suited to the 'vocational'.[37] However the influence of naturalism in England has never dominated. It has always been subservient to the transmission of 'high culture' embodied in encyclopaedism, where all pupils study 'valid' subjects, and humanism, where the moral dilemmas of responsibility are the concern of an educational élite.

Encyclopaedism and humanism find favour with those of the ideologically reliable perspective. O'Hear, who expresses views consistent with this perspective, sees an important role for inspection in a market-based system of education. Inspectors would publish 'consumer guides to schools' to enable decisions to be made by parents on the basis of 'objective comments'. By this means inspectors could ensure quality in education. He outlines the values which he feels would constitute a quality education:

> The goals of true education are to give a training in morality and taste, to inculcate certain basic abilities and attitudes, and to provide for a disinterested study of the best that has been thought and said, for those who are able or willing to profit from it.[38]

The view isolates the school from the community, because it views youth, class and popular culture as subordinate to the high culture of 'the best that has been thought and said'. O'Hear could be charged with calling for the indoctrination of pupils; how else can a child have abilities and attitudes inculcated?

The aim of such 'high culture' is to improve people, government and society. Quite whose standards are used to measure this improvement are open to speculation, although in his picture of classroom relationships O'Hear gives some clues.

> Education cannot be democratic because educating involves imparting to a pupil something which he has yet to acquire. The imparting has to be done by someone who possesses what the pupil lacks. The transaction is therefore inevitably between unequals ... Education then is irretrievably authoritarian and paternalist.[39]

Earlier, O'Hear discusses the qualities of a good teacher. These are primarily 'a sound knowledge and love of the subject' and practical skills of teaching 'acquired in and through experience and doing, rather than through talking and thinking abstractly'.[40] Here O'Hear draws heavily on another approach of English education, a form of humanism which draws heavily upon individualism and action and where 'thought is the enemy of action' and can be viewed as 'frivolous'. 'Theory is differentiated from practice and is viewed as a distinctly subordinate partner'.[41] This tradition creates schools that are strong on practical activity but weak on rationality. Here the aim of education is to communicate one's subject; other matters should not be allowed to interfere.

Oliver, in presenting a model of teacher evaluation,

concentrates upon three issues: teacher intent, teaching style and the consequences.[42] He suggests that an evaluation of these by an observer leads to problems associated with the values underlying the process. Use of phrases such as 'excessive formality of approach' or 'too little student involvement' cannot be related to precise measurements of teacher effectiveness unless the values underlying such terms as 'excessive' or 'too little' are investigated. He argues that this problem should not prevent the evaluation of teacher effectiveness. He says that, as with professional judgement, the values underlying such calibration of performance should be open to scrutiny from those with an interest in education. He argues that the declaration of these underlying values and the search for agreement may lead to imprecise measurement, but, as Norris similarly argues about competence, greater precision in evaluation causes more problems than it solves.

This literature review indicates a range of perspectives regarding teacher assessment. In order to aid analysis these perspectives can be briefly summarized as: those who view the evaluation of teacher performance as a purely technical matter where assessment objectives are determined by the needs of the economy; those who view the measurement of teacher performance as largely a matter of 'common sense', to be carried out by those who are 'experts' in their chosen field; and those who consider teacher evaluation as a social process, informing and shaping practice. It is against this background that recent legislation has attempted to introduce simple, objective measures of teacher performance.

What sort of answers are we getting?

An understanding of the 1988 Education Reform Act is central to an understanding of the nature of teacher assessment. One consequence of this act was to demand the publication of performance indicators. Performance indicators standardize information to allow comparison of schools and their teachers. The key indicators relate to the reporting and assessment of pupil performance at the ages of 7,

11, 14, and 16. These Key Stage tests (they were originally called tasks) are in the three core National Curriculum subjects of maths, science and English. They are administered nationally and the results are published in a form that allows comparison between schools. In addition, information from 16-year-olds and those at school at 17 and 18 would be provided by the examination boards through GCSE, 'A' Level and vocational results. These 'league tables' increase pressure on individual teachers to contribute to their school's performance.

In addition to standardizing curriculum content and testing in the state sector in England and Wales, the Act also introduced Local Management of Schools (LMS), which largely depends upon formula funding. This formula ties a minimum of 80 per cent of school funding to pupil numbers; in many local authorities it is well over 90 per cent.

LMS was an important innovation because the funding of schools was directly linked to the number of pupils on the school roll. An increase in the number of pupils leads to increased funding, a decline to reduced funding. However, changes in pupil numbers would first have to be agreed to by the Secretary of State. The Key Stage tests were to provide important information for the Secretary of State when making decisions about the expansion, contraction or closure, of schools. To help parents make decisions about school choice, schools were required to provide parents and local authorities with the performance indicators demanded by the 1988 Education Act.

Thus the success of a school was to be judged by outcomes. So, although the reflective perspective would view teaching as an enabling process, a school's, and consequently an individual teacher's performance was to be judged by product. These measures were much less troublesome for those who had a view of education which relied upon the inculcation of ideological reliability, or the input/output approach of the technicians.

The teacher unions in particular responded negatively to the introduction of national tests, a key performance indicator:

David Hart, NAHT General Secretary:
Compilation of the tables was 'a monumental waste of time'.

Doug McAvoy, NUT General Secretary:
We need more sophisticated tables which include measures such as school funding, class sizes, and the proportion of children with nursery education. Instead Mr. Patten has failed to recognise that, likewise, each year's group is different. His value added measure will only tell parents whether this year's vintage was different from the last.[43]

The reasons for this response are complex. In part, it was a desire to protect the status of teacher assessment of pupil progress; partly it was due to the increased workload imposed by the administration and marking of the tests; but it was also a response to Government moves towards performance-related pay, an issue explored later in this chapter.

In 1993 all six teaching associations opposed the tests. This prevented the return of the results and made them unavailable for comparability purposes. The boycott in 1994, although supported only by the NUT, resulted in fewer than one in ten schools returning results to the Government. Meanwhile, the Secretary of State, mindful that the NAS/UWT's opposition to testing was on the basis of workload, decided to provide external markers at an estimated cost of between £12 and £14 million.[44]

The General Secretary of the Secondary Headteachers Association (SHA) opposed the tables from a different perspective, 'the tables were becoming a bureaucratic monster. Mr. Patten would do better to stop simply at publishing GCSE and A level results'.[45] This view was also to be reflected in the *Sunday Telegraph* 6 June 1994 ('How to Waste £112 million'), but for the time being the Government, the Pay Review Body and the SCAA working party are moving along the road of value added. But for how long?

Opposition to performance indicators did not mean opposition to the measurement of pupil attainment. Birmingham LEA introduced target setting which would be used for individual pupils and schools to compete 'against their own previous best'. Whilst the Labour Party promised to set up an inquiry into 'ways of measuring the effectiveness of schools' – assessment procedures that detect the shortcomings in pupils' learning, rather than tests that enable league tables to be constructed.[46]

It would be a mistake to view legislation relating to schools as a number of isolated acts. Initially both performance indicators and appraisal were attempts to assess and reward teachers. The 1986 Education (No. 2) Act, along with Statutory Instrument 1991/1511, introduced teacher appraisal in all maintained schools on a phased basis from 1992.

The teachers' associations supported the developmental aspects of the appraisal process and saw appraisal as separate from procedures relating to pay and conditions, a fact reflected in some school schemes and local authority guidelines. It was the developmental nature of appraisal that Keith Joseph, Secretary of State for Education, chose to emphasize in a speech in 1985:

> To be fully effective an appraisal system would have to be complemented by better arrangements for the individual teacher's career development – including induction, in-service training, guidance on possible teaching posts and promotion. When I refer to the management of the teaching force I have this whole range of positive activity in mind.[47]

However, the difference in approach between the teachers' representatives and their employers is apparent in the discussion about the uses of appraisal. Government legislation did not stop at the outline of appraisal described above. In his speech the Secretary of State went on to say:

> I am frequently misquoted in terms that suggest that I am only concerned with the need to dismiss the very small number of incompetent teachers who cannot be restored to adequate effectiveness. That is not the case, I am concerned with the whole range of positive advantages that would flow from applying to the teaching force standards of management which have become common elsewhere.[48]

It is where the Secretary of State makes reference to 'incompetent teachers' and 'standards of management which have become common elsewhere' that the government and some commentators part company with the representatives of teachers. Furthermore, the Schools Minister said 'It is not realistic or desirable to have a Chinese wall between salary and teacher assessment'.[49] This situation was spelt out in law.

> Relevant information from appraisal records may be taken into account by head teachers, Chief Education officers or any offi-cers or advisors – in advising those responsible for taking decisions on the promotion, dismissal or discipline of school teachers or on the use of any discretion in relation to pay.[50]

The National Union of Teachers said this of appraisal:

> The National Union of Teachers has consistently supported appraisal for professional development. Introduced for this purpose, appraisal should lead to better quality teaching and learning … Introduced for the wrong reasons and linked to discretionary pay, appraisal will divide the profession and not unite it.[51]

At the NUT Conference in 1992 the union opposed appraisal if it was to be linked to pay or disciplinary matters; if the appraisal document was to be seen by governors; if it was not the sole property of the appraisee. One speaker had this to say:

> There is a new mood out there amongst some of the more bullish head teachers. Appraisal will be used by unscrupulous heads, desperate governors and local authorities keen to lose jobs. It will be used to create a climate of despair and demorali-sation. The schemes are superficial and underfunded, cheap, shoddy and ineffective.[52]

The Statutory Instrument of 1991 had already stated that a copy of the appraisal document would be kept by the head-teacher and would be accessible to the headteacher, the Chief Education Officer, the Appraisal Review Officer and the chair of the governing body.

Despite an agreement amongst teacher associations and the Government about the nature of the process of appraisal, the fundamental disagreement over the use of the end product created an uncertain picture of the implementation of appraisal in schools. There are reports of schools where the appraisal process has been geared to the demands of performance-related pay.[53] However the NAS/UWT suggest that appraisal may meet a rather different fate: 'There is more than one way of skinning the cat ... Appraisal which can involve much checking of forms would be "kicked into touch"'.[54] This paper does not attempt to undermine the value of appraisal as a developmental tool, in fact the author welcomes its use for this purpose. It is clear, however, that appraisal does not appear to be fulfilling its function of assessing teacher performance, an intention that clearly lay behind its introduction.

In addition to the introduction of performance indicators and appraisal, the nature of school inspection was changed in 1992 when the Education (Schools) Act greatly reduced the role of Her Majesty's Inspectorate (HMI) in school inspection. It encouraged a free market in the four-yearly cycle of inspection, where teams of registered inspectors would bid for the contract to inspect a particular school. One innovation was the inclusion of lay inspectors, whose main qualification was their lack of professional involvement in schools. This innovation could be seen as a method of introducing the ideologically reliable, or common sense view of education, an attempt to cut through what might be interpreted as the vested interests of the educational establishment.

The *Handbook for the Inspection of Schools* provides a framework along with guidance and advice on inspection.[55] Those who hold a technical perspective could view the framework as neutral. However, placed in the context of educational legislation since 1988, there are additional pressures to interpret the framework through the perspective of ideological reliability. These two perspectives have a summative quality: Can this person teach? How well do they teach? At the same time, the third perspective (that of the 'reflective practitioner') asks contextual questions relating to the factors which may promote 'good', 'satisfactory' or 'poor' teaching. This final perspective could lead to information from the OFSTED inspection being used in a diagnostic manner rather than as a 'consumer guide'.

The handbook itself relies upon the 'input-output' construction of the technical perspective. The standard of pupil achievement in relation to national norms and pupil abilities, along with the quality of teaching, are all graded on a five-point scale, determined by specified evaluation criteria. This leads to the use of common descriptors (very good, good, satisfactory, unsatisfactory, poor) across all OFSTED school reports. According to Russell this has often meant that

> the process of inspection has been reduced from a complex art to a bureaucratic set of checks. Some report findings are obvious and unilluminating. The twin effects of Ofsted's detailed prescription of method, and the constraint caused by competition for contracts at affordable costs, have been to generate reports whose mediocrity is not a fair representation of the talents of those who contribute to them.[56]

If one of the major purposes of inspection is the desire for accountability through 'objective' information then the 'contextualist' or 'situationist' perspective of those subscribing to the reflective practitioner model would induce caution in the production of potentially damning information. In addition, Bennet suggests that the 'inspectors, apparently, especially value teachers who are open and self-evaluating'.[57] This observation suggests that inspectors are mindful of the reflective practitioner view of teaching.

One of the central purposes of OFSTED Inspection has been 'improvement through inspection'.[58] Recommendations for change use a technical perspective, and are provided to the senior management team, including the Headteacher and Governors, who draw up an action plan. However, the quality of the assessors as well as the assessments are often considered by the school before action is taken. One reason for this is that the reports can be questioned prior to publication on the basis of factual inaccuracies, but not on the basis of disputes over judgements made by the inspectors.

The report itself cannot be used for the identification of teacher performance. However, the departmental feedback is verbal, as is the feedback at the end of the inspection prior to the publication of the report. There are unofficial opportunities for reports on individual performance, although this is strictly outside OFSTED procedures. Given that the inspection is a snapshot of a teacher's performance, the inspectors' comments would be of limited value, except where this provided further support for views already held within the school.

OFSTED inspection has a limited role in the identification and reward of outstanding teachers. The reports themselves strive for a technical perspective on a school's performance, but this is tempered by the ideologically reliable and the reflective values of those who inspect. It could be argued that the inspectors themselves are using their professional judgement in order to ameliorate the more potentially damaging effects of the technical approach. The result, for parents, are reports and summaries, which, in the main, obfuscate rather than elucidate.

The final piece of legislation to be considered in this chapter is the 1991 School Teachers Pay and Conditions Act. This had the effect of imposing pay and conditions upon teachers through a review body which was to consider these matters. It was this body which subsequently was to report to the Secretary of State for Education on the issues of performance related pay (PRP) and incentives for outstanding classroom performance. Some of the difficulties associated with the introduction of PRP were highlighted in a *Guardian* editorial:

> The [teachers] have every reason to resist Mr. Clarke's daft idea of linking pay to the crude league tables of examination results due to be published next year. Payment by results was eliminated from the school system in 1895. It is impossible to separate the various factors (home, pupils, school) let alone teacher from teacher. But a more sophisticated performance-related pay scheme is long overdue.[59]

In February 1992 the Teachers' Pay Review Body rejected the Secretary of State's request for performance-related pay on the basis that

> nobody, including Sir Graeme Day's review body, has so far devised a fair way to judge the performance of individual

teachers. The pay review body accepts that it will be several years before teacher appraisal and full national testing will be available across the country.[60]

The Secretary of State – whilst accepting that examination and National Curriculum test results, truancy and staying on rates were all indicators of performance – felt that raw data was possibly unacceptable for use in performance-related pay due to the influence of social factors. He decided that further research into the concept of value added was needed before a formula could be devised.

However, in 1994 Croydon Local Education Authority did respond to the Government's desire to link performance-related pay to performance indicators, despite a barrage of criticism. It allocated one per cent of its teaching budget to schools and individual teachers on the basis of improvements to test and examination results.[61]

Is this the best way to judge teachers?

Schools do reward classroom performance, but more often than not in an *ad hoc* manner. Allowances for Initial Teacher Training responsibility, provision of Special Educational Needs support, or responsibility for the organization of resources are more likely to be justifications of financial reward than an assessment of outstanding classroom performance. Decisions about performance continue to be made, but Government attempts to legislate into practice accountability procedures that are transparent, and responsive to market forces, are meeting with resistance. It is clear that those charged with the responsibility to implement recent legislation do not appear to be entirely at ease with these developments.

In the first part of this chapter a number of current issues in evaluation were explored as reported by several writers. Some were less explicit than others about the values that underpinned their arguments. It appears from current experience of statutory assessment that such values are a source of tension within these systems. These, at times, conflicting values determine not only the nature of the judgement, but what is worthy of judgement.

The inconsistencies of teacher assessment systems reflect the subjective nature of the values which underpin them. Similarly, Brown and McIntyre recognize the influence of subjective factors on teacher performance

> even when they have gone through the same training programmes and are employed in similar positions different personal histories, beliefs, values and concepts of themselves as teachers seem to shape the knowledge and skills on which teachers depend in their classroom teaching.[62]

Meanwhile, Goodson demands that teachers should recognize the influence of subjective experience upon their performance, and make others aware of this. '[The] teacher's voice is important because teachers import data about their own lives into discussions about curriculum development, subject teaching, school governance and general school governance.'[63] Teachers ought not to be afraid of revealing the depth and breadth of the classroom experience. There is an awareness amongst those involved in teaching and the assessment of teaching, that the classroom situation is complex and that the values of the teachers and their assessors are an important part of that complexity.

Attempts by government to assess the performance of teachers appear to be floundering. Performance-Related Pay (PRP), OFSTED, Appraisal and Performance Indicators fail to deliver meaningful judgements about the quality of teaching, to the chagrin of some, and the relief of others. These approaches to teacher assessment either misinform, are used for development purposes, or are largely ignored. Assessment of teacher performance has taken place in the past and continues to do so, but, to those outside the school community, the processes are often impenetrable and the rewards, sanctions and development unapparent. Current assessment procedures continue to mask the reality.

The representatives and agencies of government wish to assess teachers largely through indicators that quantify performance. This has met resistance from teachers. Those with the responsibility for teacher assessment also appear reluctant to apply simple measures of quantity or quality. There is a recognition that other things of value, things that are difficult to measure, are taking place in classrooms and are deserving of protection from current assessment preoccupations. However, this projection is often in the form of the old, undefined variant of professional judgement, which is being re-asserted in a manner which preserves the mystique of teaching, and does little to enable parents and the wider community to hold teachers more accountable for their performance.

Recent changes to teacher assessment are but a small part of the UK's response to major developments in the world economy. Globalization has become a cliché, but nonetheless there is likely to be a continued decline in the real wages of unskilled labour by two per cent per annum.[64] In order to increase real wages in the northern hemisphere more complex, skilled work has to be provided. This change alone is creating demands for a 'needs' orientated education system. A major feature of such a system is the emphasis upon lifelong education and the development of attitudes which promote individual responsibility for learning. These features are congruent with an education system which develops multi-skilled problem-solvers, and is one model for education. However, if the economy settles on a low skill, intermittently employed work force then the drive will be for nothing more than a basic education for the many and a 'high culture' education for the few.[65] The current drive towards competence and the simplification of educational measurement fits more comfortably with this latter model. If the majority of the future work force is simply required to follow instructions then this ability can be quantified through performance indicators. If we are to ask more of people then there is a need for greater rigour in teacher assessment.

It is not clear from the actions of those in a position to make changes to the UK infrastructure which of these two models of education they support. The aims of those who instigate educational change are not always explicit, and this lack of candour can leave teachers uncertain as to whether their own values and aims will find favour with those who wish to judge them. People enter teaching for a variety of reasons. Rarely has the author met a teacher in secondary education who is there simply in order to help children pass an exam or test for its own sake. Some see themselves involved in intellectual training; some have a love of their subject; others view their efforts as a contribution to vocational preparation; some emphasize the development of moral and social values; others have more political aims, in that they hold that education can be a key to change, or to social and economic advancement for individuals or groups. Undoubtedly other aims are left unspoken. These are often hidden behind the smokescreens of professionalism and professional judgement, and, at a time of economic and social instability, it is difficult to blame teachers for this.

Earlier, we considered Oliver's model of education which depends upon the declaration of underlying values, so that teacher intent, style of teaching and consequences can be considered. If the work of teachers is to be properly evaluated then the values that teachers hold need to be expressed, so that the communities that teachers serve can consider the worth of these values and measure their impact. In an age of accountability, a system of professional judgement cloaked in mystery is vulnerable to a charge of élitism, and recent attempts to develop performance indicators ill serve the efforts of teachers and pupils alike, as well as raise serious questions about the aims of the education system. We must look beyond the mask that assessment has become in order to evaluate our teaching. A useful beginning would be to listen to teachers. Then the broader community can begin to understand what teachers are trying to achieve and can begin to make informed decisions about the teaching we really want.

Notes and references

1. Paxman, J. My Best Teacher *Times Educational Supplement* 10 March 1995, p. 24.
2. Nevin, P. My Best Teacher *Times Educational Supplement* 15 Sept. 1995, p. 24.
3. Swindells, R. My Best Teacher *Times Educational Supplement* 17 Feb. 1995, p. 24.

4. Grace, G. (1985) Judging teachers: the social and political contexts of evaluation. *British Journal of Sociology of Education* Vol. 6 No. 1, pp. 3–15.
5. Edmonds, E. *The School Inspector* (London: Routledge and Kegan Paul, 1962), 130.
6. Ibid., 81.
7. Tropp, A. *The Schoolteachers* (London: Heinemann, 1957).
8. Ibid., 177.
9. Ball, J. (1988) Staff relations during the teachers industrial action: context, conflict and proletarianisation *British Journal of Sociology of Education* Vol. 9 No. 3, pp. 289–306. Grace, G. (1985) op. cit. Lawn, M. and Ozga, J. Unequal partners: teachers under indirect rule. *British Journal of Sociology* Vol. 7, 1986, No. 2, pp. 225–38.
10. Grace, G. (1985) op. cit., 11.
11. O'Hear, A. (1988) *Who Teaches The Teachers?* (London: Social Affairs Unit, 1988).
12. Elliott, J. (ed.) (1993) *Reconstructing Teacher Education* (London: Falmer, 1993) Schön, D. (1983) *The Reflective Practitioner: How Professionals Think in Action* (New York: Basic Books, 1983).
13. Callaghan, J. (1976) Towards a national debate *Education* 148, 22 October 1976, 332–33.
14. Schön (1983) op. cit.
15. Ball, J. (1988) op. cit.
16. Norris, N. (1991) The trouble with competence *Cambridge Journal of Education* 21, 1991, 331–41.
17. Gardner, D.E. Five evaluation frameworks: implications for decision making in higher education *Journal of Higher Education* 48, 1977, 574.
18. Ball, J. (1988) op. cit.
19. Elliott, J. (1993) op. cit.
20. Lawlor, S. *Teachers Mistaught? Training Theories of Education in Subjects* (London: Centre for Policy Studies, 1990). O'Hear *Education and Democracy* (London: Claridge, 1991).
21. Norris, N. *Understanding Educational Evaluation* (London: Kogan Page, 1990).
22. Willms, J.P. *Monitoring School Performance: A Guide for Educators* (London: Falmer, 1992).
23. Vold, E.B. and Nomisham, D.A. Teacher Appraisal in Cullingford, C. (ed.) (1989) *The Primary Teacher* (London: Cassell, 1989).
24. Ibid., 141.
25. Ibid., 144.
26. Elliott, J. (1993) op. cit.

27. Climaco, C. Getting to know schools using performance indicators: criteria indicators and processes *Educational Review* 44 (3), 1992, 295–308.
28. Elliott, J. (1993) op. cit.
29. Davis, E. (1993) *Schools and the State* (London: Social Market Foundation, 1993).
30. Council for the Accreditation of Teacher Education. The accreditation of initial teacher training under circulars 9.92 and 35.92, a note of guidance from the Council for the Accreditation of Teacher Education (London: CATE, 1992).
31. Beardon, T., Booth, M., Hargreaves, D. and Reiss, M. School-led initial teacher training: the way forward. Dept. of Education, University of Cambridge, 1992.
32. Ibid., 41–42.
33. Kyriacou, C. Research on the development of expertise in classroom teaching during initial training and the first year of teaching *Educational Review* 45 (1), 1993, 79–87.
34. Ibid., 85.
35. Beardon *et al.* (1992) op. cit.
36. Kyriacou (1993) op. cit., 85–6.
37. McLean, M. *Britain and a Single Market Europe* (London: Kogan Page, 1990).
38. O'Hear (1991) op. cit., 39.
39. O'Hear (1991) op. cit., 6.
40. O'Hear (1988) op. cit., 17.
41. McLean (1990) op. cit., 94.
42. Oliver, P. Quality in the classroom: philosophical aspects of measuring teacher effectiveness *Vocational Aspects of Education* 44 (2), 1992, 183–90.
43. Preston, B. Patten tries to woo teachers with new league tables *The Times* 8 June 1994, p. 6.
44. Meikle, J. (1994) Patten brings in external markers to beat boycott *Guardian* 2 July 1994, p. 1.
45. Preston, B. (1994) op. cit., 6.
46. Macleod, D. (1994) The vision thing *Guardian* 21 June 1994, p. 6.
47. Ball, J. (1988) op. cit., 292.
48. Ibid., 292.
49. Eggar, J. *Guardian* 4 April 1991, p. 4.
50. DES (1991) Statutory Instrument 1991/1511 (London: HMSO, 1991), para 14.1.
51. NUT (1991) *Appraisal: Your Rights and Expectations* (London: NUT, 1991), 3–4.
52. Bates, S. Teachers head for a boycott *Guardian* 20 April 1992, p. 1.
53. Berliner, W. (1991) Teacher appraisal: all on target. Wendy

Berliner on a school that is hooked on the bonus system *Guardian* 14 May 1991, p. 23.

54. Ward, D. and Meikle, J. (1993) Teacher Unions to kick appraisal into touch *Guardian* 14 April 1993, p. 2.

55. OFSTED (1993) *The Handbook for the Inspection of Schools* (London: OFSTED, 1993).

56. Russell, S. *Education* 184 (17), pp. 311–13, October 1994.

57. Bennet, P.L. (1994) Many Happy Returns *Education* Vol. 184 no. 11, p. 195.

58. OFSTED/Coopers and Lybrand (1994) *A Focus on Quality* (London: OFSTED, 1994), 7.

59. *Guardian* Beyond the battered sedan 28 October 1991, p. 4.

60. Tytler, D. Extra pain award *Guardian* 18 Feb. 1992, p. 21.

61. Young, S. Heads reject pioneer performance payments *Times Educational Supplement* 22 April 1994, p. 1.

62. Brown, S. and McIntyre, D. *Making Sense of Teaching* (London: Open University, 1993).

63. Goodson, I. Studying teachers lives: International Analysis of Teacher Education *Journal of Education and Training*, 1994, paper 1, p. 225.

64. Mintford, P. Policies and prospects in a world of emerging markets. Lecture to the Economics and Business Education Association Annual Conference. Liverpool. April 1995.

65. Macdonald, R. and Coffield, F. (1991) *Risky Business: Youth and the Enterprise Culture* (London: Falmer, 1991).

CHAPTER 5

Culture and 'Subjectivity' in the Discourse of Assessment: A Case Study

PETER SANDERSON

Introduction

The annual cycle of the release of public examination results in the United Kingdom is now regularly accompanied by controversy over competing claims of rising and falling standards. This controversy throws into sharp relief the tension generated in the process of assessment by its character, as an individual act of judgement on the one hand, and on the other as a process which is profoundly cultural, a tension accentuated by the dichotomy between ideologies which hold knowledge to be objective and monolithic, and those which believe knowledge to be contingent, relative and plural. So, for the Director General of the Institute of Management, the evidence of increased success rates at A level is in fact a demonstration that 'A levels have become a devalued currency, providing a passport to higher education, but failing to prepare individuals for the real world'.[1] Underlying this criticism is the belief that either the 'subjective' character of examiner judgement is being manipulated to generate improved results (as in criticisms of the move to favour 'authentic responses in GCSE'), or that it is the character of the 'knowledge' being examined which is suspect, with subjects being introduced into the scope of A levels which do not really 'belong' there.[2] As Phillip Brown argues,[3] although there is consistent pressure from employers' organizations and politicians to produce candidates with 'skills', the incorporation of skills into curricula is likely to devalue those curricula, 'given that the academic hierarchy remains tied to 'objective' performance in public examinations'.[4] This suspicion of new modalities of assessment and increasing pass rates for A levels appears to be deeply held, and one might infer that this suspicion coexists with equally deeply held doubts about the educability of working-class children. The consequence of these suspicions has been the proposal of the Dearing Review that the School Curriculum and Assessment Authority (SCAA) should have powers to compel exam boards to review the difficulty of all A levels with a view to making them harder to pass.[5]

Questions about the reliability of assessment come, however, not only from those apparently both sceptical and fearful of the possibility and consequences of mass access to higher education. The neutrality and objectivity of the system is also questioned by those sensitive to the apparent role of A levels in reinforcing restricted social mobility and access to higher education. At a common-sense level, the statement that 'it's all subjective' is the most persistent criticism of the assessment of public examinations.[6] Academic research has consistently appeared to lend support to the suspicion that examiners and examinations are at best of uneven reliability, from the classic study of Edgeworth,[7] through the studies of Hartog and Rhodes of the School Certificate in the 1930s,[8] to modern evidence about the SATs introduced with the National Curriculum.[9]

Much of the anxiety and controversy about assessment can be traced to the false dichotomy between 'subjective' and 'objective' judgements so indispensable to the continued legitimacy of the system, a false opposition parallel to that posed by the contradistinction between 'norm-referenced' and 'criterion-referenced' assessment. The weakness in the idea that assessment is governed by 'subjectivity' is that it is inconceivable that intelligible acts of judgement could take place, or individuals be placed in a relationship of relative merit to a population, without reference to cognitive schemata which must be cultural in origin. Consequently, the notion of pure 'subjectivity' in norm-referencing is unsustainable as a real condition. However, to elevate cognitive schemata to the status of 'objective' instruments of measurement which mimic the calibration of physical instruments is equally misguided. The statement of 'precise criteria' to guide judgement, as exemplified both by the increasing complexity of marking schemes at A levels and the influence of 'competency' and outcomes-based models of assessment in General National Vocational Qualifications are no guarantee that two individuals will agree that a given performance has met the description. Texts or performances are not, as both the traditional public examination and 'modern' models of skills assessment imply, self-evidently meaningful in themselves: observers and assessors have to make meaning out of the material. Therefore, as Alison Wolf argues, 'the process is complex, incremental, and above all, judgemental. The performance observed – directly, or in the form of artifacts – is *intrinsically* variable' (emphasis in original).[10]

Underlining the 'objective' model of assessment in the case of A levels is the view that an examination performance is to be judged as a representation of pure 'cognitive' processes, where the stimulus of the question draws a response which reveals candidates' capacities to solve a range of qualitatively different intellectual problems. The success of A levels in legitimizing distribution of social goods rests precisely in the notion that all elements of 'disposition' (or 'bias') have been expunged from the process, that what is being 'measured' so exactly is a 'pure' kind of cognition or 'knowledge'. Whilst there are few who would claim now that A levels measure 'intelligence', they can be seen instead as measuring 'attainment', a kind of cognitive mastery of tasks which is more specific and instrumental.[11] Yet this very concept of attainment indicates the fact that candidates, and their teachers, are engaged in an endeavour which is socially constructed. These activities and tasks which are the object of mastery are specific in form and vary both within (as is demonstrated by Pollitt *et al.*'s discussion of what makes questions difficult)[12] and between subjects or disciplines. This makes the overall task facing the candidate attempting more than one A level extremely complex.

This chapter explores the relationship between individuals and subjects in the process of assessment through the specific medium of sociology A level. After delineating a theoretical framework for understanding the relationship between examiner and candidate in the process of assessment, I develop this framework through a study of one specific interaction, which attempts to uncover the normally opaque processes of grappling with meaning engaged in by each side of the examination equation: candidate and examiner.

Candidates and examiners: a theoretical framework

The key concepts in this framework of analysis are drawn from Bourdieu's work on linguistic markets and cultural capital,13 and from sociolinguistic writing on discourse and genre.14 Both sets of concepts provide a means of articulating the relationship between individual linguistic performances and the social worlds within which they are inscribed.

I have already argued that the answers which candidates write in response to examination questions cannot be viewed as acts of 'pure' cognition. Candidates are not just attempting 'tasks' or solving problems, they are representing themselves as the kind of person who can solve problems. In terms of speech act theory,[15] the formulation of scripts can be viewed as perlocutionary, a series of performative acts. However, there is this distinction: in everyday interaction the rhetorical character of texts can be negotiated: misunderstandings arising from context or culture can be clarified, or, (to use the linguistic term) disambiguated. In writing, on the other hand, understanding is dependent on mutual adherence to rhetorical formulations which are commensurately understood by each party to the communicative act. This fact has a dual significance in relation to an examination answer. It is difficult, particularly in some of the humanities, to decide whether the 'knowledge' or 'skills' on display are authentic, or simply the consequence of skilled paraphrase; one of the persistent concerns of examiners is the 'well-rehearsed' answer. Secondly, lack of skill, or what Michael Hoey describes as 'rhetorical ineptness'[16] can render it difficult to perceive in a candidate's writing the degree of 'skill' or 'knowledge' that is actually there.

The cultural character of the academic prose which forms

the ultimate goal (for which A level acts as a kind of filter) is revealed through a number of studies of the difficulties of second language learners,[17] but it can be argued that for many native language speakers the difficulties are as acute.[18] In particular, the role of prosody in reducing the ambiguity of speech is substituted in writing by devices which are complex at a general level and require considerable rehearsal; but they are also particular, in that they are framed by their precise context. The presence or absence of structural factors varies widely across different writing contexts,[19] and the precise form which these features take may be governed by ground rules which are specific to given subjects or disciplines.[20]

For example, text linguists are particularly interested in the way in which texts are organized. This concern has recently been echoed by the Schools Curriculum and Assessment Council in their paper on quality of language: whilst much of their rationale for examining quality of language is based on issues of spelling, grammar and punctuation (already examined in GCSE), their sample texts and commentaries refer extensively to other 'structural' devices for 'linking' sentences and paragraphs.[21] Few of their examples, however, are structural in the sense that might commonly be understood, that is, providing a clear and unambiguous link between propositions (analogous to that of mathematical operators). These kinds of links, the kind described by Halliday and Hasan in their scheme of 'cohesive ties'[22] as conjunction ties (words like 'however', 'whilst', 'furthermore' and so on) do not generally depend on their context for meaning (which is why they could be used 'correctly' in the construction of meaningless sentences). By contrast, the bulk of devices for organizing text depend heavily on context and their relationship to lexical, rather than syntactic, elements to achieve their function.[23] Even when analysing the texts of skilled writers, it has been necessary for researchers to read passages aloud to each other so as to enable an enunciation of the prosody to determine whether a particular linguistic item is or is not 'cohesive'.[24] So even at the level of textual organization, let alone semantics (difficult as it is to separate the two), ambiguity is a constant rather than occasional feature of writing, and the means of reducing ambiguity for the purposes of making a judgement have to involve recourse to cultural experiences and assumptions which draw on a far wider field than that defined by the syllabus or the marking scheme.

The theoretical framework within which we need to place the relationship between the examiner and the examinee is one that places the text (produced by the candidate and judged by the examiner) within this wider field of cultural exchange, a field which includes a 'general' discourse of assumptions about language and its manifestation in writing, and a more specific discourse which is conceived as being particular to a 'subject' or discipline. Within this wider cultural field, communication occurs between examiners and candidates, although it is a curious, rather fractured communication, and one which is mediated by a complex market structure.

Markets, discourse and 'recognition'

Bourdieu's use of the term 'linguistic markets' is sometimes seen as a kind of metaphor, a parallel with economic markets, though Bourdieu himself is quite explicit in arguing that 'linguistic exchange – a relation of communication between a sender and a receiver, based on enciphering and deciphering, and therefore on the implementation of a code or a generative competence – is also an economic exchange. This exchange is established within a particular symbolic relation of power between a producer, endowed with certain linguistic capital, and a consumer (or a market), and is capable of procuring a certain material or symbolic profit'.[25] The instance of GCE examinations in the UK may be seen as a paradigm of the way in which linguistic, or symbolic, and economic markets may be seen as collapsing into one another. In terms of syllabus, the 'frame' of subjects and disciplines (to use Bernstein's terminology[26]) has progressively weakened with the incorporation of the notion of 'skills' into A levels (and with, ironically, the expansion of the volume of syllabus materials), and this movement has encouraged the development of a flourishing 'market' in texts, supporting materials, tutorials, 'student conferences', and teachers' conferences (sponsored on at least one occasion by publishers).[27]

Some actors in this market conform to Bourdieu's description of 'a body of specialists competing for the monopoly of cultural reproduction',[28] in that teachers may also examine for Examination Boards, write textbooks (and advertise their credentials as examiners in the publishers' fliers) and speak at conferences: this phenomenon indicates the symbiotic relationship between the Examination Boards, who may be considered as the key agents in defining the theoretical specifications of the discourse or 'discipline', and the market, which determines its realization in practice. A leading player in 'the market' has expressed the point thus:

> In developing a new product (syllabus) to compete in an estab-lished market (16+ educational institutions), a manufacturer (board) has a choice between going for substantial redesign and innovation, and producing an improved version of what is already available. The former usually carries the greater finan-cial risk. In the case of the educational market-place, there is an inertia embedded in textbooks, teaching styles, past examina-tion papers and sheer habits of thinking and of practice, that makes the option of large-scale innovation a particularly risky one.[29]

The tension between the quasi-legislative authority of the boards and the relative autonomy of the market produces areas of ambiguity which are exacerbated by the tortuous circle of communication between boards and candidates. Whilst the secrecy which once surrounded the aims and intentions of boards[30] has been converted into a qualified regime of 'freedom of information', the key process which determines the status of each individual candidate's communication, namely the standardization (or socialization to use Wolf's terminology) and the actual allocation of a mark to a script, takes place in private. The conversion of this judgement into a public form (a grade) renders it to a level of generality which is of little use to a candidate who wishes to revise her or his performance. So whilst the broad market of Sociology A level is characterized by apparent openness and ambiguity, with authoritative texts representing different views of what should be in the 'canon', different interpretations by key members of the 'canon', and different approaches to 'skills', make the final act of judgement absolute.

The absolute character of the judgement is clearly essential, given that the ultimate objective of the examination process is to render a complex human communication into a number: as the number can be seen indisputably as having an objective relationship with all the other numbers, so, logically, must the acts of judgement be seen as having an equally objective relationship with each other, and with acts of judgement which have taken place in other years.[31] In their communications back to the candidates, or more probably their teachers, in the form of Examiners' Reports, the examiners, by curious tricks of expression, transform their acts of judgement into the clear objective characteristics of candidates. So one report for history states that, 'it was once again evident that the more successful candidates have undertaken readings of up-to-date material', whereas the same point could equally and possibly more accurately be expressed as 'this year we examiners have once again rewarded highly references to recent material'. Readings of reports for different subject areas tend to produce a range of different qualities of judgement which examiners attempt to embed as absolute properties of candidates. In the case of English, the concern is often with 'style', under which rubric, structural properties of text are often confused with 'content', as in this example: 'the virtual absence of paragraphs in the body of a piece of writing results in turgid, undifferentiated content'. What appears to be the actual judgement here is that this examiner found it hard to perceive structure or meaning in a text without the support of paragraphing, but the quasi-legislative authority of the role allows the statement an unchallengeable authority. Bourdieu's critique of the Chomskyan use of the term 'competence' is brought to mind here:

The shift in vocabulary conceals the *fictio juris* through which Chomsky, converting the immanent laws of legitimate discourse into universal norms of correct linguistic practice, sidesteps the question of the economic and social conditions of the acquisition of the legitimate competence and the constitution of the market in which this definition of the legitimate and the illegitimate is established and imposed.[32]

This conversion of the normative into the 'objective' is an aspect of the way in which, as Bourdieu argues, the 'established order' comes to be viewed as natural through the 'disguised (and thus misrecognised) imposition of systems of classification and mental structures that are objectively adjusted to social structures'.[33] Clearly, however, unless a subject is examined by one sole examiner, this process of 'misrecognition' cannot be achieved by *fiat*, but we must rather look for complex processes of socialization which enable groups of examiners to judge often ambiguous texts with a sufficient degree of consistency. The concept of the linguistic market in itself does not seem precise enough for this purpose, so within the context of the linguistic market, let us look at the concepts of discourse and discourse community.

Examinations as discourse

John Swales defines a 'discourse community' as having common public goals; mechanisms for intercommunication amongst its members, which provide information and feedback; the use and possession of one or more 'genres', that is 'a class of communicative events, the members of which share some communicative purpose' and which 'exhibit various patterns of similarity in terms of structure, style, content and intended audience';[34] specific lexis; and a threshold level membership.[35] It is important to stress that it should not be seen as coterminous with Bourdieu's conception of the linguistic market. Our A-level candidates can be seen as actors in the linguistic market through their consumption of published resources and (through entry) examinations; like all consumers they can produce changes in the general paradigm of the linguistic market. They cannot, however, shape the key features of the discourse of A levels, since judgements about the legitimate features of that discourse (genre and lexis in particular) are exercised in an arena which is beyond their reach. The judgements about whether any individual examination script achieves a status of 'prototypicality' in the genre and discourse field are the province of examiners, who represent the 'parent' discourse community, operating behind closed doors.

The social process of establishing a 'discourse community' amongst an examining team is unlike those experienced by most of the discourse communities described by Swales, where the communication between members of the community is consistent over time, and the output generally public, and authored by members of the community themselves. In the case of A levels, the output is private, and decisions about 'prototypicality' are made by a parent discourse community none of whose members are likely to have produced an example of the genre very recently (and some of whom may never have produced one). The core of the socialization process is the examiners' standardizing meeting, where a common standard of judgement, and interpretation of the 'marking scheme' (which attempts to outline criteria which will support the acts of individual judgement) is attempted. This is often achieved through the common marking of 'sample scripts' by all the examiners, and the pronouncement of the 'correct' mark by the Senior or Chief Examiners. (These photocopied 'sample scripts' subsequently become points of reference for examiners when marking on their own.) The prolonged process of linguistic acculturation that may be characteristic of, say, the editorial board of an academic journal, is in this instance, therefore, considerably condensed.

The product of this process of acculturation should be the internalization of a set of perceptual 'schemata'[36] which allows judgement of texts to take place, and it is this set of schemata which characterize the discourse field. These schemata are not, I would argue, the 'criteria' as specified by the Examination Board in the marking scheme, but a framework drawing on an examiner's knowledge of the linguistic market and broader cultural phenomena (perhaps a view of what 'good students' are 'like') which enables her or him to operationalize the criteria. Bourdieu argues that these kinds of 'classificatory schemes', which in a sense 'embody' social structures, operate below the level of consciousness,[37] and indeed, even quite experienced examiners, when called upon to articulate their reasons for judgements of quality, find it difficult to do so. Therefore, retrieving them involves a kind of archaeological exercise. I have attempted to achieve this by recording examiners in the process of marking texts.

In the case of Sociology A level I would argue that the following schemata apply at a general level, though their application may, or the relative emphasis accorded to each will, vary from examiner to examiner (and from 'discipline' to 'discipline'). The definitions are supported by illustrations from the oral comments of an examiner, recorded whilst in the process of awarding a mark to an essay on social policy.

The first schema is concerned with structural elements in the text that one might associate with both macro-structural properties (such as Meyer's notion of 'hyper-structure'[38]) and micro-structural properties (the presence or absence of devices like cohesion ties or logical operators), and could be seen as relating to the idea expressed by the particular board whose syllabus we are considering as 'well-craftedness': 'If you don't tie it into the essay question to start with you'll lose it as you go'; 'She doesn't actually say the two things are connected'; 'We haven't had a separate paragraph'; 'That should be a new paragraph'. This schema appears to be used more in the process of reviewing a script than in the summary process of reaching a judgement.

The second schema is concerned with semantic reference, and appears to focus on the author's ability to express an unambiguous meaning to the examiner: 'It doesn't say anything in particular'; 'She's saying I agree with the question but'; and a concern with specificity that perhaps fits into this category: 'She needs to be more specific there where she says …'.

The third schema deals with 'truth claims' – evidentiality, veracity, relevance (or 'accuracy' as it is generally referred to in marking schemes). These elements, which are not exactly synonymous, appear to mingle in the process, but all refer to whether the text is 'right' in some way, whether arguments are supported, whether they are supported by material the candidate believes to be 'true', and whether they are supported by material which is 'accurate':

'Whether she can substantiate that with the reality of women doing that'; 'I'm going to need a few statistics here, a few figures or I'm going to start getting irritated'; 'Absolutely NO reference made to any sociological study, figures' (evidentiality)

'She or he is saying institutions were criticised by Goffman as being, but I'm not sure that it's relevant to the question' (relevance)

'I have to assume she's telling me the truth here' (veracity)

'Yet another one of those students who can't get their history together'; 'Enoch Powell is the first confusion' (accuracy).

This schema does seem to feature in the summary process of judgement.

The fourth schema concerns 'discourse integrity' – whether the discourse matches the preferred model internalized by the examiner, that is whether it appears as 'genuine sociology'. This schema appears to have a number of sub-elements some of which cross-reference to other schemata. For example, the issue of 'evidentiality' could be seen as one of the core elements of 'sociology' (whilst 'authenticity' is a contrasting quality in English), certainly in contradistinction to 'common sense', but there are other distinct elements, like 'naming', 'referencing', 'defining' (concepts, positions), and 'keeping to discourse boundaries'.

'Absolutely no reference made to any sociological study, figures and real sociological argument – they may discuss gender or the welfare state in general' (specific sociological evidentiality)

'I also see people's names mentioned which may or may

not be appropriate'; 'I would give this a tick. "Functionalists see this as." Well they certainly do – I would have liked a little elaboration on Townsend actually' (naming, referencing)

'This is a sociology essay but it feels as though it's a social policy essay'; 'We've got to the bottom of page three and so far we've had a little bit of history, then a little bit of description of where the elderly are but not the disabled or children specifically mentioned by the question, and now we've got a little bit about current social policy' (keeping to discourse boundaries)

'So what's that got to do with the state of the art?' (perhaps defining, though maybe this elides with the category of 'accuracy' above).

These elements of the text tend to receive considerable attention in the summary comments, and could be seen as a fulcrum around which other perceptions are turned.

The fifth schema concerns 'discourse textuality' – elements of the texture of the script which are indicative of the degree of congruence with the textual 'model' for the discourse, or for particular 'text types' within the discourse:

'Dump? What kind of word's that?' (writes 'slang')

'As I get older do I want to be compared to a prisoner? It's an insult, I can see what she means but it's a poorly chosen example ... it's inappropriate – you know?' (this seems to be to do with lexis – 'are the words appropriate to the context?' and this sense of appropriateness could be considered in relation to Halliday's[39] concepts of 'tenor' and 'mode')

'There's a lot of description there, she's just describing how it is for the elderly ... that's what I'd say anyway, rather than say, the question seems to be asking for you actually to describe what current social policy is assuming' (this seems to be about text-type, say 'descriptive' as opposed to 'evaluative' or 'discursive/expository').

This set of categories also receives quite considerable attention in summary comments, often with specific reference to the written criteria in the marking scheme, which also concern themselves with these elements in script.

Finally, I would argue that there is a schema concerned with 'propositional validity and propositional density', often referred to as 'points' by examiners. There appears to be a distinction between this field and the 'semantic'. Most sentences including 'She's saying ...' mark an identified proposition. The following passage summarizes a series of linked propositions:

'They got the difference between institutional and the reasons for it and I know she didn't say who these critics were but she did comment on that, the family was going to be depended on for community care, but Enoch Powell is the first confusion'. Written comments appear to focus more on propositions, than spoken comments, which range over a wider span of fields of judgement, e.g. 'Interesting, but the govt. policy was not predicated on Goffman's ideas but does tie in with your intro.'

The function of these schemata is to enable examiners to sort and differentiate text, to interpret text in structural terms, and to reach a judgement about text in terms of its 'prototypicality', the degree to which it conforms to the genre of a 'Sociology A level answer'. Whilst the aim of the overall process of judgement is to place text on a graded continuum of quality, the fact that these schemata are often applied to the text in order to decide on whether it either fits or doesn't fit the prototype, whether it is 'genuine' sociology or 'just' common sense, whether it is contrasting ideas or 'just' juxtaposing them,[40] leads to examiners looking for a 'sense' of appropriateness (and the words 'appropriate' and 'inappropriate' frequently recur in Examiners' Reports). This search for 'sense' is all the more important because of the ambiguity of much of the text. This ambiguity in turn is both a function of the relative lack of skill of the candidates in terms of clarifying ambiguous patterns deriving from speech by the use of 'linguistic devices' (such as logical operators, or 'discourse markers'), and also a function of the uncertainty created by the particular character of this 'discourse community'. It has been argued that our capacity to comprehend text is affected by our capacity to make 'causal bridging inferences',[41] to fill the space deliberately left by authors between sentences: some rhetorical devices (such as that described by Nash[42] as 'the Stack') depend precisely for their effectiveness on this space. Our judgement as to whether such an inference can be made, however, is dependent to a degree on the assumed status and attributes of the author, and the importance of the examiners' 'sense' of the qualities of the candidate is in the degree to which candidates will ultimately be 'given the benefit of the doubt' in instances where the text is ambiguous.

Consequently, there is a very real sense in which the script of an A-level candidate is a performed subjectivity: its author is trying to speak directly to another individual, even though this may not be in her or his own voice, but in one which is borrowed, so to speak, for the occasion. The degree to which this voice is viewed as 'appropriate' will ultimately determine the grade. The process is therefore intersubjective, but in a curious way. In everyday discourse, the subject forms and reforms in a process of continuous interaction with one or more interlocutors, and even in most forms of written communication, processes of adaptation occur in response to direct or indirect feedback. In the examination process, as we have already demonstrated, such feedback is very remote, delivered on a formative basis throughout courses by teachers attempting to mimic examiner judgements,[43] and on a summative basis, at a general level, through the opaque statement of a grade, and by examiners' reports (which few candidates will ever read). The communicative task candidates face in representing themselves favourably in text must therefore be seen as acutely difficult. Equally, examiners face a difficult task in establishing to their own satisfaction what candidates 'really' mean and what they are 'really' like.[44]

Examinations as intersubjectivity: a worked example

I now want to trace this process by examining both sides of the equation: the candidate's attempt to, as Bourdieu describes it, 'encipher' meaning, and the examiner's attempt to 'decipher' it. The following discussion is based on an investigation using a genuine A-level candidate (though one at the end of the first year of a two-year course), and an even more genuine A-level examiner working within his marking period. The 'candidate' (Martin) was asked to write a timed response to a question from a genuine A-level paper, and then was interviewed about what he had been trying to achieve in his writing (producing a taped 'protocol').[45] His script was then given to an A-level examiner (Dennis) who was currently marking scripts which included responses to the same question. The examiner marked the script and gave a taped protocol of his marking. This method provides an unusual account of the efforts of both sides to cope with this curious form of communication. The question concerned was worded as follows: 'How useful are official statistics for measuring class differences in criminal behaviour?' In discussing the evidence, I shall concentrate on the strategies employed by candidate and examiner in their complementary tasks, rather than the substantive issues. (Where appropriate I will provide details in the notes.)

The marking scheme provided by the Board defines the parameters of the discourse for this question in the description for the top markband: these boundaries are in terms of the 'canon' ('names' included are Chambliss, Merton, Cloward and Ohlin), a definition of the 'core' of the question 'the relationship between class and types of crime, and how these are constructed in the process of production of official statistics', and a definition of 'quality': 'well-crafted analyses' and material organized and 'focused on critical evaluative discussion'. This particular construction of the discourse probably leans more on some of the standard A-level texts than others. (The methodology of collecting statistics is placed off-centre in this account, as it is in the 'main' A-level text,[46] whilst it is absolutely central to one of the 'specialist' deviance texts.[47]

The first point of interest is the extent to which Martin was aware of an audience at all in constructing his answer; his awareness is in fact emphasized at several points through his narrative reconstruction of writing the answer. He signals this awareness on several occasions through expressions of uncertainty: 'I wasn't sure if this was really the rich vein I was supposed to be mining at this point'; 'It seems like perhaps this is not quite what they are looking for'; and by repeated use of modal auxiliaries, as in 'I should have begun the paragraph'. On two occasions he refers directly to teaching staff as a source for this awareness, and it seems to be clear that his teachers are trying to pick up criticisms of rehearsed answers and communicate to their students the examiners' demands for analysis and evaluation: 'I've always been told this is what we're trying to do, not to give lots of information but to give pieces of information that illustrate our understanding'; 'People have pointed this out that information seems to come in from nowhere and I haven't said why I've done this'. This sense of an imperative deriving from a sense of the discourse field is also present in some of the comments on substantive comment, particularly where he refers to 'getting things in', though as we can see when we get to the Examiner's comments, his interpretation of what the field is 'about' isn't necessarily a good guide.

Martin's opening comments make clear that he is sensitive to the need for a clear hyper-structure, the notion that writing scripts is about 'crafting', though simultaneously it is clear that the path to a well-crafted answer is by no means clear: 'The instant problem was picking out the elements that relate to class and show a balanced account'; 'I was pulling out the main areas that came to mind and trying to put them in some kind of order. I don't know if that worked to be honest'. Throughout the protocol he refers to structural elements and to strategies for working his way around the structure: 'I was trying to lead off by saying ...'; 'I was trying to get in/get out quickly'; 'The point about that last bit at the bottom is to return to the starting point and to round it off and move on to the next stage. Give that section a beginning and an end and move into the next section'; 'There was the weighing up I was thinking about. That is something else I've missed in an essay before'.

Interestingly, Martin identifies specific linguistic features as serving the function of 'adding meaning' to his text, and solving the 'just juxtaposition' problem: 'Mebbe I was trying to write too much information without saying why. I managed to get a "however" in more or less – "Marxists on the other hand"'. In response to a question about whether that kind of feature was a part of his conscious writing strategy, he replied (and it is worth quoting this passage at length) that he wanted

> to lead into why I'm saying this rather than 'that stops and this starts' and then 'that stops' and something else ... I need to put a few words at the beginning of this to say that these people don't agree with these people or this perspective would look at something as well as this perspective. Just to say where the links are and what the differences and connections are between the things I'm talking about rather than listing them. I should form a more coherent sentence around it all. I don't know if that really was a problem or not – often it's the English that defeats me 'cos I know what I'm trying to say in the sense that I know what you're wanting me to clarify but it's difficult to do on the day.

He subsequently goes on to describe strategies for 'marking' similarities and contrast, though when the actual text is examined, the commonly-accepted strategies for marking text for meaning seem rather thin on the ground. Nevertheless these reflections indicate self-consciousness about his position in relation to the 'academic language of the discourse community'.

This self-consciousness, the sense of measuring his own performance against the judgement of 'another' is reinforced in several other passages referring to structural and semantic elements of the text: 'Reading it now it seems as though I'm struggling to justify what I put in instead of it being something which is relevant'; 'I was trying to get in and get out quickly without writing too much about each specific thing'. So he appears to have a strategic and performative view of what he is trying to do in the essay. He is not simply responding to a question as a cognitive exercise, but rather as a rhetorical one, though interestingly, the language which he is using to describe his working strategies, of 'bringing in' and so on, suggests that the 'cognitive work-bench' model developed by Britton and colleagues in relation to text-processing might usefully be redeployed to help understand the writing process.[48]

Martin appears to place a great deal of emphasis on the field referred to in the earlier protocol as 'discourse integrity', in particular the areas of defining, referencing and naming. A key strategy appears to be to make the answer revolve around the headlined approaches or 'perspectives' (Marxists, Functionalists and Interactionists. This approach is thought to be characteristic of the dominant A-level text by Michael Haralambos, and has frequently been commented on negatively in Examiners' Reports). In discussing the issues of strategy, he makes it clear that one function of the 'speed' strategy that he mentions is to be able to widen the scope of the 'naming': 'I tried to say who's done the study, what angle it's coming from, name something – give it a specific label it's supposed to have so I've correctly identified it, named it and said why I'm saying it without taking way too much time'. One difficulty that he perceived in his problems with writing competence was the restriction that this placed on the range of material he was able to use: 'I didn't actually use many examples, just one or two from any one thing – the internal criticism then the external criticism, but it did seem to be going – I did take too long doing it. I ran out of time anyway and if that's an indication then I did'. The naming also referred to specific studies and their authors (the definition of the 'canon' distinctive to sociological discourse), and references in the interview together with the manuscript of Martin's plan appear to indicate that the propositional structure of the answer revolves around this definition of the canon for each individual question. A confirmation of this appears in the section where he explains the appearance of a supplementary paragraph (covering Cicourel's theory of the 'negotiation of justice') which is added on to the end of the answer:

> That footnote – I think that's because I got through broadly what I wanted to get through but realised I'd missed something off the plan which I hadn't gone back to – the language negotiation of justice. Which is broadly a class thing because if people can manage to talk themselves out of it they're not going to

appear in the statistics because of their class because of the way they interact with people. That's worth a paragraph.

However, the 'canon' is interpreted as relevant not just to the 'naming' element of the discourse integrity field, but also in terms of the field of propositional density/validity. Much of the retrospective interview is given over to reiteration of the 'items' as propositions, which Martin sees as a clear need to tie together, and discussion of the propositions as propositions in themselves, not just signs to be deployed in aid of convincing an examiner of discourse familiarity. On occasions, as with the case of the 'crime as a right-wing tool' element, the propositions appear to become blurred and difficult for him to understand: 'I don't know if I've actually said that to be honest but to say that some people are seen as criminal and some are not and that crime is in some circumstances a right-wing tool, blah blah. I don't know if that's really clarified what I was trying to say or not'.

However, when Martin was given the opportunity to review the piece overall, he concentrated on a 'missing item' from the 'canon': 'Well I know there are a couple of things I should have mentioned. I should have named the "Dark Figure", the "criminal iceberg"', and the 'balance of the structure' rather than the propositional elements. In a sense this is to be expected, as he would quite naturally be inclined to take the validity of the propositions for granted. The contrast with the examiner's 'summing up' is in the absence of criteria other than the 'canon' against which to weight the work.

In terms of process, it is interesting to try to trace the process of planning and constructing the answer. Martin's plan seems to indicate that the first strategy is to retrieve the names of the 'canon' and the arguments associated with them, in summary form, set them out on paper, construct links between the items using non-verbal cues like lines and ties, and progress from there. If the hyperstructural elements were an element of his planning, they appear to have been 'silent'. The plan includes no comment on the question or its developed meaning, and Martin's discussion of his 'start' appears to imply that he was using words in the title as cues for known lines of argument rather than viewing the title as a proposition in its entirety:

> I know when I first saw the question I thought it was going to be OK as we'd already covered quite a bit of ground in official statistics but the weak spot was class, and the instant problem was picking out the elements that relate to class to show a balanced account of how they can be useful ... so when I was doing the first scribbles before I started writing I was pulling out the main areas that came to mind and then trying to put them in some kind of order.

Having 'pulled them out', Martin then appears to have laid them on a 'cognitive work-bench' to which he periodically returns as the writing progresses. As Britton and colleagues argue, a key problem with text-processing is 'overload' or having too much on 'the bench'. That Martin suffers from this problem is evidenced by the fact that he leaves a key item off, and has to rush back at the last moment to get it. This homology with a model of text-processing is not coincidental, in that candidate strategies will probably include processing a recalled 'text' of some kind, whether this is derived from a textbook, class notes, revision notes and so on.

Sally Mitchell has argued that the 'rhetorical bias' embedded in the performance required for the three-hour exam in sociology inhibits the use of what she describes as 'cognitive ability'. Martin's critique of his own weakness in developing semantic elements in his essay structure are mirrored in Mitchell's perceptions of a common fault of A-level writing.

> Examples as a result often remain in the form of lists, tacked onto concepts without really illuminating them. These lists ... can find their way into written work, fulfilling the rhetorical demand for supporting detail, but without indicating any cognitive ability to connect by abstracting.[49]

Though perhaps, as Martin appears to argue powerfully on his own behalf, it is not the need to subordinate argument to rhetorical form which produces this phenomenon, but the difficulties of translating argument into writing. Not self-restraint but self-expression is the root difficulty.

The most immediately striking feature of the examiner's (Dennis's) response to the answer is that Martin's high profile for the 'canon' has been successful in one sense, in that Dennis has noted and absorbed it, but that it appears to have had the opposite effect to that Martin intended. The 'perspectivist' approach is immediately noted, as are all the 'names' and 'naming exercises' throughout the answer, but the effect appears damaging. So the statement about functionalism which opens the answer is 'pretty bald', the mention of the Cohens goes awry 'the wrong Cohen – which doesn't build up great confidence'. The cumulative effect of listing the canon without 'addressing the question' is noted 'Moves into Merton and nowhere yet have we had a statement of what exactly the relationship is between classes in official statistics'. A reference to functionalists' views, intended I suspect as a kind of 'comparison and contrast' is dismissed: 'Functionalists "pay little attention to class struggle" – well they wouldn't would they?' Criticisms of Martin's 'naming strategy' include inaccuracy (the 'wrong Cohen', 'Gouldner not a psychologist'[50]); irrelevance ('Some sort of vague reference at the bottom of the page, line 25, to Cloward and Ohlin suggested the subcultural approach. That did not clarify the class issue much further. Quite what that's doing there I'm not quite sure'); a heading which is hard to label but which is something like 'travesty', and which seems to come under the schema of discourse integrity ('There's really no excuse for people coming up with this kind of over-simplified view of labelling theory'); an implication that the account of the theory or author doesn't accurately represent its object, but not as a result of a mistake, but because the 'sense' is not there, and the theory has been transformed from 'sociology' into something else.

A less trenchant criticism of the attempt at discourse integrity is embodied in the criticism that 'Miller crops up and so then the interactionist stuff isn't developed much further'. The word 'development' also crops up regularly in the marking scheme for the Board which sets this question, normally in relation to deficits in answers ('needs development' for example). The idea of 'under-development' appears to embrace different aspects of text quality: a lack of articulation of ideas (the 'links' that are referred to by both the candidate and the examiner in this instance); an under-elaboration of the theory; and a failure to refer the theory directly to the question.

However, it is clear that Dennis's judgement strategy does include continuing to look past the impression for positive pointers, because as the commentary moves on to the last page, the comments include many more positive notes:

> At least there is some sense now that we're beginning to answer the question in linking class and official statistics through this kind of explanation and then there's quite a nice link to the Marxists ... The idea that the lower orders are criminalised to keep them from seriously damaging the *status quo*, and a sense that some people would dispute the truth of official statistics on class grounds ... Well it's going in the right direction anyway ... then a sense that white collar crime.

It is interesting that Dennis uses the term 'a sense of', several times in the more positive remarks in the second half of his commentary. I have referred above to the importance of the 'sense' an examiner gets of the candidate, but the fact that the qualities Dennis is attributing to the answer aren't clearly there possibly underscores the ambiguity which Martin felt was created by his difficulties with 'English' and the problems of 'making it flow'. Intended meaning and perceived meaning appear to converge as the essay progresses, along with Martin's use of discourse markers. The 'nice link' with the Marxists is underscored by a contrast marker combined with a new paragraph, with the following sentence using a subtle form of cohesion found in what Nash describes as the rhetorical device of 'the stack',[51] which I mentioned above as a possible source of ambiguity.

Dennis's final judgement is based on an attempt to construct a line of argument out of the material, a positive searching for some structure through the separate instances of what appears to him to be 'rehearsed material', and the most crucial factor appears to be 'the sense of the production of statistics and the influence of class on the production of statistics' which produces 'an attempt at a sustained answer to the question'. The line of Martin's argument is therefore not obscured by language in the way he appears to fear, though its ambiguous and occasionally obscure expression appears to create for Dennis a view that the positive qualities of the script are all qualified. Dennis uses a large number of qualifications 'Quite good', 'Quite a nice link', 'Reasonablish insurance and fraud', 'Not that brilliant an example', 'Forgotten note on Cicourel which again is quite good', 'Trying to answer the question, not that clearly, not particularly well', 'It's not very good'.

Martin's striving in this communication is to meet the demands which he believes examiners make for evidence of 'knowledge' and for its construction into argument, and his handicaps are the self-confessed confusions about the means to these ends. These confusions are partly about real difficulties of self-expression in writing, and partly about a problem of cultural competence: knowing how to represent himself as 'a sociologist'. Dennis's problems are the mirror image of these: trying to discern the line of an argument through apparently confused prose and a disjointed text structure, and trying to evaluate whether the text represents 'real sociology'.

Conclusion

This chapter has explored the relationship between the judgement of the examiners, exercised within a relatively coherent and socialized framework of discourse, and the attempt by candidates to produce appropriate text, working from a far more diffused sense of what is appropriate. The debate over standards is perhaps significant more in terms of its general effect on pedagogic approaches than in terms of its substance. In spite of the introduction of increasingly elaborate specifications of skill into syllabuses, a principal complaint of examiners in their reports is the rigid adherence of candidates of heavily rehearsed material. A sample of comments from the Reports for Summer 1995 from the Associated Examination Board serves as illustration:

'Candidates were not adapting their knowledge and skills to the demand of the particular questions. It must be stressed that over-rehearsal and preparation of answers ... is not a helpful or efficient examination strategy. Rather candidates should regard the examination as a problem-solving exercise ... Rote-learned and rigid sets of answers rarely deal with examination questions appropriately or efficiently.' (Psychology)

'Too often there is a sense that candidates write down everything they know about a topic without tailoring their knowledge and understanding to the specific demands of the question.' (Communications)

'The general pre-prepared answer is still occasionally seen.' (English)[52]

With some variation, depending on the character of the discipline's discourse, poorer responses by candidates are typified as ones which depend on descriptive accounts of rehearsed 'knowledge'. Sally Mitchell argues that this is a consequence of the rhetorical demands of composing written exam answers, reinforced by teachers' stress on 'structure' rather than 'argument',[53] but if we search for the influences which shape this rhetorical imperative, it is possible to discern the outlines of the convergent model of knowledge, where value is attributed to what can be known and repeated rather than what can be known and used. The powerful sense that this is the dominant ideological view of knowledge circumscribes the work of both teachers (who see a syllabus as something to be 'got through' or 'got over') and students, who therefore perceive the accurate reproduction and paraphrase of texts as one of the highest skills to which they can aspire.

Another major feature of the discourse of A levels is the central role of 'the appropriate' in the feedback provided by examiners. The key 'skills' of 'analysis' and 'evaluation' which are common to many A-level syllabuses are extraordinarily difficult to illustrate, and are more often the subject of cultural exhortation than of detailed guidance in examiners' reports. I have argued that this is partly the consequence of the fact that the means by which examiners reach their judgements are not the precise criteria defined in marking schemes, but their sense of 'appropriateness' which is derived from the broader linguistic market. The concept of the market employed here would clearly suggest that, as Martin and other 'genre theorists' argue,[54] this process privileges the discourse of more successful social classes and groups.

If one goal of an assessment process is to achieve greater equity, is there a remedy for this condition? Certainly the moves to greater openness on the part of examination boards through the publication of sample materials and marking schemes, combined with in-service training for teachers, has rendered the culture of the judgement process more transparent, but a major difficulty remains in the fact that the linguistic market and its technical intricacies, the vehicle for the skewed distribution of success in examinations, is poorly comprehended in the education system. 'Subject' teaching seldom involves explicit teaching of the skills of writing the 'genre' of the subject.[55] Whether such teaching would redress the balance remains an open question. It is also arguable that the more explicit specifications of criteria which characterize outcomes-based curricula such as General National Vocational Qualifications can eliminate the cultural character of the assessment process. Whether the detailed criteria have been 'met' or not remains a cultural judgement. (It is noteworthy that, at a professional level, the introduction of 'skills assessment' into training for the Bar brought with it increased accusations of racial bias in assessment.) As Bourdieu argues, the influence of the social structure through the examination system is more powerful than merely in its effects on those entering:

> In every country, the inequalities between the classes are incomparably greater when measured by the probabilities of candidature (calculated on the basis of the proportion of children in each social class who reach a given educational level, after equivalent previous achievement) than when measured by the probabilities of passing.[56]

The irony is that challenges to the skewed effect of the cultural character of assessment, through increased openness and efforts to reward candidates for achievement, rather than penalize them for failure, are likely to lead to ideological assaults on the effects of these innovations on reliability, and to efforts to reinstall the privileged culture in the criteria (in the form of 'quality of language' or some other proxy) in order to preserve 'standards'.

Appendix

MARTIN'S ESSAY

The essay is produced with abbreviations as in the original, and with the line numbers referred to by the examiner in brackets in the text. There is no way of reproducing the paralinguistic features of the text (handwriting and graphic presentation), but the examiner does not explicitly refer to these.

(1) The official statistics (O.S.) on crime are interpreted in different ways by different sociological perspectives. The Functionalists would try to 'science out' the O.S. as facts without questioning (5) their validity. Theorists such as Durkheim would have seen the stats as facts and interpreted them as such, and this tendency is continued now. Some Functionalists (F.), however, do consider class distinctions when (10) doing this. Cohen as an example interpreted the w/c tendency to commit crime as 'status frustration' which relates loosely to what we would call class. In his study of mugging and media he suggested the existence (15) of a 'moral panic' when faced with sensationalist headlines. Merton further interpreted the actions of the w/c in U.S.A. as seeking to achieve 'the American Dream' and they 'innovate' to move towards (20) it – they steal! He did state that the m/c and lower m/c would 'ritualise' in that they live for red tape and for rules, but only because they aspire to be u/c. Cloward and Ohlin suggested the (25) subculture approach, but did not clarify the class issue much further.

The Functionalists see the O.S. as a true answer & then look for the question, but pay little attention to (30) class struggle. An Interactionist account may clarify some aspects of how class is reflected in O.S. In the form of Becker's 'labelling' theory (although he regretted using the term so (35) forcefully afterwards) he did say that if a label is applied it will stick. After the Primary deviance & the label being used, it leads to secondary deviance & the 'criminal' goes on from there. This 'labelling' was (40) applied to crimes such as theft & burglary, but more so to murder and rape. These are less class related and Gouldner (psychologists) criticises Becker for treating the labelled criminal as a passive victim – we are all (45) social animals who create our reality around us. (see Note 1 at end*). Miller viewed w/c crime as a symbol of w/c culture – toughness, smartness, & excitement were seen as the premium status aspirations on the w/c. Therefore they have not (50) accepted the legitimate means of society & gain their status through other means. If this is a class issue it would go some way to explaining the O.S. being skewed the way they are. How?

(55) Marxists, on the other hand, would argue in a completely different context. If the owners of the means of production are to protect their interests they must keep the w/c divided, but reasonably happy. They do (60) this by criminalising any activity which they see as a threat. Gouldner would point out that the definition of what is criminal is left to the people with power. If they treat it as criminal, then it (65) appears in the O.S. Chambliss studied the Seattle organised crime syndicates & found that the banks and gov. officials were corrupt & money laundering for them (for a price). Pearce saw crime as (70) a R/wing tool in the economy. So the State and Industrialists/businessmen are supported by the law & criminal justice is there to serve the bourgeoisie. If the O.S. see the w/c as more criminal than the m/c (75) or the u/c it is because they are criminalised to keep them from seriously damaging the status quo. Unlike F. & Interactionists, Marxist Soc. would dispute the truth of the O.S. on economic/class grounds. Around £21 million worth of insurance claims (80) in 1 year is balanced against £3

billion worth of fraud, so it is plain to see that the white collar crime (which is mostly(?) undetected) makes up the larger criminal activity, but is seen as second to street crime in (85) importance. If the same resources were used to detect & catch m/c (white collar) crime the O.S. would reflect very different characteristics indeed.

(90) * note 1. – Cicourel would also argue that in the 'negotiation of justice' there are no objective facts, just interactions, and the m/c are better equipped to do that negotiating than the less eloquent and persuasive (95) w/c. Partly because of the sub-cultures outlined earlier the w/c are more likely to show 'toughness' than cooperate and 66% of uncooperative suspects are arrested against 23% of cooperative ones according to studies.

Notes and references

1. *Daily Telegraph* 17 August 1995 p.1, col. 1.
2. The leader article in the same edition of the *Daily Telegraph* suggests that 'vocational' subjects such as expressive arts, media studies, photography and leisure studies should be 'stripped out and redesignated as General National Vocational Qualifications', p. 16.
3. Brown, P. Cultural capital and social exclusion *Work, Employment and Society* 9 January, 29–51.
4. Brown, ibid., p. 45.
5. First reported in the *Independent* 6 March 1996, p. 1.
6. When trainee teachers are initially exposed to the extraordinary variability of judgements of a piece of text amongst themselves and their peers, their initial response is to blame 'subjectivity', and to assume that standardization is impossible.
7. Edgeworth, F.Y. (1890) The element of chance in competitive examination pp. 400–75, 644–63 in *Journal of the Royal Statistical Society* 53, September/December, cited in Rowntree, D. (1987) *Assessing Students: How Shall We Know Them?* (2nd edn) (London: Kogan Page, 1987), 191.
8. Hartog, P. and Rhodes, E.C. *The Marks of Examiners* (London: Macmillan, 1936).
9. English seems to have presented particular difficulties, as reported in Wolf, A. *Assessment Issues and Problems in a Criterion-based System* (London: FEU, 1993), 16, and exemplified by the London Association of Teachers of English reaction to the 1995

SAT results, *Times Educational Supplement*, 20 September 1995, p. 3. The reliability of the tests were also questioned by SCAA in their *Evaluation of the Quality of External Marking of the 1995 Key Stage 3 Tests in English* (Hayes: SCAA, 1995).

10. Wolf, ibid., p. 16. Or as Wittgenstein argues 'if language is to be a means of communication, there must be agreement not only in definitions but also (queer as this must sound), in judgements', (1972) *Philosophical Investigations* (Oxford: Blackwell, 1972), **242**, p. 88e.

11. For example, see Pollitt, A., Hutchinson, C., Entwhistle, N. and de Luca, C. *What Makes Exam Questions Difficult?* (Edinburgh: Scottish Academic Press, 1985).

12. Ibid.

13. Bourdieu, P. (1991) *Language and Symbolic Power* (Cambridge: Polity, 1991); Bourdieu, P. and Passeron, J-C. *Reproduction: In Education, Society and Culture* (London: Sage, 1977).

14. In particular, John Swales *Genre Analysis* (Cambridge: Cambridge University Press, 1990).

15. Though it needs to be acknowledged that these are not the 'pure' performative utterances to which Bourdieu refers in his discussion of Austin and pragmatics (1991, op. cit., 73–74).

16. Hoey, Michael *On the Surface of Discourse* (London: Allen & Unwin, 1983).

17. For example, the studies cited in John Swales, op. cit., p. 66.

18. See Gunter Kress *Learning to Write* (2nd edn) (London: Routledge, 1994), 21 where he argues that unequal access to the development of writing skills is a key feature of the role of writing in the social system.

19. Biber, D. *Variation Across Speech and Writing* (Cambridge: Cambridge University Press, 1988).

20. See Edwards, D. and Mercer, N. *Common Knowledge* (London: Routledge, 1987) and Sheeran, Y. and Barnes, D. *School Writing* (Milton Keynes: Open University Press, 1991).

21. Schools Curriculum and Assessment Council (1995) *Assessing Quality of Language* (London: SCAA, 1995), 6.

22. Halliday, M. and Hasan, R. *Cohesion in English* (London: Longman, 1976).

23. See Michael Hoey's arguments in *Patterns of Lexis in Text* (Oxford: Oxford University Press, 1991) for a discussion of 'lexical bonding' as an organizing principle.

24. See for example Lovejoy, K. and Lance, D. Information management and cohesion in the study of written discourse *Linguistics and Education* 3, 1991, 315–43, or Neuner, J. Cohesive ties and chains in good and poor freshman essays *Research in the Teaching of*

English 21 (1), 1987, 92–105.
25. Bourdieu, P. (1991) op. cit., p. 66.
26. Bernstein, B. *Class, Codes & Control* Vol. 1 (London: Routledge and Kegan Paul, 1971) in particular, Chapter 11, 202–230.
27. The 1994 conference of the Association of Teachers of Social Science was sponsored by Collins Harvill. The standard A-level text, which sells between 10–12,000 copies a year, is published by Collins Harvill.
28. Bourdieu, P. (1991), op. cit., p. 165.
29. McNeill, P. Developing a new syllabus *Social Science Teacher* 22 (1), 1992, 17.
30. Whilst it was the case that up to the mid-1980s examiners' marking schemes were treated as secret documents, it is now regarded as good practice to publish them and make them readily available to teachers.
31. Hence the dogged determination of examination authorities to argue that examination standards are being maintained, even when changing disciplinary paradigms mean that different performances from different dates could clearly not be commensurate.
32. Bourdieu, P. (1991) op. cit., p. 44.
33. Ibid., p. 169.
34. Swales, J. (1990) op. cit., 57–58.
35. Swales, J. (1990) op. cit., 24–27.
36. The concept of schemata has been used extensively in studies of text comprehension, see for example Anderson, R.C. (1980) Schema-directed processes in language comprehension. In Hartley, James (ed.) *The Psychology of Written Communication* (London: Kogan Page, 1980), 26–39.
37. Bourdieu, P. *Distinction* (London: Routledge and Kegan Paul, 1984), 468.
38. Meyer, B.F. (1985) 'Prose analysis: purposes, procedures and problems' in Britton, B.K. and Black, J.C. *Understanding Expository Text* (Hillsdale: Erlbaum, 1985), pp. 11–64.
39. Halliday, M.A.K. *Language as Social Semiotic* (London: Arnold, 1978).
40. In looking at the way in which 'stigmatising' categorisations tend to be partial in their view of what they judge, Bourdieu comments that 'those who are surprised by the paradoxes that ordinary logic and language engender when they apply their divisions to continuous magnitudes forget the paradoxes inherent in treating language as a purely logical instrument and also forget the social situation in which such a relation to language is possible.' (1984) op. cit., p. 476.
41. See Singer, M., Halldorson, M., Lear, C. and Andrusiak, P. Validation of causal bridging inferences in discourse understanding *Journal of Memory and Language* 31, 1992, 507–24.

42. Nash, W. *Designs in Prose* (London: Longman, 1980), 12–13.
43. On unreliability of predictive grades, see Delap, M.R. (1994) An investigation into the accuracy of A-level predicted grades *Educational Research* 36 (2), 1994, 135–48.
44. Sandra Stotsky argues that our interpretive capacities are very much influenced by our previous experiences (1983) Types of lexical cohesion in expository writing: implications for developing a vocabulary of academic discourse *College Composition and Communication* 34 (4), 1983, 430–46.
45. This is a method of researching and analysing the writing process which has been extensively used by Flower, L.S. and Hayes, J.R. The dynamics of composing; making plans and juggling constraints, in Gregg, L. and Steinberg, E. (eds) *Cognitive Processes in Writing*. (Hillsdale: Erlbaum, 1980), 31–50, and (1981) A cognitive process theory of writing *College Composition and Communication* 62 (4), 1981, 365–87.
46. Haralambos, M. (3rd edn) *Sociology, Themes and Perspectives* (London: Unwin Hyman, 1990).
47. Moore, S. (1991) *Investigating Deviance* (London: Collins Educational, 1991), 129–42.
48. Britton, J., Glynn, S. and Smith, J. Cognitive Demands of Processing Expository Text: A Cognitive Workbench Model. (1985), in Britton and Black *Understanding Expository Text* (Hillsdale: Erlbaum, 1985), 227–47.
49. Mitchell, S. Learning to be critical and correct *Curriculum* 14 (1), 1993, 48–56, p. 55.
50. Gouldner is in fact a famous American sociologist whose work is only marginally relevant in any sense to the question being discussed. The professional labelling of 'names' is an interesting topic on its own, and appears to be a response to comments sometimes made in Examiners' Reports about candidates' lack of familiarity with the distinction between disciplines. In this case, as in others, the attempt to meet the examiners' criticism seems to exacerbate the problem rather than solve it.
51. Nash, W. (1980) op. cit., p. 12.
52. Associated Examining Board (1995) Examiners' Reports, Guildford.
53. Mitchell, S. (1993) op. cit.
54. Martin, J.R. *Factual Writing* (Oxford: Clarendon Press, 1989).
55. Ibid., p. 75, for example.
56. Bourdieu and Passeron (1977) op. cit., p. 153.

CHAPTER 6
Assessment, Evaluation and the Effective School

CEDRIC CULLINGFORD

The time that is spent on the testing of individuals is time taken away from teaching and learning. One of the major complaints of teachers when testing at Key Stages 1 and 2 was introduced was that they were spending hours establishing what they already knew but being expected to do better whilst deprived of the means of doing so. The growth of the examination industry has been matched by the huge investment in a vast machinery of inspection. Never has the belief in measuring success and failure, as a means of improving the education system through competition, been so clearly demonstrated as in the Office for Standards in Education (OFSTED) and the publication of league tables.

Making judgements about people and institutions, whether formally or informally, is, of course an ancient phenomenon, both within and outside the education system. For many years Her Majesty's Inspectors had an automatic right to enter schools, judge their performance and subsequently disseminate what they thought. Local education authorities relied on teams of inspectors and advisors to monitor their school's performance.[1] But there has been a recent sea-change in the tone and attitude of inspection. The ambiguity between the role of the 'advisor' and the role of the 'inspector' arises from the tensions between making crucial judgements and in trying to support and help schools and the teachers in acting on them. HMI wanted to see improvements. Criticism was balanced by praise with the underlying assumption that they were pointing the way towards action. There is a clear distinction to be made between those aspects of appraisal which are constructive and contain clear advice, and the primitive judgements that brand particular schools as failures.

There is no doubting the impact of OFSTED, although what this impact is appears rather different from the intention. What does emerge from a series of small-scale studies of the local effect of OFSTED inspections is that the crucial phase is the anticipation of inspection rather than the aftermath.[2] The 'threat' of an inspection is very powerful. It causes a great deal of stress. It creates an enormous amount of work in preparing documents and directs attention away from teaching towards the justification of teaching. It is as if it is more important to demonstrate that one has taught, and how, than actually to teach. For some, as in the case of new headteachers, the impending inspection is an opportunity to introduce change. Some have even gone so far as to suggest that a great deal of money could be saved if there were an OFSTED 'detector-van'. Knowing that there is the likelihood of inspection is enough in itself.

About the results of OFSTED inspections there is more doubt, except of course in those cases where the schools are threatened with closure. There is little evidence that what the inspectors say makes any different to the school. This is partly because there is a very rigid formula for inspections, often out of tune with the way that schools operate. The very effect of an inspection results in a period of recovery from the trauma where little action is taken. But the most powerful reason for a lack of subsequent change is that all attention is focused on the 'rating', on the grade the school receives. The publication of the judgement is a terminal point. It exposes rather than improves the school. Anything that happens as a result of the report will be overshadowed by the report itself. All the attempts to induce action by charging the governors with a series of measures to act on do not appear to have the same effect as the desire of the teachers within the school to make changes.

OFSTED inspections can have traumatic effects. Whether there are any results, in terms of improvements, is quite another question. In terms of league tables it could be argued that the results themselves are all that matter. After all it is the assessment itself that is supposed to clarify the success or failure of the school. All the government documents stress accountability and information. The concern is with measuring standards. Any improvements will, it is assumed, be made through the workings of the market, through choice and competition.

The idea of the 'market' involves parents. They are the people who are to make choices. It is to them, ultimately, that OFSTED inspections are geared since they are seen as making judgements for themselves. The majority of the documents in the Parent's Charter are about the assessment of 'effective' schools, regular reports from inspectors, performance tables, the school's prospectus and the annual report from governors. It is as if parents themselves were being asked to make the judgements. Certainly a lot of information is delivered to them.[3]

This new role for parents leaves them somewhat bewildered. It is not only teachers who are bombarded with information. Inspections and governor's reports, parent's charters and league tables are all supposed to be of crucial interest to parents in their judgements about choice, competition and effective schools. From OFSTED's point of view parents are there to support them as 'stakeholders'. But however parents are cited, the parents themselves express a quite different point of view. They are cynical about choice, dismissive of league tables and suspicious of the amount of inspection.[4] The reason for this is that they experience what is happening in schools and personally know the difference between the theory of choice and the reality. They witness the substantial amounts of stress exhibited by teachers faced with inspection and by their children undergoing assessment. They have the impression that the demands of the National Curriculum and its emphasis on the measurable acquisition of knowledge have taken from teachers all chance of creative and stimulating teaching. As the research makes clear, parents have a far more jaundiced view of the educational system since the Education Reform Act than they do of the schools which their children attend.

Parents' views of the effectiveness of the schools they know, indeed parents' evaluation of schools, demonstrates their belief that they have improved over the years.[5] They also feel that the changes made through the National Curriculum and through the concomitant series of measurements of its effects are threatening the improvements. It is not only teachers who feel beleaguered. Far from feeling empowered by all the new responsibilities and rights over schools, parents feel sympathy for what they see as the professionalism of teachers, and do not like to see it taken away. Despite the cajoling of the government, only a quarter of parents wish to see the reports of OFSTED inspections, and only a quarter go to meetings in school to discuss the results.[6] Attendance at parents' meetings remains low all over the country, even whilst parents appreciate the willingness of teachers to talk to them. It is the formal, official inspectorial role that they do not like. They prefer to see themselves as partners.

This results in a great deal of parental suspicion of OFSTED inspections. In research commissioned by OFSTED itself,[7] parents see the inspectors as the 'enemy', bringing threats, rather than help, causing stress rather than improvement. Whilst the principle of knowing more about the school is welcomed it is clear that parents think this is best done through direct talks with teachers. The idea of involvement is appreciated, but it is through partnerships rather than control that it is best expressed. Most parents surveyed were unsure whether the school had been at all affected by the OFSTED inspection – including the preparations made for it. Half the parents remain unsure about OFSTED despite the amount of what could only be described as propaganda on its behalf.

In the OFSTED assessments of schools there are clear distinctions to be made between the anticipation and preparation of inspections and the outcomes, and between the judgements made against a set of criteria (some politically motivated, such as the way reading is taught) and the desire to improve the effectiveness of a school. The question remains: what is being measured and what is it being measured for? We are left with final judgements of many schools. Some are deemed satisfactory and others not. And then? Does making such assessments actually change anything? When it comes to evaluating schools the stress is not so much on measurement as on finding out what activities, and what kinds of approach, lead to improvement.

Making judgements is not only an age-old activity but one which comes easily. More difficult is the action that arises from such judgements. Nothing could be more clear than the studies of what makes effective teachers. After all, there cannot be anyone who does not agree that some teachers are 'better' than others; but how does one measure teaching, or appraise it; and more pertinently, what does one do to improve the performance of those teachers labelled by the Chief Inspector as below standard? If the proper answer were instant dismissal, like the instant closure of the least successful schools, would it not have been done by now?

There are some who believe that teacher effectiveness is very difficult if not impossible to measure, or rather who assert that there is no established connection between teaching skills and learning outcomes, given all the other socio-economic factors.[8] The difficulty lies in the measurement, in the exact detailing of all the variables that support success, given the complexity of individual personalities. That there are certain teachers who have made a great difference to pupils is clear.[9] That pupils enjoy certain subjects and dislike others according to teachers who take them, is also well established.[10] The problem is that there are relationships involved which are not factors which can be isolated, since they include personalities. In shared teaching when one takes a class for the morning and another for the afternoon, some pupils respond much more positively to one than to the other; but the reasons are difficult to identify and measure.

Nevertheless there are certain qualities in good teachers that are clearly established.[11] These qualities go beyond individual traits of character. Just as it is clear that some are better than others, so it is clear what makes them so. The successful teacher, for instance, will be fair and consistent, will praise more than blame, will be clear and patient, will ask questions and listen, rather than shout and present repetitive exercises.[12] Even those who are too fastidious to suggest that good teaching can be easily taught admit to certain qualities that make the successful teacher, like the art of providing their pupils with as many opportunities to learn as possible. But this is to observe quite properly the effects of good teaching, to realize that however difficult these are to measure precisely, the pupils themselves recognize the necessary qualities. Children clearly spell out what makes a good teacher. They do not sentimentalize about personality. Indeed they are not deceived about the distinction between the likeable person and the good professional teacher. They prefer the one who is firm and keeps her distance. They like the charisma of the teacher who understands the authority of the role as well as the ability to break out of that role for moments of humour.[13]

It is not only pupils who have a clear view of what makes teachers effective. As with studies of effective schools there is an undercurrent of agreement on what these qualities are. Some might seem obvious but all reveal that the good teacher, like the good school, is clearly interested in the improved results – the learning of the pupils, rather than the demonstration or the theatricals of the teaching performance in itself. The characteristics cited include clarity and enthusiasm, questioning skills, a variety of teaching approaches, not wasting time, and always making sure that the pupils are thinking rather than learning testable information.[14] In Bennett *et al.*'s closely observed and critical study of teacher performance there were many signs of all these effective characteristics going astray, for one reason or another.[15] They witnessed undemanding lessons, with emphasis on quantity, with many uniform tasks which did not fit the abilities of the class. They observed a great overemphasis on spelling and punctuation as if they were an end in themselves rather than a means to expression. They saw countless repetitive tasks, especially in arithmetic and writing. The children both knew what was going on, and had to put up with it. 'Children seek to please teachers by delivering the goods teachers appear to want. Children learn what teachers want by monitoring what they reward. Thus, neat work, full pages, procedures evidently followed –

all these attract teacher's praise.'[16] One can understand the external pressures on teachers, like the National Curriculum, that make low level routines part of a 'coping' strategy. But what makes such observations disturbing is that bad teaching is avoidable. The difficulty is that teaching is such a subtle thing. It is impossible to measure it purely in terms of results, of outcomes. There is a distinction between the good teacher and automatic success. Yet the good teacher can be observed as such. The irony is that one of the characteristics of the good teacher is the attempts to bring out the best in the pupil. Given that is what she is striving for it is, perhaps, no wonder that the conclusion will be drawn that the only true measure of success is the assessable outcome. The problem is that this is not so.

Nowhere is the distinction between knowing what makes a successful teacher and finding a means of measuring and demonstrating the fact made more clear than in teacher appraisal. This also has a long and difficult history. The intentions behind appraisal were, from the beginning, both positive and negative: to reward, celebrate and learn from the good and to punish the bad. The problem has always been, since its inception in the United States, that it is far easier to set up a series of criteria against which to measure performance, than to translate insight into improvement.[17] As with a series of competencies, the greater the demand for precision, for inviolable categories, the more real 'quality' is left out. What happened in the United States is instructive. As the battery of objective measures became more comprehensive so they measured smaller and more precise behavioural objectives. Almost inexorably, the kinds of demands being made to show 'competence' in the face of such appraisal became lower and lower. Assessment itself drove out quality. But then, as in the Cannell controversy, the same was true about the measurement of performance of schools. In order to be able to report 'above average' results, it was found necessary to lower the standards of what was meant by 'average'.[18] In the end 'the law of performance indicators states that too many questions drive out good answers'.[19] The complex but real qualities of good teaching can be recognized and agreed, but not easily measured. This is an important distinction. To 'know' what is effective is different from assessing it because the underlying aim is quite different. We come again to the distinction between measuring something for the sake of placing it in a rank order, or as a prelude to some kind of punishment, and judging or diagnosing performance so that something can be done to enhance it. Blaming teachers does little if anything to enhance success. On the contrary, as with the pupils of the same teachers, constant criticism is a most successful means of undermining performance. The art of successful teaching is clearly recognizable, but it is subtle and not simply measured.

If it is possible to know a good teacher it is also possible to know a good school. Again, the attempts to assess and explain what makes an effective school have a long history.[20] In its wake is a growing body of effective school research, attempting to clarify exactly what the factors are that make some schools, with similar social and economic conditions, so much more successful than others.[21] It is fair to say there is a strong measure of agreement about what makes a 'good' or 'effective' school. But even such a seemingly bland statement is controversial. Not only is there a distinction between the 'good' and the 'effective' which begs the question of who is making the judgement and against which criteria, but there is also a deeply held suspicion about the extent to which a school can make any difference at all, given the impact of socio-economic factors and the effects of parenting. Even those who are deeply immersed in defining the factors of effectiveness recognize that the differences between schools are halved when home background is taken into account.[22]

Schools are not institutions isolated from their environments. One of the factors that is recognized as a pre-condition for success is the acceptance of this fact. When the conditions of healthy schools are diagnosed one of the central elements is the relationships set up with parents – as partners rather than controllers – and a sensitivity towards the early experiences that the pupils bring with them. Thus socio-economic status is not simply a factor to set against the school, for however strongly urged the belief in genetic and immutable factors that dominate and explain away people's lives, many studies have accumulated a body of knowledge that points to school effectiveness. This should be both an encouragement and a burden on teachers. Far from being helpless in the face of powerful social forces they are a significant influence on the life chances of pupils.

The studies of school effectiveness have been carried out particularly in Great Britain, the United States and in developing countries. It is instructive to detect the measure of agreement. The two well-known British research studies were in secondary schools in the first instance and then in primary schools.[23] Rutter's work was quickly attacked since it was one of the first to undermine the sociological notions of helplessness and school importance. But as in Mortimore's later work, when all kinds of factors were taken into account, there emerged a strong sense of what makes an institution work. The picture includes staff working well with pupils and with each other, with a strong sense of shared mission, with clear and supportive leadership promulgating a sense of firm discipline and high academic standards. The reports are as revealing for what they do not mention as for what they do. They do not parade the idea of the strong autocratic headteacher imposing his or her will on the school. They do not speak of sudden changes or the missionary preaching of dogma. They do not make mention of the centrality of assessment. Nor do they speak of marketing, or inspections, or the control of governors.

The British studies suggest something about the subtleties of a cohesive social institution where each person has a significant part to play and yet where all share a collective sense of purpose. This is not something that can either be imposed from outside or created overnight. After all how can one convince people instantly to change their attitudes? And yet it is on subtle matters, such as that useful but slippery term 'ethos', that a school depends. When, for example, some American studies were summarized it was found that school effectiveness depends on motivations and

intentions, as, for instance, teachers having high expectations of pupils, staff having good interpersonal relations and
sharing a mission, and pupils and parental involvement in
the school.[24] These are matters that could not possibly be
introduced instantly were they to be missing, if that is what
an OFSTED inspection decided. Those factors that might,
on the face of it, be quicker to introduce, like the head's
powerful academic leadership, consistent rules and reward
systems, and a forum for public praise, themselves depend
on the agreement and unity of staff and pupils.

In every study, whatever the research instruments and
however the findings are analysed and expressed, certain
clear conclusions are reiterated. Naturally they all centre on
people, that unmechanistic fact that can be described but
not instantly reproduced. The warm climate for learning
and teaching, a 'pervasive' and broadly understood academic goal, teachers who have high expectations who believe
their pupils can learn, the head's concern with the quality of
teaching and a constant attention to self-improvement,
these factors emerge again and again.[25] But they are not
confined to one country or one set of circumstances. They
inform the way in which schools of all types operate, when
successful; the factors are not those that can be assessed in
terms of measurable outcomes, although they do have
improved outcomes in the end. Terms like 'trust' between
pupils and staff, 'involvement' in learning, 'understanding'
the purpose, 'sharing' the agenda by all children, and 'challenge' echo the points made in many studies.[26] The fact that
the words might appear imprecise should not indicate
anything more than the fact that they are attempting to
summarize many complex organizational arrangements and
relationships. They point out those almost immeasurable
factors which schools need to improve and develop. Above
all it is the sense of shared values, values created and developed by the community of the school, rather than imposed
from outside, that is most significant.[27]

As the most elaborate review of all modern educational
assessment made clear, there is a big difference between the
judgements formed by summative assessment and diagno-

sis. To find the way of making judgements is not the same in seeking out means to effect improvements.[28] The studies briefly cited so far indicate how much work has gone into defining what makes an effective school. But there are also many attempts to discover the ways in which schools can be helped to be made better. Of course this rests on the assumption that schools can make a difference, that they can improve and change, that the judgement is not in itself terminal. Even the HMI after an experience of visiting schools in the United States suggested that progress was more significant than attainment, and that the performance of schools should be measured against a wide range of criteria and not just test results.[29] In the projects which seek to improve the quality of schools the most successful strategies for change clearly reflect those qualities which already result in good schools: the importance of involving all staff, and the community; the teachers' sense of 'ownership' of the innovations; and the unity of vision which provides the best for each pupil, rather than for those who are deemed to attain the best results.[30] It is recognized that real change (for the better) takes time.[31]

When school systems are evaluated in the light of a desire for improvement, certain ground rules emerge. This is as true of developing countries as of the developed. Change is incremental. Successful reform focuses on the school as a whole rather than one particular factor such as the curriculum, or teacher appraisal.[32] It is a matter of subtle change, of shared vision and purposes, of change in which all are involved. Whilst it is change that can be introduced by outside agencies it cannot be imposed from outside. Effective schools depend on the people within them, and 'people' is an all-inclusive term reaching into the supporting community and embracing each individual. Some clearly have more influence and set the tone. But the idea is to bring out the best. The point at which inclusiveness ceases to have coherence is the point at which judgements are made from a potential perspective of enmity, of external blame, rather than the responsible concern to make things better. No amount of inspection will in itself make any difference. If the headteacher and the staff wish to make changes they will use any external agency available, since the changes are still in their hands. But external changes against the will of the school community will either end in no improvement or with the cost of closure.

All this depends on accepting the fact that there is a potential for a shared vision, that teachers actually want to see improvements, that they welcome true evaluation. Given the way teaching operates it would be perverse if they did not. That dependency on shared concern has a solid base, and has been proved all over the world. How, then, can change for the better be brought about, not just in a single school, but in a whole system? Again, there is no lack of evidence.[33] Again, the findings are consistent. We find the same coastal shelf of agreement. However expressed, from whatever sources, from whatever country – the way to help schools improve rests on certain immutable principles. These include:

- The sense of the school as a centre of change
- The teacher's feelings of responsibility or 'ownership' over change
- The close involvement of parents and the community
- Good clear systems of communication, sharing and support
- The willingness to make changes happen over time
- The encouragement of teacher motivation and commitment
- The support of teachers through in-service education
- Trusting schools to develop their own policies and motivations without undue outside interference or detailed external control and inspection.

Clearly there are some factors which change an education system for the better and some which do not. Tight inspection and control are counter-productive. The assumption that schools are resistant to reform is untrue. The desire to make systems of assessment so tight that teachers carry out the directives mechanically is disastrous. Instead the support for schools is vital, and the support of teachers and parents, with shared commitment and a shared sense of purpose, is essential.

It might have struck the reader that there is at least one country which goes against all these principles, that, in the face of all the evidence, pursues a path which, on its own admission, leads to 'falling standards'. How can this be?

The answer lies not just in human folly but in the nature of the debate about distinctions between assessment and evaluation. The idea of a tool of measurement for its own sake might seem unattractive to those to whom it is a personal starting point for improvement. But there is always a distinction between the idea of a 'good' school, which for example brings out the best qualities of all its pupils and the 'effective' school which fulfils the criteria laid upon it, however servile they might be.[34] Silver describes the history of the search for effectiveness and reveals how much public examination has been used as a controlling tool.[35] Assessment is an obvious means of control, and control is an obsession for its own sake. But underlying the concern with assessment, with inspection, with league tables and the comparison of one school to another, lies not the imposition of market forces, with the new empowerment of parents or of choice, but a new locus of blame. In this style of thought the results between schools do not matter as long as there are differences, as in the football league. So if some, like factories, cannot keep up with the market, they fail. They go out of business and so do their pupils. But this is 'competition'. The point behind this thinking is that it is the fault of the school. There was a time when it was argued that schools and the teachers within them made no difference. The argument was that it was socio-economic factors that were the essential determinant of success or failure. But now at last the teachers and the educationists have their wish. The value of schools is recognized. Teachers can make a difference. And they are the ones blamed for failure, not the social environment, nor poverty nor racism.

Such an obsession with the judgements that follow accountability are not confined to the world of education. Indeed they are a reflection of a belief in the efficacy of market forces that affect or have been imposed upon virtually all sectors of the economy. The idea of citizens' rights follows the consumerist view of society. The Citizen's Charter, of which the Parent's Charter is a part, lays down, for instance, precisely what is to be expected from the railways and lays down a series of punishments – in this case fines – if the trains do not meet their targets. One of the outcomes of this of course is the lowering of the standards that are to be expected for if high expectations are not met there will be such an amount and number of fines that there can be nothing left over for investment. So the spiral of decline is absorbed into the system.

In schools the notions of accountability are presented not only in terms of information against which to judge the school but in terms of 'entitlement'. There are performance targets against which schools are judged. Some are deemed to fail. But whose failure is it in the real sense? When schools 'fail' pupils it is pupils who suffer. Notions of competition suggest certain schools and the people in them should be allowed to 'wither on the vine'.

One result of this is both a fascination with, as well as horror of, failure. The burgeoning research on assessment includes studies of ineffective schools.[36] There is a growing awareness of the extreme difficulties that some schools face. The problem is that the solutions being presented to them, like better marketing strategies, do not help.[37] The presentation of the raw scores of examination results causes anxiety to teachers as well as parents. Knowing how little choice parents outside the private sector really have, it is no wonder that the correlations between high and low socioeconomic circumstances and high and low test results pass them by.

It is on the children that the results of all these experiments will fall. There are signs that the future looks bleak. The association of schools with testing and with little more than the core curriculum, seems to lead to more negative attitudes.[38] Teachers and parents already notice the shift of emphasis from learning to knowing, from thinking skills to a concern with demonstrating what can be tested. Like schools and like teachers children need to be evaluated. And evaluation, as a part of teaching and learning is a very different matter from examination results. Children have always seen the distinction between work rate and success and compared themselves to others. But never have they had so much information against which to judge themselves as now.

Notes and references

1. The tension between the notion of the 'inspection' and the notion of the 'advisor' is explored in Winkley, D. *Diplomats and Detectives: LEA Advisors at Work* (London: Royce, 1985).

2. Most of the material from which this conclusion is drawn derives from a series of Master's dissertations which examined groups of inspected schools, at secondary but more particularly at primary level.

3. Department for Education *Our Children's Education: The Updated Parent's Charter* (London: HMSO, 1994).

4. This research is discussed fully in Cullingford, C. (ed.) *Parents, Education and the State* (Aldershot: Arena, 1996) See also Hughes, M., Wikeley, F. and Nash, T. *Parents and their Children's Schools* (Oxford: Blackwell, 1994).

5. Ibid.

6. Ouston, J. and Klenowski, V. *The Ofsted Experience: The Parents' Eye View* (London: Research and Information on State Education Trust, 1995).

7. Tabberner, R. *Parents' Perceptions of Ofsted's Work* (Slough: NFER, 1995) (A report for OFSTED).

8. See Silcock, P. Can we teach effective teaching? *Educational Review* 45 (1), 1993, 13–19.

9. See for example the chapters on children's and parents' views of teachers in Cullingford, C. *The Inner World of the School* (London: Cassell, 1991) and Cullingford 1996 op. cit.

10. See research reported in *Towards Employability: Addressing the Gap Between Young People's Qualities and Employer's Recruitment Needs* (London: Industry in Education, 1996).

11. Cullingford, C. *The Effective Teacher* (London: Cassell, 1995).

12. SET *Research Information for Teachers* No 2 1995 Unit 10.

13. Cullingford 1991 op. cit.

14. Rosenshine, B. and Furst, J. *Teacher Behaviour and Student Progress* (Slough: NFER, 1971).

15. Bennett, N., Desforges, C., Cockburn, A. and Wilkinson, B. *The*

Quality of Pupil Learning Experiences (London: Erlbaum, 1984).
16. Ibid., p. 211.
17. Vold, E. and Nomisham, D. Teacher appraisal. In Cullingford, C. *The Primary Teacher* (London: Cassell, 1989), 131–47.
18. See Gray, J. and Wilcox, B. *Good School, Bad School: Evaluating Performance and Encouraging Improvement* (Buckingham: Open University Press, 1995).
19. Ibid., p. 26.
20. See Silver, H. *Good Schools, Effective Schools: Judgements and their Histories* (London: Cassell, 1994).
21. Jansen, J. Effective Schools? *Comparative Education* 31 (2), 1995, 181–200.
22. Gray, J. and Wilcox, B. op. cit., p. 18.
23. Rutter, M., Maughan, B., Mortimore, P. and Ouston, J. *Fifteen Thousand Hours* (London: Open Books, 1979).
    Mortimore, P., Sammons, P., Stoll, L., Lewis, D. and Ecob, R. *Schools Matters: The Junior Years* (London: Open Books, 1988).
24. Galloway, D. Effective schools In Reid, K. (ed.) *Combating School Absenteeism* (London: Hodder & Stoughton, 1987).
25. Levine, D. and Lezotte, L. *Unusually Effective Schools: A Review and Analysis of Research and Practice* (Madison: NCESRD, 1990) A summary of many US studies.
26. Cooper, P. and McIntyre, D. Commonality in teachers' and pupils' perceptions of effective classroom learning *British Journal of Educational Psychology* Vol. 63, No. 3, 1993, pp. 381–99.
27. Lightfoot, S. *The Good High School: Portraits of Character and Culture* (New York: Basic Books, 1983).
28. Black, P. (Chair) Task Group on Assessment and Testing. A Report. (London: Dept of Education and Science, 1988).
29. HMI 1991.
    See Hargreaves, D. and Hopkins, D. *The Empowered School: The Management and Practice of Developmental Planning* (London: Cassell, 1991).
30. Ibid.
31. Fullan, M. *The New Meaning of Educational Change* (London: Cassell, 1991).
32. Lockheed, M. and Verspoor, A. *Improving Primary Education in Developing Countries* (Oxford: Oxford University Press, 1991).
33. Dalin, P., Ayono, T., Blazen, A., Dibava, D., Jahon, M., Matthew, B., Rojas, M., Rojas, C. *How Schools Improve: An International Report* (London: Cassell, 1994).
34. Silver, H. op. cit.
35. Ibid., 17–18.
36. Reynolds, D. The future of school effectiveness and school

improvement *Educational Psychology in Practice* 11 (3), 1995, 12–21.
37. Brown, S., Duffield, J. and Riddell, S. School effectiveness research: the policy maker's tool for school improvement? *EERA Bulletin* 1 (1), 1995, 6–15.
38. Davies, J. and Brember, I. Attitudes to school and the curriculum in Year 2 and Year 4: changes over two years. *Educational Review* 46 (3), 1994, 247–58.

CHAPTER 7

How Primary Schools Deal With Assessment in the National Curriculum
VAL WOODINGS

Introduction

The focus of this chapter is the discussion and analysis of National Curriculum assessment through the case study of a school, in Oxfordshire. Whilst it is essential to acknowledge the contributions of parents, governors, LEAs, inspectors, governmental bodies (setting boundaries, priorities and funding) and academic commentators to the assessment process, there is insufficient space to discuss these in detail. We shall, however, touch on the much neglected concept of school morale and how that is reflected in the teaching profession.

Although the National Curriculum has undergone many changes since its inception in 1988, assessment is still informed by the same principles identified by the influential Task Group on Assessment and Testing (TGAT).[1] The purposes of assessment were to be diagnostic, formative, summative and evaluative. It was the intention that the diagnostic and formative functions were to be teacher-controlled and directly linked to the process of teaching and learning. These two assessment processes would inform the teacher of what is established in the child's learning bank and, from this, inform forward planning of the curriculum.

The summative process is concerned with nationally controlled tests (Standard Assessment Tasks [SATs]), set to test the National Curriculum near the end of the academic year. The resulting quantitative scores, TGAT suggested, could provide information on the performance of pupils, teachers, schools and the educational system as a whole. This information is required for two reasons: to provide a basis to establish whether or not educational standards are rising or falling; and to provide the means by which parents are able to judge the effectiveness of schools before making their final choice of school for their child.

The tension that has arisen between the diagnostic/formative and the summative/evaluative assessments has given some commentators cause to suggest that the emphasis has moved towards 'teaching to the test' (SATs) to the neglect of the formative aspect.[2, 3] Black, meanwhile, states that 'good formative assessment can be a powerful tool for raising standards of learning, but that it is in general badly underdeveloped in schools. There is therefore a tremendous opportunity for improvement'.[4]

We will seek to question the extent of teacher involvement in assessment through our case study. We will argue that, although teachers experience the tension between the formative and summative assessments, it is the positive models of formative assessment which have informed the organization, and ethos of practice. Whilst the teachers administer the Key Stage 1 and 2 SATs, the educational significance, as suggested by TGAT, is questionable.

Clearly, Dearing's recommendations, in his final report in January 1994, changed the face of the National Curriculum and its assessment. But primary schools saw very little change in Key Stages 1 and 2. In spite of the worries in the original debate that the curriculum would be assessment driven, and that a 'prescribed curriculum in much detail would make assessment easy', this would get very close to the kind of 'behavioural objectives curriculum model which was already discredited'.[5] Dearing has shown himself to be very aware of some aspects of that problem and offers less detailed prescription. But primary teachers will still have 80 per cent of their school day taken up with prescribed content.

A further difficulty is that 'while Mrs. Shepherd is known to be fighting the Treasury for extra resources to prevent further worsening [of teacher numbers] next year, her officials maintain that marginal increases in class sizes had no effect on the quality of education.[6] In spite of the debate in HMI affirming that it isn't the size of the class that matters but the quality of the teaching, and whilst no teacher would contest the second point, most teachers would endorse the case for smaller classes, which is based on more than anecdotal evidence.

Functions of assessment

There are three functions of assessment, as argued by Professor Black:[7]

1 direct assistance to learning: formative assessment
2 the certifications of individual students: summative assessment
3 public accountability of institutions and teachers.

In the case study we will be arguing for a number of variations in each category, in particular by demonstrating how assessment is tackled in Year 4.

We have already mentioned the participants in the assessment process. The critical one is the child. It is here that the foundations of self assessment are laid. By learning to assess their own performances, children are able to be instrumental in their own educational progress – academic, social and emotional. Next in the assessment process are the teachers and parents (those most closely involved with the child) and the headteachers, the governors, the LEAs, the inspectors and the academics who help to train teachers. All these individuals contribute to the assessment process, its use and its power over the schools, in the public arena.

Towards a model of assessment

Since assessment has become a political football (in terms of method and content) between the parties who design it, those who administer it and those who perform its tasks, definitions are a minefield of contradiction. For the purpose of this chapter, we will take the definitions set out in Thomas's paper on assessment and evaluation.[8] He suggests that 'assessing learning, should involve not only terminal or summative assessment but should also be a diagnostic process embracing learning as it proceeds'. He further states that 'assessment of learning often leads to qualifications such as certificates or diplomas, which in reality act as 'access cards' to employment or higher education'.[9]

We take this definition of assessment to mean assessing the performance of pupils by some quantitative measure. How this is done will be explored in the case study, but Robert Stake's labels of antecedents (learner background), transactions (learner/teacher) and outcomes (learner) provide the basic framework.[10]

In his discussion, Thomas adopts Wahlberg and Haertel's definition of evaluation as 'a careful and rigorous examination of an education curriculum, programme or institution.[11] So when teachers design the materials to teach the Programmes of Study as laid down in the National Curriculum, they are looking at content not the pupil's learning achievements.

We suggest, therefore, that evaluation should be seen as the what, where and how of learning, while assessment should be understood as monitoring cognitive performance.

Case study

We will now investigate how one school endeavours to operate the system laid down by government and, in particular, take examples of Year 4 responses, plans and practice. But first, in order to illustrate the magnitude of the task (for we are dealing with a very large primary school) we will outline the structure of the school and see how a jigsaw of tasks has to be fitted together to provide continuity and progression.

STRUCTURE

This county primary school is one of the largest in Oxfordshire. There is a student population of approximately 450 which increases and decreases not only as a result of local demographic changes, but as a consequence of league-tables' market forces.

The school's teaching and administrative organization consists of a headteacher, a deputy head, fourteen teachers, [two teachers for each year band], and learning support assistance. In addition there are two office staff, one the head's secretary, the other the finance officer organizing LMS, and the usual catering and caretaking staff. The head and two teachers are on the governing body.

CURRICULUM

Each member of staff (with the exception of newly qualified teachers) is responsible for a particular curriculum area. They prepare and present a policy document as part of a small team, inform the other staff of current thinking on their specialist subject, and organize in-service training and informational advice.

MANAGEMENT TEAM

There is an on-going developmental dimension to all areas of the curriculum and a management team is responsible for setting up a series of plans for the whole school to ensure progress and continuity. For example the topic of 'electricity' is found in Year 3 autumn term and then is revised and developed in Year 6 autumn term. This meets the statements of attainment and assessment targets as set out in the National Curriculum.

Once the master plans have been decided, the year teachers do their own research into each topic in order to produce a series of worksheets (some teacher-designed, others from commercially produced packs) for all areas of the curriculum for each half term. For example, Year 4 could be tackling topics on the Tudors in history, poetry in English, measurement in maths, the pavanne in dance, rugby in PE, and so forth. The plans are then submitted to each curriculum co-ordinator and a copy retained in a year folder for future reference. The curriculum is organized in this way in order to prevent duplication, for in a large school, sharing teacher ideas by direct contact is not easy.

In addition to these plans, a bank of formative and summative assessments are being compiled in a school portfolio, giving examples of assessments for each level and each curriculum target. This can then be referred to should a teacher or parent wish to establish 'exactly' to what an example of, say, Attainment Target 3, Level 4 English should conform. Each assessment takes considerable time to prepare since there have to be meetings of the teachers, curricular co-ordinators and assessment co-ordinator in order to make a decision. Whilst this is excellent for cross-fertilization of ideas amongst teaching staff and peer support, taking into account all the individual issues concerning a child is complex.

YEAR TEAM MEETINGS

Since the school is organized in year groups, the subject matter of the ten areas that make up the National Curriculum is allocated to each year at the appropriate level. This subject matter has to be differentiated in order to cater for the needs of a mixed ability group. Inevitably there is a large degree of overlap to ensure continuity and progression. The teams from each year band meet weekly to reflect on the week's work, to amend and adapt, if required, and to plan the following week's work in detail. This also enables teachers to evaluate whether they are on target according to the termly plan. These meetings also provide an opportunity to discuss individual children, to share ideas on curriculum content and behavioural problems and, most importantly, to develop staff relationships.

STAFF MEETINGS

There is a rolling programme of staff meetings throughout the school. It is set out as follows

Week 1 Domestic   These meetings inform the staff of important diary events in the school, enable exchanges of information on how in-service training plans, social events and matters individual staff members wish to raise.

Week 2 Curriculum   There is a constant need for updating planning, assessment and ideas managements. Since time is limited, all areas of the curriculum cannot be debated at once, so a focus for the term is agreed. Once this is set, the curriculum leaders are joined by other members of staff, to debate the issues, produce a report and present it to the staff at a subsequent curriculum meeting.

Week 3 In-service training   The in-service co-ordinator sets the programme in response to the school development plan, the needs or requests of staff members, or as part of a curriculum focus. The meeting is usually a twilight in-house session (between 4 and 6 p.m.), and is sometimes conducted by a co-ordinator, at other times by county advisory staff.

In order to argue the case of how the reality of practice measures up to the official National Curriculum dictates, it is important to observe the degree of administration that is required. For example, maintaining notes on classroom happenings for future reference, curriculum planning, updating of profiles, report writing and preparation of worksheets. All these mean that less time is available for working with the children.

PARENT/TEACHER LINKS

These links are very strong at the school. Parental contributions to curriculum planning, classroom assistance, outside school activities, extra curricular activities and fund raising are major contributions to the school. In addition parents are involved, by invitation to weekly surgeries, in the assessment of their child's work. Approximately four parents per teacher each week discuss their child's progress as recorded in the profile. This profile is compiled in order to highlight success, share problems and prepare action plans. The latest version of this profile has moved away from box-ticking (so disliked by parents) to a more 'user friendly' approach where parents feel not only in control of what is being said, but also that they are contributing to their child's learning. Parents have the opportunity to assess their child's work and raise questions.

At the end of each academic year, a detailed analysis of each child's work is prepared as an annual report. This document can then be discussed by parents with the teachers should there be issues to explore. A copy of this report is kept by the parents and another copy is filed in the child's profile folder. This is then passed to the next year teacher which aids assessment of the needs of the child. Documents relating to academic or behavioural problems are also kept in the profile. Included in this remit, therefore, is a joint responsibility of teacher and parents in the education of the child.

Having discussed the structure of the school, we must now move to the two kinds of assessments, in-house designed assessments and Standard Assessment Tasks (SATs).

But before these can take place, the learning intentions must be established. Shirley Clarke suggests:

Knowledge: what do we want the children to know?
Skills: what do we want the children to be able to do?
Concepts: what do we want the children to understand?
Attitude: what do we want the children to be aware of?[12]

It would be useful to make some general comments on assessment at the outset – where it is to take place and how it is to be conducted. Although the *Handbook of Guidance* issued by SEAC stated that SATs were not to disrupt the general day-to-day running of the class, we shall see how this contrasts with the in-house methods which are part of the planning and day-to-day routine. Once a child is removed from the classroom, from peers and from the teacher – that is, from all the familiar conditions for learning – the harder it is for a child to perform to standards expected by the teacher. The child is also aware of the standards and may become distressed at not meeting them. We shall subsequently argue the value of the implicit in-house assessment as opposed to the explicit assessment of SATs in its present form.

A number of methods of assessment, as practised at the school, are set out below.

Brainstorming This can be conducted in a group, or as a class. The idea is to establish what is known about a concept, to note down the relative information (for example, on a poster) and then to re-examine it to eliminate duplications of language and headings; '... this will provide vital planning information for the teacher: the differentiation range – from the child who has not heard the word "Roman" to the child who knows more about the Romans than the teacher!'[13] If this is conducted at the end of term in preparation for the next term, as Clarke suggests, 'it means that activities can be planned which will meet the needs of all abilities in the class if the two extremes have been defined'.[13]

Discussion   This can be conducted in small groups with a scribe who writes down the findings; then the groups come together as a class and share what they have found.

Conferencing   A concept is discussed with a child on a one-to-one basis. This requires careful handling since interviews with a teacher can be overpowering. However, if handled carefully, conferencing can be most productive. This method is used in reading interviews. The disadvantage is that the interview should not be disturbed so an assistant of some kind should be there to field diversions.

Questionnaires   are a quick and easy method of establishing the information that is required to inform the next step.[14] They are obviously more successful with older children who have a greater command of the written word but infants, given outside help, are seen to make good efforts. There are two kinds of questionnaire. One is teacher-designed and the other child-designed. The ideas to be judged have to be established by the teacher but the content, once the children have had the opportunity to practise the method, can be organized by the children. This method is of major importance when considering self-assessment.

Having looked at methods of assessment, it is important to make a note on the styles of assessment. Intuitive assessment needs to be treated here so that it can be seen how it applies to the variety of assessments.

Intuitive assessment takes account of all dimensions of the child that are available to the teacher. The teacher is not only looking at the written word but at classroom atmosphere, oral and social participation, relationship with teachers, reactions to work, language development, behaviour and so forth. This 'holistic' approach to assessment as opposed to the somewhat reductionist box-ticking exercises in the National Curriculum represents a significant change in style. This form of assessment is diametrically opposed to SATs.

FORMATIVE ASSESSMENT TASKS (ANTECEDENTS) OR 'FATS'

These tasks are designed to establish what the child knows about a topic at the beginning of the course. This is not simply a memory test, but a process analysis also. How did the child get to the point that he/she reaches? Where on the prepared curriculum ladder of ideas is she/he to be placed?

An example of this is poetry in English as treated in Year 4. The initial assessment was in the form of a brainstorming session to establish what the children knew and to build that into the 'Poet's Pack' for use during the topic. (The Poet's Pack was a list of verbal devices such as metaphor, alliteration, metre, onomatopoeia and so on.) The child would then explore a genre of poetry that would enable him or her to either reinforce a concept, explore a new one or revise a device that had been forgotten. In addition to this, the children read a great number of poems, brought their favourites to class discussion, had them photocopied and prepared a class collection. This topic included all three 'in-house' methods of assessment, as will be seen.

CONTINUOUS ASSESSMENT TASKS (TRANSACTIONS) (CATS)

These tasks are designed to enable a teacher to monitor learning and to see where to go next. They can involve a discussion on a concept, marking work and discussing outcomes, guidance on finding information, sharing ideas with a group and many more. Since these are the largest portion of tasks and constitute the main body of learning, it

135

would be useful to see how the child views assessment of the work. Pollard *et al.* suggest that over half the children questioned gave positive answers to the question, 'Do you like it when the teacher looks at your book?'[15] This was because the children received positive feedback, so that their confidence and self-esteem were boosted. However, there were many children who also dreaded showing their books, 'in case I have to do it again', 'because I'll never be super', 'I worry in case it's wrong' and so on. Neither kind of answer, however, indicates the level of ability of the child. The most confident child, for example, may be producing inferior work, but the teacher is able to judge that potential by daily observations. There may be something blocking progress and therefore the teacher must act to promote confidence. There are many ways to tackle such an issue but first it is essential to establish the factors that may be inhibiting the child's progress. These might include a family problem, a friendship problem, a personal problem, lessons being perceived as 'too difficult' to name but four. All the children, however, rely on the teacher's positive feedback and 'smiley faces' and 'ticks' figured strongly in the responses.[16] Pollard *et al.* further argue that when confronted with such questions as, 'Why do some children do better at school work than others?', children's response was strongly influenced by their perception of their peers' ability. Such phrases as 'Nick is very clever at maths' or 'Rachel is a brilliant artist' are typical.

The children spend a great deal of time on CATs. There is a small amount of time allocated at the beginning and ending of a topic to establish what a child knows and then what he or she has been learning. But the major learning time is spent on interactive tasks. These are seen by the child as very important because they are able to judge progression by the increasingly difficult material being presented to them. Conversely, the child who is having difficulty has the opportunity to reinforce or restate their learning in order to progress.

SUMMATIVE LEARNING TASKS (OUTCOMES) (SLTS)

These tasks are designed to assess the teaching and learning of the child and can be produced in a number of ways. Problem-solving exercises, quizzes in groups, paper and pen exercises, games, using the learning material presented to produce a definitive work (as in the poetry topic) and so on. Brainstorming and discussion group findings could be compared with those constructed in the formative tasks at the beginning of the topic.

STANDARD ASSESSMENT TASKS (SATS)

These are the official government tasks designed in Key Stage 1 (Year 2) to test knowledge of English and mathematics, and in Key Stage 2 (Year 6) English, mathematics and science. These are summative tasks. In Key Stage 1 they pick up on the learning over two years, in Key Stage 2 over three years. This is the present version. There have been many others.

Behind SATs 'It is clear that the political priority is still parental choice, despite evidence that choice does not improve standards overall',[17, 18] but does increase the performance gap between schools.[19] It is argued that parents should be free to choose which school their children should attend. The problem is how to provide an independent yardstick to measure schools. That yardstick is SATs and the practice of SATs can only be understood in terms of assessment results for the market accountability of schools, that is league tables.

But the way that league tables are constructed contradicts the 'fair testing' element we teach children in National Curriculum science. Raw data, which is the material of league tables, denies social, cultural and regional diversity, and language barriers; in other words, the value added element. In addition, to this value added element, which takes account of intuitive assessment, already described – a *Qualitative* assessment, SATs is concerned with 'right' or 'wrong' answers – the *quantitative*. In other words, SATs is not about 'fairness', it is about outcome. Torrance comments that conducting SATS goes against everything else that happens in school and is as far removed from good primary practice as it is possible to get. We are constantly helping and encouraging children. Then suddenly all this changes for the test times. The children have a problem and we cannot help them with it.[20]

SATs creates a further problem if the class is vertically grouped, as was the case at the school during the first tests. What happens to the children not taking SATs whilst the teacher has to focus exclusively on the SATs group? They have to be presented with a variety of tasks that can be self-governing. The difficulty of designing a totally foolproof worksheet is practically impossible, since the child may, for a variety of reasons, need the teacher's support. So the children outside the SATs group become detached from their peers and the teacher. Re-forming the class after SATs wastes valuable teaching time.

Standardization of presentation in tests is another problem observed by Pollard *et al.* They observed SATs material being presented as, for example, a competition with reward (housepoints and sweets), as a Continuous Assessment Task (CAT) and as a straight test. They found that in the face of excitement, stress and anxiety, the results of these variations, as would be expected, produced major differences in responses from the children.

With all these variations and changes, by the time Dearing came to his review in 1993, the move from the original TGAT version of a

combination of continuous assessment and SATS which would not be old fashioned unreliable paper and pencil exercises, which enlightened teachers regarded as a waste of time, but would be carefully constructed examples of good teaching and learning with built-in opportunities for standard assessment

had been 'diluted to such an extent that they were very close to the obsolete paper-and-pencil tests'.[21]

Conclusion

Through discussion and case study, this chapter has explored assessment and evaluation; the different methods employed; and how one school attempts to assess the National Curriculum.

In contrast to the intuitive, holistic approach that teachers have developed systematically, we have outlined the official assessment practice of SATs. It can be seen that assessment *per se* is far from being what teachers object to; after all, intuitive assessment has informed their pedagogic practice for generations. Their objection is to the implications of the official assessment of SATs in terms of real value to the child. It would be more than useful to think of assessment as not 'always to be a simple summative judgement between success and failure', but that it 'can have a formative purpose helping to identify aspects of work where action can be taken to improve'.[22]

But at this stage, we must return to the tension that is created between the rhetoric and the reality of practice. SATs conflicts directly with the professional judgement of the teacher.[23] The ideology of dedication to children and commitment to doing the best for every child comes into direct conflict with National Curriculum assessment because these ideas derive from different sets of principles. The first is the concern for the learning of the child, and all that that means. The second is the concern for market accountability.

The concern for the child's learning embraces all the 'value added' elements detailed, in particular the social and emotional well-being of the child, for without this security the child is not going to perform to his or her potential. SATs, it is suggested, runs against the ethos of good primary practice in that if there is a problem in today's classrooms, we want to be able to 'work it through'. The children are encouraged to talk about tasks, share expertise and develop language skills. All of which promote confidence and self-esteem. What better way is there for a teacher to judge understanding than to observe one child teaching a task to another.

As has been seen at the case study school, the reality of practice, assessment is not a problem; it is vital to the continuity of progression, academically, socially and emotionally. Assessment is part of the daily routine of any teacher and in the final analysis Clarke suggests that 'it is a process to make explicit the children's achievements, celebrate their achievements with them, then help them to move forward to the next goal'.[24]

Maybe we should let Cockcroft have the final word: 'no one has ever grown taller as a result of being measured!'[25]

Notes and references

1. Black, P. (Chair) Task Group on Assessment and Testing (London: DES, 1987). See chapter 3, this volume.
2. Troman, G. Testing tensions: the politics of educational assessment *British Educational Research Journal* 15 (3), 1989, 279–95.
3. Gipps, C. *Assessment: A Teacher's Guide to the Issues* (London: Hodder & Stoughton, 1990).
4. Black, P. Can teachers use assessment to improve learning? *British Journal of Curriculum and Assessment*, 5 (2), 1995, 7–11, p. 7.
5. Lawton, D. What kind of national curriculum and assessment after Dearing? *British Journal of Curriculum and Assessment*, 4 (3), 1994, 8–12, p. 9.
6. Carvel, S. and Wintour, P. Assessing significant achievement in the primary classroom *British Journal of Curriculum and Assessment*, 5 (3), 1995, 12–16. One should question whether numbers such as 40 in a class are 'marginal'.
7. Black, P. 1995 op. cit., p. 7.
8. Thomas, E. *Assessing Learning* Unit 11 MA and Diploma Course in Distance Learning (London: Institute of Education, University of London, 1990).
9. Ibid., p. 37.
10. Stake, R. Language rationality and assessment In Bently, W.H. (ed.) *Improving Educational Assessment* (Alexandria: Association for Supervision and Curriculum Development, 1969).
11. Wahlberg, H. and Haertel, G. (eds) *International Encyclopedia of Educational Evaluation* (Oxford: Pergamon, 1990), 38.
12. Clarke, S. Assessing significant achievement in the primary classroom *British Journal of Curriculum and Assessment*, 5 (3), 1995, 12–16, p. 13.
13. Ibid.
14. Mortimore, A. Using questionnaires in formative assessment. Part 7 of *Strategies for Classroom Assessment*, from the project *Assessment, Teaching and Learning in the Primary School*, National Primary Centre (South West), 1991, 1–8.
15. Pollard, A., Broadfoot, P., Croll, P., Osborn, M. and Abbot, D.

Changing English Primary Schools? Impact of the Education Reform Act at Key Stage One (London: Cassell, 1994).

16. Ibid.
17. Adler, M. *An Alternative Approach to Parental Choice* NCE Briefing 13, 1993.
18. Miliband, D. *Markets, Politics and Education* (London: IPP, 1991).
19. Lawton, D. op. cit., p. 12.
20. Cited in Pollard *et al.*, op. cit., p. 209.
21. Lawton, D. op. cit., p. 9.
22. Parker-Rees, R. Why are we doing this? Part 1 of *Strategies for Classroom Assessment*, from the project *Assessment, Teaching and Learning in the Primary School*, National Primary Centre (South West), 1991, 1–8, p. 7.
23. See Pollard *et al.* 1994.
24. Clarke, S. op. cit., p. 12.
25. Department of Education and Science 'Cockroft Report', *Mathematics Counts* (London: HMSO, 1982).

CHAPTER 8
Practical Assessment and Testing in a Secondary School

GRAHAM HERBERT

All too often the terms assessment and testing become confused. Recently the government had to change the title of the Standard Assessment Tasks to the Standard Assessment Tests, belying a lack of care over its own terminology. The word 'assessment' is a more far-reaching term than the word 'test'.

But what is assessment? Assessment can be defined as an estimation or judgement of the value of a pupil's achievements. This estimation or judgement will have more meaning if it is based on evidence. Achievements can be seen as gaining mastery of certain skills, knowledge or understanding in any piece of work. Evidence of this mastery can be collected at any time and does not rely upon a form of test at the end of a unit of work. Assessment then is not something that is collected at the end of a unit of study – that is a test. Assessment is not something which is bolted on to the end of a unit of study. Testing is indeed not the only method of assessment. Assessment includes a variety of tasks, tests, practical activities and observations by teachers and pupils' peers, as well as the individual pupil. For assessment to be effective, it must be part of the learning process. The outcomes of the assessment must then be fed back into the programme of learning as learning objectives. In this way, assessment is part of the learning process itself and does not detract from teaching and learning.

The value of assessment is that it

> lies at the heart of the process of promoting children's learning. It provides a framework in which educational objectives can be set and pupils' progress charted and expressed. It yields a basis for planning the next educational steps in response to children's needs. By facilitating dialogue between teachers, it enhances professional skills and helps the school as a whole to strengthen learning across the curriculum and throughout the age range.[1]

142

This definition of assessment has, then, far-reaching implications for schools and the different ways in which they assess pupils.

Classroom implications

Assessment is part of everyday teaching and learning. It is a continuous process, not a separate activity which necessarily requires the use of extra tasks or tests. Most teachers already assess informally beyond the confines of the National Curriculum as they try to evaluate a pupil's progress and the success of their own delivery. Informally, teachers make comments about a pupil's attitude to work or a pupil's efforts. Teachers also make comments about a pupil's presentation skills or certain characteristics which militate against or support a pupil's ability to learn. Assessments are already used to record 'quantifiable' attainment in the form of descriptors of levels in the National Curriculum, or the cognitive aspects of attainment. However, teachers also pass comments about a pupil's personal achievements, or the affective aspects of development, sometimes called achievement.

That teachers are making assessments all the time in order to function effectively is beyond doubt. These assessments use a variety of criteria at any one time. This process has been summarised by Ruth Sutton: 'Assessment is a human process conducted by and with human beings and subject to the frailties of human nature. However crisp and objective we might try to make it and however neatly quantifiable may be our resutls, assessment is closer to an art than a science'.[2]

Assessment can be made on cognitive ability and the mastery of knowledge and skills, but judgements are also made on personal qualities in order to structure and plan for each individual's future progress, or formative assessment. The National Curriculum and the SATs which measure a pupil's progress in it, address the cognitive attainment of pupils. A pupil's affective development is addressed in the form of the cross-curricular themes and

143

dimensions. However, progress in these areas of learning do not form part of the SAT. As teachers we contribute to other areas of development on a continuous basis. In practice, assessment in schools concentrates on assessing the cognitive elements of the National Curriculum, the product of education – not its process. If pupils are to develop an understanding of their personal and social development, or self-awareness, beyond the limiting confines of the cognitive elements of the subject specific National Curriculum, these other areas cannot be ignored in the classroom.

Statutory requirements

The 1988 Education Reform Act emphasizes the summative purposes of assessment: 'The curriculum ... shall ... specify the arrangements for assessing pupils at or near the end of each key stage for the purpose of ascertaining what they have achieved in relation to the attainment targets for that key stage'.

However, assessment has other educational purposes:

1. To assist pupils in their learning by enhancing motivation, recognizing achievements, ensuring continuity and progression, reviewing progress and setting appropriate targets.
2. To identify pupils' strengths and weaknesses in order that teachers may review their delivery of their curriculum to fit the needs of the pupils.
3. To supply information through which the school can assess the quality of its provision.
4. To provide information on individual pupils and/or the whole school as appropriate.

If a school is to meet the educational needs of its pupils as well as meet its statutory duties, then it is more meaningful if the assessment of the process of education is formalized. By formalizing assessments in this area we create a common vocabulary for teachers, pupils and parents. Such a vocabulary allows us to chart an individual's progress across a key stage, not only in terms of the cognitive, but also in terms of the affective development of the pupil. Such a vocabulary also facilitates a dialogue between teachers, pupils and parents about the learning process itself. By specifying the terminology, we also provide a more meaningful framework for the evaluation of courses, materials and pupils' progress. Such an assessment requires other methods than tests at certain key stages. This is because what we are assessing are the ways in which pupils learn. In other words we are assessing the process of learning and not merely its product.

Within the context of the National Curriculum, a pupil is expected to develop diverse skills, knowledge and under-standing as well as attitudes, which need to be recorded and based upon evidence. This cannot be left satisfactorily to a summative method of assessment, for such an assessment cannot take account of the diversity of a pupil's achieve-ments. To do this, evidence must be gained from a variety of sources including self-assessment, peer assessment, course evaluation and teacher assessment of written, oral and practical work as well as tests.

This is because the National Curriculum as a set of subjects is, of necessity, a limited view of what and how chil-dren learn. We also have to take into consideration the ways in which children learn. They learn by watching, discover-ing, telling, investigating, questioning and so on. This happens across subjects and is not the prerogative of one subject alone. Other important aspects of the ways in which pupils learn are also cross-curricular. This includes such things as use of language, imagination, aesthetics, citizen-ship, problem-solving and so on. Any learning is therefore a three-dimensional, not the one-dimensional process as presented by the subject specific National Curriculum and the testing of progress in it by the national SATs.

Possible areas for assessment: a philosophical perspective

The following areas for use in assessments are based upon Pring's ideas about the development of self in pupils.[3] These are chosen to avoid the simplistic concentration on the cognitive elements of a pupil's development, presented as level descriptors in each subject area, and to highlight the affective elements which are often overlooked or given merely a cursory mention by teachers. Nevertheless, these are areas for which pupils can be given credit and helped to develop. They help in providing a common vocabulary by which to assess the processes of education. Developing approaches for assessing through these area also provides a way of tackling personal and social skills, the cross-curricular themes and those important characteristics which are outside the prescriptive National Curriculum. The resulting matrix can then be used as a basis for a planned programme of systematic guidance.

1. **Intellectual competences:** those skills and abilities that allow accurate observation, clear thought, hypothesis, logical argument and exposition. These can be found in the level descriptors in such subjects as English, maths, history, geography, science and RE.
2. **Practical knowledge:** this is necessary for 5 (below) to operate. It relates to the practical nature of learning in a variety of environments both inside and outside school. This involves an understanding of appropriate methods of working in different environments such as a workshop, a laboratory, a library, an art room, a formal classroom, a field trip, a museum and so on.
3. **Theoretical knowledge:** the concepts, insights, beliefs and principles afforded through theoretical study. This relates to the theoretical nature of all subject levels as well as to aspects of the cross-curricular themes.
4. **Character traits:** those qualities of the will such as perseverance, courage, tenacity, patience and so on which pupils must exhibit to complete a task and thereby experience some form of achievement.
5. **Social competences:** these are the skills which make the above operational. They include oral and numeri-cal skills as well as the ability to interact with other people, to work within the parameters set down by an organization and so on. Such skills and personal quali-

ties arise in all aspects of school life and across the whole curriculum. When their delivery is planned and written into schemes of work, these too can be assessed. This might, for example, refer to the way a pupil collaborates with peers in a particular situation, or perhaps how one individual can encourage a more reticent pupil to take part in a particular task. Although the methodology putting this theory into practice is fraught with problems, some schools have managed to achieve this.

6. **Personal values:** this would include those values which are appropriate to an individual such as a particular religious belief or being a vegetarian. It is of course dangerous to attempt to quantify such values, but because they can have a profound effect upon a pupil, it is also dangerous to ignore them.

7. **Personal characteristics:** this includes dispositions such as modesty, self-confidence, kindness, assertiveness and generosity. These dispositions can be manifested in many ways, particularly in life skill courses, active tutorial work or PSE. The assessment of such dispositions is often carried out by pupils' peers, since they are more likely to see these dispositions, or a lack of them, than are teachers.

In the assessment process, areas 1, 2 and 3 are more readily 'quantifiable', but areas 4 to 7 can be assessed using a common vocabulary and rewarding progress. However, pupils should know when and upon what criteria they are being assessed. Not all of these areas will be assessed at all times, but need to be considered when planning the curriculum and carrying out assessments of it.

However, is this philosophical perspective sufficient to give us a three-dimensional matrix which will fairly reflect the processes of learning which a pupil experiences? Will it develop into a process designed to foster social control or will it achieve its aim of encouraging pupils to learn?

Possible areas for assessment: a sociological perspective

Watkins adopts a different paradigm yet comes up with similar results.[4] His approach to the content of PSE is student-centred, 'picks up time honoured themes of adolescent development ... and is framed at a sufficiently general level to engage the vast majority of teachers'. His approach combines the general with the specific aspects of PSE, giving a 'whole-person' result. He too divides the self into seven areas:

1. **The bodily self**: understanding change and growth, the impact and variety of bodily changes, the uses and abuses of the body, maintaining the body, eating and health care of the body, the links between the body and the environment.
2. **The sexual self**: an awareness of and coping with rapid changes during adolescence. Understanding that a range of sexual lifestyles exists in society; examining the role of sexuality in relationships, the processes in sexual attraction, the processes in sex-role stereotyping of young people, sexuality, procreation and choice, STDs and choice.
3. **The social self**: communication skills in the family, with friends and in the community. Giving and receiving feedback. Making sense of other people, stereotypes and prejudices. Understanding other's points of view. Presenting oneself in a variety of social settings. Making, keeping and ending relationships. Assertiveness, handling conflicts and resolving conflicts. Relationships in the family, with authority, with others. Working in groups and teams, co-operating, negotiating, collaborating. Managing stress, coping with loss and separation.
4. **The vocational self**: understanding influences on vocational decision-making. Examining choices and options. Understanding different lifestyles: paid, unpaid and so on. Adult roles in the home, the community and at leisure. The impact of jobs on lifestyles. Handling tran-

sitions to other lifestyles and to other aspects of education. The changing nature of lifestyles and the impact on job opportunities. Evaluating the quality of information on prospective job opportunities. Rights and responsibilities in the work place.

5. **The moral/political self:** assessing the effect our actions and inactions have on others. Understanding the value of another's point of view and the principles or beliefs that underlie it. Identifying conflicts of principles, handling dilemmas. Understanding the principles underlying different beliefs. Examining the impact of the law on different beliefs and behaviours. Examining the impact of change at all levels of a democratic and pluralistic society. Understanding how and why codes are developed in different situations and how these can change.

6. **Self as a learner:** to reflect on present study modes to explore the demands of various learning tasks. To organise and plan responses to learning tasks. Using other people as a resource in learning. Developing effective self-assessment skills. Understanding and responding to assessment feedback. To engage in group activities for the purposes of learning. Managing time and coping with anxiety. Organizing independent work. Developing a greater range of learning strategies. Target-setting as a means of learning.

7. **Self in the organization:** to learn how to cope in a new organization. To use organizations in constructive ways. To be an active participant in organizations. To gain access to help in any organization. To handle transitions between organizations. To identify opportunities and choices within any organization.

Such a view of the development of self presents teachers with an enormously complex system which it could be argued, is impossible to implement. However, by using pupils and their responses as basic resources, some schools have managed to satisfactory incorporate such views into their PSE provision.

Both of these perspectives provide a view of the self which is far broader than that which the National Curriculum specifies. Both perspectives also support the view that development of the self cannot be divorced from the role of the individual within any community – family, school, local community, national community, global community. What is surprising is that these important areas can be assessed and individuals can improve their performances in these areas by acting upon the feedback from their assessment.

The following examples give sufficient evidence to show that pupils can work in such a system by analysing their strengths and weaknesses, setting appropriate targets and working towards them.

Michael, a Year 8 pupil identified that he was not using his homework diary correctly. To help him improve his organizational skills, he agreed, along with his form tutor, to keep his diary up-to-date for one week. Having achieved this feat, he was given an award of a merit. His subsequent target was to maintain this for a further three weeks. His success was once again rewarded. Such a process involved him in being in control of his own behaviour and allowed him to change it without recourse to any negative feedback in school.

Katy, another Year 8 pupil, identified as a weakness her inability to work with pupils who were not in her close circle of friends. This was agreed by both her peers and her form tutor. To improve this aspect of her work, she set herself the following target. During the next project in tutorial lessons, she would work constructively with a group of pupils with whom she did not normally work. The group she named was asked if they objected to her presence. They did not. Subsequently, Katy worked alongside some people with whom she had not worked before. Although she found this irksome, she collaborated with the 'alien' group and was rewarded for doing so. This approach is of course open to abuse. Cynical pupils may well block the approach adopted by Katy, but usually, with pupils who are in their first two terms of secondary schooling, this does not happen. Once the patterns and ground rules have been set and acted upon by the majority, then the rest usually fall into place.

Problems occur when pupils new to the form appear in the same year and deliberately disrupt the proceedings. Problems can also occur with this system when younger pupils find little or no currency in the reward system adopted by the school and the majority of pupils. When this occurs it requires intensive reviewing on the behalf of the form tutor to bring the pupil back into the fold.

If such an approach to assessment is to assist pupils in their learning by motivating, ensuring progression and continuity and recognizing achievement then the personal and social aspects of assessment cannot be ignored by a teacher in the classroom. If this happens, teachers will be ignoring the context in which learning is taking place. We cannot rely solely on anecdotal references to a pupil's laziness or lack of organizational skills or whatever else a teacher may blame for a pupil's poor performance or failure to progress. To secure sound assessment we must make a more systematic use of the vocabulary which the school adopts to describe and inform the assessment system.

Management and classroom practice

To help teachers in the task of assessing and recording achievement, two things must happen. First there must be an over-arching framework in which assessment takes place. This means that there must be an assessment policy in place in the school. More precisely this would refer to a set of assessment procedures. Expressed as procedures it implies that something is actually happening rather than a statement which may then simply gather dust. By providing a set of procedures in a school, we can allow individual departments to determine how those procedures will impact upon assessment practices in each subject area. Furthermore, teachers must take account of the processes of learning rather than merely assessing the product of learning.

A POSSIBLE MANAGEMENT FRAMEWORK

The following represents a summary of documents which already exist in schools and local authorities. It is not intended to be a definitive framework, but one which shows the principles underlying the management of assessment in any school.

1. *Introduction* The assessment process cannot be divorced from the recording, reporting and reviewing processes in school. The principles underlying Records of Achievement will be consistent with the assessment procedures.

2. *Aims* To promote the quality of learning and improve teaching methods.
   To provide information to pupils about their progress, their means of improving and their achievements.
   To provide information to the staff about the progress of individual pupils, the effectiveness of teaching strategies, the planning and effectiveness of the curriculum.
   To provide information to parents, the next stage of education, potential employers.

3. *Principles* Assessment will meet with statutory requirements.
   Assessment will make use of a variety of methods.
   Assessments will be an integral part of the learning process and not a bolt-on addition to it.

Such a framework can then be fed to departments which might wish to provide their own guidelines as follows. Again, the guidelines given here are based on a number of instances already working within schools and local authorities.

Guidelines for departments The department will ensure that schemes of work will have appropriate assessment practices as an integral part. These assessment practices will take the following into account:
- The assessment will inform upon and improve the quality of the learning provided.
- The assessment will be carried out with pupils, not done to them.
- Pupils will view the experience of assessment as a positive one.

- The assessment will differentiate between pupils and take into account the differing aptitudes and requirements of pupils.
- Not all learning will be assessed (this is not possible).
- The criteria upon which any assessment is based will be made explicit to pupils before the assessment takes place.
- The assessment of the academic aspects of education will form only a part of the whole of a pupil's achievements.

Implicit in such procedures is a recognition of the depth and complexity of the curriculum. Personal and social skills, so necessary for effective learning to take place, must be made explicit to pupils before assessment of them takes place.

IMPLICATIONS FOR CLASSROOM PRACTICE

What are the implications of this for the teacher and learner in the classroom? All too often, under the constraints of time, the teacher can only assess the product of the learning. That is to say the teacher 'marks' and grades a pupil's work and records the results. However, this does not have to be the total of assessment in a classroom. We can also include the individual pupil's self-assessment as well as the assessment carried out by the pupil's peers.

How can the individual pupil or a group of the pupil's peers begin to assess what is happening in terms of the National Curriculum and level descriptors? By using as a starting point the vocabulary common to the school, which has been explained to the pupils and their parents and is understood by all teachers, meaningful assessments are possible by both individual pupils and their peers.

This can be done by introducing a set of personal and social factors which will have an impact upon the learning of an individual. If these factors are written in the form of 'can do' statements, it is easy for the pupils to complete as well as easy for the pupil's peers to assess. The statements will also

153

Table 8.1 Personal and social skills and attitudes which promote learning

	Ready	Sometimes	Usually	Always
1. Personal Skills				
I bring all equipment to lessons				
I arrive on time for my lessons				
I use my student diary correctly				
I stick to deadlines				
I copy any work I have missed				
I carry out all tasks which are set me				
I try my best				
If I do not understand, I ask for help				
I set myself challenging targets				
2. Social Skills				
I can work constructively in a group of friends				
I accept other people's points of view				
I can stick to agreed rules				
I encourage others to join in set tasks				
I can co-operate with people who are not my friends				
I can collaborate on a group task				
I can listen to others				
If I see someone being bullied I help to stop it				
3. Attitudes				
I tolerate people who are different from me				
I help those who need it				
I share things with other people				
I ask if I want to borrow something				
I treat other people with respect				
I can control my emotions				
I can speak to other people appropriately				
I avoid associating with bullies				

help in the formative process for the completion of the National Record of Achievement by Years 10 and 11. Table 8.1 represents one school's attempts at producing a matrix for ease of assessing the achievements of its pupils. This is not a definitive document, not will it be imported into other schools and used by them. This particular matrix was used by pupils in Year 8. Schools may find it necessary to use a different matrix and a different set of skills and attitudes for older or younger pupils.

Pupils can complete such a matrix quickly. Following this, it is possible for each pupil's peers to check the individual's assessment. It is important that this is carried out by the pupil's peers, for if teachers were to check such an assessment, it is possible that they would be assessing the school's norms and not the individual pupil.

From the original assessment, pupils can set themselves targets, negotiated with a form tutor or subject teacher, which relate to the improvement of a particular skill or development of attitude. It is useful to reward the pupil for the achieving of such targets, by means of a merit or star, or whatever reward system is in operation in the school, much as was outlined on page 150 by both Michael and Katy. Reward systems lose their currency the older pupils become. However, by linking rewards to agreed targets, the 'confetti' syndrome, associated with such reward systems, is avoided and pupils develop the habit of setting targets, so important in Years 10 and 11 for the Records of Achievement process.

An assessment system which uses such a matrix, or one similar to it, is beginning to address the complex nature of the learning process, as well as making peer and self-assessment central to the assessment process. It is not a difficult process to introduce, nor is it difficult or time consuming for teachers to administer. Importantly, any assessment carried out by the teacher can be diagnostic in terms of the pupil's personal and social skills as well as subject content. Further, it allows pupils and teachers to assess the affective as well as the cognitive aspects of education and recognizes explicitly the complex nature of the learner and the individual.

Process of Implementation

To begin the process of implementation of such a view of assessment needs a carefully thought out plan. Figure 8.1 suggests a method that could be adopted, although other models may be appropriate as well.

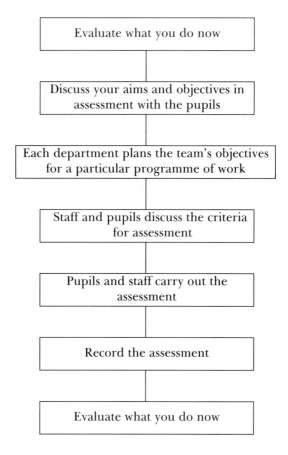

Figure 8.1 Seven steps to better assessment

Conclusion

Such a view of assessment, although more complex than the view of testing or other summative tests, at least allows pupils to be rewarded for learning. This view of assessment also reflects a multi-faceted view of the learning process. If assessment is to mean anything, then it has to be linked to the concept of the development of self. Expecting assessment to reflect merely the absorption of a body of knowledge or a part of some understanding is to deny the worth of the educational process itself.

Notes and references

1. Black, P. (Chair) *Task Group on Assessment and Testing* (London: DES, 1987).
2. Sutton, R. *Assessment: A Framework for Teachers* (London:Routledge 1992) .
3. Pring, R. *Personal and Social Education* (London: Hodder and Stoughton 1984) .
4. Watkins, C. *Whole School Personal and Social Education: Policy and Practice* NAPCE Publications, University of Warwick, Coventry, 1992.

CHAPTER 9

Evaluation: Trinkets for the Natives or Cultural Change?

DAVID HOPKINS, DAVID JACKSON, MEL WEST AND IAN TERRELL

We have distinguished elsewhere between three approaches to evaluation and their link with school improvement.[1] These are evaluation of school improvement, evaluation for school improvement, and evaluation as school improvement. In the later stages of this paper we explore, through an example of research in schools, the current relevance of this taxonomy of evaluation. In particular we explore the extent to which the schools we have studied have been able to make use of external evaluation data to inform and generate school improvement strategies. We begin, however, be defining our conceptual framework for school improvement, enlarge upon the link between evaluation and school improvement, and explore more fully the evolution of evaluation approaches introduced above.

School improvement

The world wide school effectiveness research movement has become increasingly sophisticated at producing lists of the characteristics of the 'effective school' – at school, teacher and student levels. These lists of quality indicators, competencies, performance indicators and output measures are useful descriptors and have helped to inform the framework on which schools and teachers might be evaluated. However, there remains a gap between the establishment of common understandings about characteristics that predispose schools towards effectiveness and the implementation of processes and strategies for generating improvement at the individual school level.

In his book *Improving School from Within*, Roland Barth distinguishes between the two different approaches towards school development that we have generally called 'school effectiveness' and 'school improvement' movements.[2] He parodies the different sets of assumptions and opinions, the first as follows:

- Schools do not have the capacity or the will to improve themselves; improvements must therefore come from outside the school.
- What needs to be improved about schools is the level of pupil performance and achievement, this measured by standardized tests.
- School improvement is an attempt to identify what school people should know and be able to do, and devise ways to get them to know and do it.

These assumptions (selected from Barth's more detailed list) imply an approach which encourages someone to do something to someone else; it is about measurement and control rather than growth and self-directed learning; it is about external interventions rather than internal development.

Barth goes on to argue that a 'community of learners' approach to school improvement generates a radically different set of assumptions from those above. Some of these are:

- Schools have the capacity to improve themselves, if the conditions are right. A major responsibility of those outside the school is to help provide these conditions.
- When the need and purpose are there, when the conditions are right, adults and students alike learn and each energizes and contributes to the learning of the other.
- What needs to be improved about schools is their culture.
- School improvement is an effort to determine and provide conditions under which the adults and youngsters who inhabit schools will promote and sustain learning amongst themselves.

These assumptions capture the essence of our approach to school improvement. It is an approach strongly influenced by involvement with the OECD International School Improvement Project (ISIP).[3] Van Velzen defined school improvement as 'systematic, sustained effort in changing learning conditions and other related internal conditions in one or more schools with the ultimate aim of accomplishing educational goals more effectively.' Whilst this definition has stood the test of time, it is rather abstract and for our purposes needs some further explanation. Much has been learnt about the process of change over the last ten or fifteen years. Although it is neither appropriate, nor is there space, to cover this issue in detail, the following points are relevant to the context of our research.[4]

- Change takes place over time. Realistic or undefined time-lines fail to recognize that implementation occurs developmentally. It is a process, not an event.
- Ownership and understanding of the change are important – both the reasons why it is happening and how it will bring about improvement.
- Shared control of implementation is important – top-down is not all right.
- Organizational conditions within and in relation to the school make it more or less likely that school improvement will occur.
- It is very difficult to change education without also changing the school as an organization, without enlisting the co-operation of fellow teachers and without the advocacy of school leaders.

It follows that school improvement is therefore about curriculum development, the strength in the school organization, the teaching/learning process, and a developmental approach to evaluation. Such an approach to evaluation focuses attention on the process of strengthening the school's capacity to deal with change and ensuring a belief in the school improvement agenda.

It will be evident from this last definition that our particular ideological position places evaluation as an integral element in school improvement. We would agree with Stenhouse when he argues 'against the separation of developer and evaluator' and in favour of integrated research. He continues: 'Evaluation should, as it were, lead development and be integrated with it. Then the conceptual distinction between development and evaluation is destroyed and the two merge as research'.[5] We perceive the fusion between evaluation and school development as defining the central axis of school improvement processes and roles. We are committed to development and to the use of evaluative data to illuminate, inform and guide this process.

Six or seven years ago, when we first proposed the model in Figure 9.1, we also argued 'if evaluation of school improvement is done well, this leads inevitably to evaluation for school improvement, which in turn provides the substance for evaluation as school improvement'.[6] Our research work with schools over the last few years, both in the evaluative and developmental fields, suggests that the reality is rather less straightforward. The cycle implied in the model (or the continuum in the description) is perhaps less inevitably sequential than we then suggested. The three approaches might be better represented as three overlapping but interdependent aspects of evaluation, the first providing descriptive or analytical data, the second representing our capacity to make appropriate judgements on which to design school improvement approaches, and the third representing a continuous process of data collection and

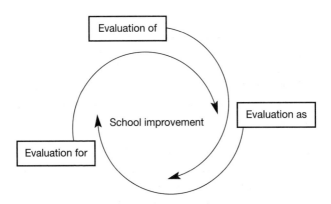

Figure 9.1 Evaluation and school improvement

school improvement response which is integrated, inter-dependent and mutually enhancing in the manner described by Stenhouse (Figure 9. 2).

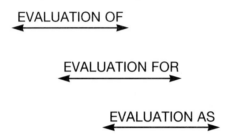

Figure 9.2 Rethinking evaluation and school improvement

With these background patterns established, we can now turn to an analysis of evaluation of, for and as school improvement.

EVALUATION *OF* SCHOOL IMPROVEMENT

'Evaluations *of*' are usually concerned with evaluating the outcomes of improvement effort or a particular initiative. These will tend to be built around the question 'What aspects of previous practice would we expect to see changed if this programme or innovation is to be effective?' Inevitably, therefore, 'evaluations of' will tend to be 'product' evaluations, dealing primarily with quantitative and statistical data. Where 'process' evaluation is employed it, too, will tend to be a search for 'process outcomes'. This focus on the results of an initiative lends to the evaluation data many of the characteristics of school effectiveness research. Summative data produced as a result of evaluating school improvement activities will have limited transferabil-ity to other innovations or to the distinctive cultures of other schools. It is inherent in our definition of school improve-ment that it is an 'adaptive, evolving and problem-coping' process rather than one in which fidelity to other initiatives – however successful – plays a large part.[7]

What is implied is clearly an evaluation schema that

reflects the evolutionary, relatively autonomous nature of school development – and which is part of the development culture itself. This statement clearly leads us forward into the next stage of the cycle or continuum.

EVALUATION *FOR* SCHOOL IMPROVEMENT

The sense of what is meant by evaluation *for* school improvement is perhaps best captured in the commonly understood phrase 'formative evaluation'. This is evaluation conducted for the purpose of bringing about improvements in practice. The critical features of this evaluation approach is that its prime focus is the facilitation of change. In this mode, though, the evaluation and the change remain distinct. There are two major issues raised in the literature that relate to the effectiveness of evaluation for school improvement. The first is its lack of integration with our knowledge about change and implementation processes. The second is the problem of communicating, utilizing and gaining ownership of the data.

In order to do 'evaluation *for*' properly, Fullan argues that data would need to be gathered also on elements of the change process itself.[8] In order to generate information on which judgements and actions might be based, there would need to be three aspects of evaluation for school improvement:

1. a definition of the change itself
2. a description and assessment of the factors influencing change
3. an evaluation of the outcomes of the change (both anticipated and unanticipated)

In order to outline the potential complexity of 'evaluation *for*' design purporting to facilitate improvement, Fullan and Park suggested that the following dimensions would need to be incorporated:

1. alterations in structure
2. use of new materials
3. the acquisition of new knowledge

4. the introduction of new teaching styles
5. the internalization of new beliefs.[9]

It will be obvious, we hope, that an evaluation design based on these implementation components would readily provide a framework for effective development.

We also outlined the communication of evaluation data as a concern with the 'evaluation for' approach. The meaningful outcomes of evaluation are usually presented in a written report or in statistical analyses. These are particularly inappropriate methods for communicating about development, and the written form is a particularly difficult medium for moving the hearts and minds of school leaders and teachers. This communication problem has been shown to be significant, and this is particularly the case when evaluation activities are conducted by external researchers.[10]

The limitations of space preclude a full discussion of this issue, but it is probably sufficient to state that studies have shown that 'evaluation for' activities can give rise to greater ownership when they focus on user issues; involve users in the process; develop a pedagogy for learning from evaluation; and make explicit the integration between evaluation and development.[11] This last point leads naturally into the next section.

EVALUATION *AS* SCHOOL IMPROVEMENT

In many ways this heading is self explanatory. Evaluation as school improvement occurs when the evaluation has an explicit school improvement purpose and when those who will be involved in the development are engaged also in the evaluation. The process of evaluation and school improvement is one and the same thing.

In the 1980s we saw the introduction of GRIDS in Britain and other similar school-based review activities throughout Europe. These were examples of 'evaluation *as*' activities.[12] Similarly, school self-evaluation, school development planning, action research and a variety of other school-based research activities are current examples of the integration between evaluation and development activities. Evaluation has the potential to be a change process in itself: to change teachers through their professional growth; to change the culture of the school in which it takes place; to increase the knowledge base about the school; and to lead to further school improvement.

Based on our own research in schools and the research literature in this field, it appears that 'evaluation as' school improvement becomes increasingly effective when it:

- is 'owned' at the school level
- is free from accountability implications
- utilizes a systematic and conscious methodology
- relates to perceived needs at the school level
- embraces a clear perception and definition of process and roles
- is integrated into on-going school improvement processes
- receives external support

Evaluation and the local management of schools

In the previous sections we have described a broad classification of the different purposes served by and perspectives on the evaluation process. Though we still feel that this offers a useful overview of the evaluation process itself, it is clear that the educational reforms which have been implemented over the past eight years have altered the balance between these perspectives.

Whilst the previous decade saw much attention paid to the evaluation of initiatives intended to improve schools, the relevance of external, *post hoc* evaluation has been more difficult to discern in the newly established 'educational marketplace'. There are a number of factors contributing to this. One has been the change in central government policy with regard to systemic change. The use made of 'trialling' new ideas and approaches in a small number of educational authorities or schools has diminished sharply. Many of the important developments of the 1970s and 1980s were introduced in this way (e.g. pupil profiling, the Technical and Vocational Education Initiative, Schoolteacher Appraisal).

Implementation limited to a small part of the school sector was evaluated, most often with a range of partners, and any lessons emerging could be assimilated before national implementation. Generally, this approach to educational change was successful, and evaluation certainly played a part in the success. However, since the late 1980s the British Government has favoured a rather more rapid implementation, and change has tended to stem from legislation which affected all schools simultaneously. Subsequent evaluations have been commissioned (and some have led to modifications in policy) but the majority of schools may well feel that they were aware of the problems/difficulties associated with particular policies long before an 'evaluation report' became available. In that sense, the role played by systematic evaluation of policy implementation over the previous decade has been eroded, and such reports are now as much concerned with the demonstration of public accountability as the improvement of practice.

A second factor is the demise of the local education authority (LEA) as a significant partner in the development of the educational system. Local management, with its transfer of funds and decision-making into the school, has left the LEA with less influence and fewer resources. The district-level evaluation of educational change has also declined sharply in this climate: LEAs do not have the funds to commission evaluations and, even if they had, schools might not be inclined to cooperate as they did in the past.

Third, there has been a growing dissatisfaction with the point of focus of 'externally' commissioned evaluations. In part, this relates to the concern of central government to establish that policies have been implemented, rather than that policies are achieving the purposes for which they were brought forward. Studies of implementation hold less interest for teachers than studies of impact. In part, it is related to the failure (sometimes) to establish success criteria before implementation. This often results in 'evaluators' simply describing what they find rather than monitoring for specific outcomes. In such circumstances evaluation is phenomenological rather than deliberate.

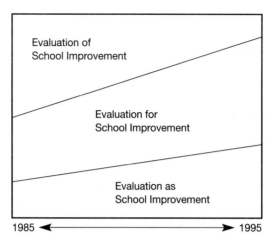

Figure 9.3 The change in balance of evaluation activities in the United Kingdom over the past ten years.

But this reduction in the evaluation of the impact of school improvement initiatives has been offset by a widening of evaluation used *for* school improvement and evaluation *as* school improvement (Figure 9. 3). Again, we can identify factors which have contributed to this development, the two principal ones being the new pressures on schools to demonstrate their own effectiveness and the growing understanding of what local management means at school level.

The recent emphasis on school performance, fuelled by the production of a variety of 'measures' – such as the league tables of public examination results and the testing of all pupils using the standard attainment tests (SATs) tied to the National Curriculum – has made schools acutely aware that in the educational marketplace results count. Indeed, the climate of potential expectation which has been generated by this emphasis is such that the school may feel that even to maintain performance – however satisfactory the level – is not good enough. In a climate where continual improvement is looked for by parents, to stand still will appear to equal going backwards. Consequently the quest for continuing improvement brings with it a need for new measurement. Schools need to know more about how they are doing, and where they might improve so that evaluation for improvement is often seen as a major priority.

The second factor is associated with the new pressures and opportunities which come with self-management. It is now increasingly recognized that the future of the school and its ability to develop (or, in some contexts, simply to survive) will depend on the quality of decisions which school managers are making now. Insofar as evaluation is, above all, a process which seeks to influence the quality of decisions about the future (here we can distinguish between evaluation, with its commitment to influence future decisions, and research, which, though it may influence decisions, is concerned principally with explanations of the past) it is understandable that those responsible for decision-making in the school are looking to evaluation as a source of knowledge and understanding.

The level of activity associated with evaluation for school improvement has increased markedly in the post-Education Reform Act period. Two examples of this emphasis which involve all schools are the adoption of Development Planning and the imposition of formal external inspection under the supervision of the Office for Standards in Education (OFSTED). Development Planning, which all schools now carry out annually, is a continuing cycle of review, planning, implementation and further review.[13] This process helps schools to take stock of strengths and weaknesses, identify priorities for development, plan a review of those priorities, and evaluate their success. In the majority of schools this cycle of action and review is becoming the dominant approach to planning, so that evaluating what needs to be done to improve the school is an activity to which most teachers will make some contribution. Unfortunately, schools seem to have mastered the review element more quickly than the planning or implementation elements, so that whilst most schools could offer a grounded picture of what needs to be done to move the school forward, it is less certain that they will have plans which will enable this to be done, or the capacity to implement plans in a way which does move the school forward. Nevertheless, there is clear evidence within individual schools' development plans that schools can now systematically evaluate their own performance and identify action points, a large step forward from the mid-eighties.

The school's commitment to use evaluation to identify opportunities for development has been reinforced by inspection. The inspection process is clearly documented: it identifies a range of areas which will be scrutinized and, for each, a set of criteria which will be applied in reaching judgements about the school's performance.[14] Following the inspection, a report is produced according to the format set out in the *Handbook for Inspection*, as seen in the following section.[15] This report is a public document. It is available to the school staff, to parents, to the local community, and it requires a public response, the school's Action Plan which follows inspection.

Despite our reservations about the inspection process it is clear that it is seen as an important review of how the school is functioning, and that the 'key issues for action' are seen as areas where a response must be made.[16] To this extent, inspection is clearly an important vehicle, conveying evaluation *for* school improvement onto the agenda of all schools.

The trend away from evaluation *of* towards evaluation *for* is, then, an important one. It transforms schools and teachers from objects of the evaluation process into partners within the evaluation process. But, as we hint at above, our own feeling is that the most exciting and, thus far, underdeveloped use of evaluation within schools lies in the third strand. It is evaluation *as* school improvement which offers schools the best opportunity to build a continuously developing culture. It is evaluation *on* school improvement which can best help the school constantly to improve its ability to meet the needs of students and to renew itself in the fact of ever increasing demands from government and expectations from parents. Though, as yet, only a minority of schools have embarked upon a systematic programme of evaluation and improvement, interest and activity is certainly growing.

We have been fortunate to work with some of the schools that are leading the way.[17] Over the past five years, we have been able to test out these beliefs in Improving the Quality of Education for All (IQEA) Project, based at the University of Cambridge.[18] At the outset of IQEA we attempted to outline our own vision of school improvement by articulating a set of principles that provided us with a philosophical and practical starting point. Because it is our assumption that schools are most likely to provide quality education and enhanced outcomes for pupils when they adopt ways of working that are consistent with these principles, they were offered as the basis for collaboration with the IQEA project schools. In short, we were inviting the schools to identify and to work on their own projects and priorities, but to do so in a way which embodied a set of core values about school improvement. Originally, there were ten such principles, but during our period of working with the schools we have found ourselves reorganizing these into the following five statements. They represent the expectations we have of the way project schools will pursue school improvement. They serve as an *aide-mémoire* to the schools and to us.

The five principles of IQEA are:

- School improvement is a process that focuses on enhancing the quality of students' learning.
- The vision of the school should be one which embraces all members of the school community as both learners and contributors.
- The school will see in external pressures for change important opportunities to secure its internal priorities.
- The school will seek to develop structures and create conditions which encourage collaboration and lead to the empowerment of individuals and groups.
- The school will seek to promote the view that monitoring and evaluation quality is a responsibility which all members of staff share.

We feel that the operation of these principles creates synergism. Together they are greater than the sum of their parts.

They characterize an overall approach rather than prescribing a course of action. The intention is that they should inform the thinking and actions of teachers during school improvement efforts, and provide a touchstone for the strategies they devise and the behaviours they adopt.

During this time we have also been able to look closely at schools that are deliberately using evaluation as a strategy for school improvement. We have observed that evaluation as improvement requires substantial numbers of teachers (if not all) to see themselves as responsible for evaluating and improving their own practice, albeit in dialogue with, and with support from, others. This is not easy to establish and it is harder to maintain, but if it can be maintained then we begin to see evaluation merge seamlessly into planning and into implementation, in ways which enhance teachers' thinking and practice.

In the first part of this chapter we outlined one way of classifying evaluation processes, a way which we feel helps us to make important distinctions between strands of evaluation activity according to their different purposes and audiences. We have then gone on to suggest that over the past ten years we have noticed a shift in emphasis between the different strands, with a movement away from evaluation *of* school improvement efforts and a new emphasis on evaluation *for* school improvement. We have suggested that evaluation *as* school improvement has also increased, though not by any means to its full potential. Indeed, we see in this strand the major opportunity for evaluation to contribute to the development of schools and schooling.

In the remaining sections of the chapter, we report research carried out recently in one local education authority. This research was conducted to test out our assumptions about the directions in which evaluation is moving, and the response of senior staff to evaluation activities and data of the various kinds. We first briefly outline the background to the research and the methods used and then report our findings. Finally, we draw some conclusions and speculate about the possible evolution of links between evaluation and school improvement.

Background and methodology

We illustrate this evaluation framework by reference to a small scale evaluation study conducted in a range of schools within one English LEA, Essex.

Each school chosen to participate in the study had experienced two major external evaluations within the previous eighteen months: A Technical and Vocational Education Initiative (TVEI) summative evaluation and an OFSTED inspection. We will begin by describing some of the significant features of each of these evaluations, and then provide an outline of the research methodology.

TVEI IN ESSEX

This work developed from an earlier study conducted by the University of Cambridge Institute of Education, who were commissioned by the Essex LEA to conduct a small-scale evaluation of the Phase 3 TVEI.[19] TVEI was a large-scale educational project initiated and supported by central government. Each LEA in the country took part, designing their own project brief within a fairly broad framework provided by the centre. The project was supported by targeted funding allocated in response to detailed implementation plans.

Within Essex LEA, each school planned a programme of development, lasting over five years, to meet its own needs and those of local and central government. Participation in the project was organized through the involvement of schools in different phases of the project's life. The third and last phase involved 43 schools in the county. These were LEA, grant-maintained and special schools and included selective, denominational and non-selective comprehensive schools.

In view of the cessation of the TVEI project funding in March 1995, the Essex TVEI extension programme commissioned an external evaluation of the impact of TVEI on students' learning in the Phase 3 institutions. Earlier phases had been evaluated by a number of different means and drew on the expertise of external evaluators. The focus of the evaluation was two-fold. The first aspect was the impact of TVEI on learning outcomes of students as a result of the development work. The second was the internal conditions that enhanced teaching and learning. In view of the current interest in school improvement, the report was intended to provide a response to the question: 'What can the LEA and participating schools learn from the TVEI experience to support further work in school improvement?'

The findings were presented in a detailed report which was circulated to all participating institutions and was available to the LEA and its schools as a basis for further school improvement initiatives. An executive summary distilled the main findings as set out below.

1. Learning outcomes

   - TVEI introduced and enhanced curriculum relevance.
   - TVEI has supported student involvement in the assessment and reporting process.
   - Student learning opportunities, activities and experience have been considerably enhanced by TVEI.
   - TVEI has helped schools provide appropriate resources for learning, especially IT, printed learning packages, and networks with industry.
   - Through providing new opportunities for success, TVEI has helped to develop a broader concept of student excellence.

2. As regards school development

   - The planning process was well developed and disseminated by TVEI in Essex.
   - TVEI has been a major stimulus to the quality and quantity of school self-evaluation in Essex.
   - TVEI staff development has had a major impact on school development.

3. Analysis of the data suggested differences between schools

   - There appear to be slight but consistent differences

between schools on both learning outcomes (defined as learning environment and student learning) and school process dimensions (defined as reflection/ enquiry, planning and staff development). Special schools report slightly higher levels on both dimensions than secondary schools.

- There is a positive relationship between staff development, planning and evaluation, and staff perceptions of student learning. This is an area where Essex TVEI has focused much of its development effort.

4. In summary

A key aspect of TVEI was that it helped participants to engage in and to learn about the process of change. Where it was most successful, TVEI was a major contributor to the emergence of a development structure within schools, but enabled them to manage change and sequence innovations over time. Collaborative planning, staff development and reflection/evaluation were the main features of this emerging development structure and the main focus of development work was on student learning.

OFSTED INSPECTIONS

The past ten years have seen an increasing concern about the levels of achievements attained by pupils in maintained schools in England and Wales. Despite extensive changes following the 1988 Education Reform Act the concern remains. The more formal means of holding schools accountable for their performance is now through the Office of Standards in Education (OFSTED) and their inspection function.

OFSTED, under the direction of Her Majesty's Chief Inspector (HMCI), was established by the provisions of the 1992 Education (Schools) Act, and is responsible for the inspection of schools. Independent inspectors, trained and registered by OFSTED, work to the criteria and procedures which have been published in the *Handbook for the Inspection of Schools.*[20] Initially, their task is to inspect each of the 25,000 (approx.) maintained schools in England (with parallel arrangements for other parts of the UK) within a four-year cycle. Reports of each inspection, which are public documents, must be made available to interested persons by governing bodies on request. The *Handbook*, which outlines procedures, also sets out the purpose of inspection which is:

> to identify strengths and weaknesses in schools so that they may improve the quality of education offered and raise the standards achieved by pupils. Particular attention is to be paid to pupils' standards of achievements which are better or worse in any subject or area of learning than the average for their age, and to the reasons for such differences.

As we have seen earlier, the essence of this model is that the inspectors will make judgements on schools based upon the school's perceived effectiveness at the time of the inspection. The report has a standardized format and requires inspectors to state their main findings in relation to these categories, together with supporting evidence, and to list the key issues for action.[21]

1. Introduction, including school data and indicators as set out in Section 1 of the Record of Inspection Evidence
2. Main findings and key issues for action
3. Standards and quality
4. Efficiency of the school
5. Pupils' personal development and behaviour
6. Subjects of the curriculum, including all the subjects of the National Curriculum, religious education where appropriate, and other curricular provision
7. Factors contributing to these findings.

...

19. The summary of the report should contain the main findings and key issues for action, a summary of the standards of achievement judged against national averages and pupils' capabilities in the subjects of the curriculum, and basic information about the school.

20. The Registered inspector is responsible for checking and, where necessary, correcting the data presented on the headteacher's Form. The completed Record of Inspection Evidence (*Handbook* Part 7) including subject summary sheets, lesson observation proformas, school and subject judgement summary statements and the Headteacher's Form (*Handbook* Part 8) must be sent to OFSTED's agent with the report and summary.

So far approximately one third of the schools in England and Wales have received an OFSTED inspection. HMCI, in his Annual Report, describes the final evaluation criteria for making overall judgement:

> Judgements on aspects of schools are summarised for OFSTED on a seven point scale from the best to the worst, the mid-point of the scale indicating a balance of strengths and weaknesses. In this [annual] report schools are described as 'favourably judged' when their strengths in a particular aspect outweigh any weaknesses; conversely, schools where weaknesses outweigh strengths in any particular respect are described as 'unfavourably judged' in that aspect. Schools which attract either the highest or the next highest mark on the scale are described as 'highly rated' and those which attract the lowest or the next lowest marks are termed 'low-rated'. Schools on the mid-point of the scale are described as judged 'neutrally'.[22]

This parallels the principle used in evaluating more specific aspects of schools, for example judgements on lessons, where rating scales are applied to the quality of teaching, the quality of learning and the appropriateness of the work seen.

Inevitably, in commenting on the effectiveness of schools, OFSTED are also identifying areas of 'ineffectiveness'. Perhaps it is irresistible, once such data exist, to offer generalized statements on the 'state' of English schools. Thus in a recent report by HMCI, it was pointed out that the early experience of inspection suggested that

> Less effective schools have weaknesses in one or more of the four aspects ... and a number of schools are judged to be weak in each. Standards are poor in approximately one school in ten. As would be expected, the schools most likely to be judged as

'failing' or as 'likely to fail' to give an acceptable standard of education are those in which the quality of education, school ethos and financial efficiency are also weak. About 2% of schools have weaknesses which outweigh their strengths in all four aspects and a further 3% in three.[23]

Weaknesses are markers for under-achievement. A report that a school is 'failing' or is likely to fail will trigger a sequence of actions which may require 'special measures' as detailed in the 1993 Education Act (Sections 204–228).

Where the judgement on a school is that it is under-achieving, this is recorded in the main findings of the inspection report. By contrast, under-achievement in specific aspects of the school's functioning is identified and incorporated in the section of the report on 'key issues for action'.

METHODOLOGY

The two significant evaluation studies experienced by the schools in our research were conducted by external researchers or inspectors. Both had an overall objective of providing evidence and information that could be used for school improvement work. In the case of the TVEI evaluation the individual school was part of a wider, summative evaluation study and it was intended that the generalized findings contained in the evaluation report would be of benefit to schools in their future planning as well as to the LEA in its strategic development work with schools. As the project had reached its conclusion, there could be no mandatory requirement for schools to respond to the findings and recommendations.

Whilst the OFSTED inspections also place the individual school within the context of a wider sample of inspected schools, the OFSTED report is individualized and presents a very full picture of the research team's findings. Specifically, there is both the intention and the legislative back-up to insist that schools respond to the action points with an appropriate action plan.

As will be clear from this summary, the TVEI evaluation was a summative one, and therefore one which can be clearly classified as *'evaluation of'*. It also had the specific intention of acting as *'evaluation for'*. Similarly, the OFSTED inspections are in part *'evaluation of'* but are much more sharply focused towards providing *'evaluation for'*. Our interest in the *'of, for* and *as'* classifications, and in particular the assumptions about the relevance and effectiveness of the different types of evaluation in generating school improvement, led us to consider using this previous work as a basis for some further investigation.

We visited eight of the eleven schools who were part of the Phase 3 TVEI Evaluation and which had also been inspected by OFSTED. The contents of the TVEI Evaluation Report were well known, as members of the research team (based at the University of Cambridge Institute of Education) had also been involved in the TVEI evaluation. Both the individual results for each school and the final evaluation report provided background knowledge to inform the research. Similarly, the OFSTED reports for each school were obtained by the researchers and studied in order to provide background to the questioning.

For each of the schools in the study interviews were organized with the headteacher, the deputy headteacher responsible for OFSTED arrangements and follow-up, and a middle manager (usually a head of department), who was closely connected with TVEI development and the OFSTED inspection. Quite detailed interviews were conducted using an open response interview schedule which allowed for supplementary questioning. Interviews were taped but not transcribed. Participants were assured that no transcripts would be made, that no names would be used, and that no individual school would be identified.

Key themes from the interviews were noted both during the interview and on subsequent listening to the tapes. Quotations or encapsulations supporting or disagreeing with themes were selected to provide examinable data. A range of these are reported in the Appendix.

The analysis of data from the interviews was tabulated using a framework which was broken down in three ways:

1. Using the '*of*, *for* and *as*' framework to classify data for each school.
2. Further dividing the data into TVEI or OFSTED.
3. Further dividing the data into positive or negative in each of the above categories.

The questions asked during the interview were about the impact of TVEI evaluation as an external summative evaluation, as a stimulus for school improvement or as a valuable process in itself. The questions asked of OFSTED related similarly to its value as an external summative evaluation, its usefulness as a stimulus for school improvement and the value of the process itself.

From the analysis of the data it is possible to identify a number of findings which are set out in the next section and that are elaborated in the Appendix. In the final section we go further to draw some provisional conclusions and propositions from the findings.

The research findings

As outlined in the previous section, we have chosen to use the analysis of 'Evaluation of, for and as' both as the framework for processing the data and for presenting the findings. In each case the findings are further broken down into those relating to the TVEI evaluation and those relating to OFSTED. These, too, are broken down into positive and negative findings.

TVEI: EVALUATION *OF*

Negative findings

1. The external evaluation was frequently perceived as irrelevant, narrowly focused and had received very limited circulation or attention within schools.
2. Schools generally felt little ownership of the evaluation. As it was external and common to a number of schools, they viewed it as something belonging to the local authority.
3. Schools saw little relevance to the TVEI evaluation and largely ignored it.

Positive findings

1. The TVEI summative report was viewed as a celebration of what had been achieved.
2. It was seen as an endorsement of an effective value for money innovation.
3. The TVEI report was seen as having value for the LEA in its strategic function for planning. In that strategic sense it was seen as evaluation *for* development.

OFSTED: EVALUATION *OF*

Negative findings

1. It was viewed as a waste of money, demonstrating lack of value for money.
2. There was some teacher resistance (including resistance by heads and deputies).
3. There was a view that the OFSTED framework narrows the focus of the school's work towards the easily inspectable.
4. OFSTED was viewed as a 'snapshot', forming judgements at a specific point in time.
5. The OFSTED experience was viewed as disruptive, and sapping of staff energies.
6. One or two schools expressed the view that it was possible to put on a performance for evaluation such as OFSTED.

Positive findings

1. Where OFSTED was viewed positively, it was seen as a boost to morale, and that it re-energized staff.
2. The scope of OFSTED was valued because it was a whole school evaluation.
3. Some staff, particularly headteachers, like the objectivity of having external evaluators.
4. Heads in particular found that the information about the school gave them a lever that was helpful in making managerial decisions.

Negative findings

1. The TVEI report was viewed as being external to the school's development agenda, on the periphery of things.
2. The lack of a broad knowledge-base about the evaluation and its findings amongst staff was an insuperable barrier to its effectiveness for school improvement.
3. Implementation was at the discretion of the school, and therefore required the advocacy of the head and deputies and a receptive school culture if it was to be undertaken.

Positive findings

1. The TVEI summative evaluation was seen as a useful experience by some schools in preparing for OFSTED!
2. Where the TVEI report harmonized with the school development agenda, it was a useful additional impetus for change.
3. The recommendations about changes to school structures contained in the report resulted in positive action by some schools.
4. Schools which saw TVEI itself as an agent for institutional growth developed long-term relationships with the project and its personnel. This in turn enabled them to deal with summative evaluation more in the light of consultancy, and therefore supportive to their improvement efforts.
5. TVEI summative evaluation was seen by some as a validation of the regular formative evaluation that was intrinsic to the project.

OFSTED: EVALUATION *FOR*

Negative findings

1. Many schools (probably a majority of schools) claimed that OFSTED revealed little that was not already known.
2. OFSTED was perceived (quite strongly in a number of cases) as identifying weaknesses without providing

strategies, support or resources for improvement.

3. The OFSTED action points paid no attention to the internal capacity of the inspected school to respond to the report's recommendations.
4. The OFSTED report was seen as having missed some key issues, or as being incorrect on some item, which limited its credibility in some schools.
5. Negative attitudes towards OFSTED on the part of the staff were seen as providing an excuse for some to resist taking ownership of the outcomes.
6. Those schools which have been identified as having serious weaknesses saw the lack of support (point 2 above) and continued threat of further inspection on progress as a major barrier to school improvement.
7. Schools with serious weaknesses felt that OFSTED's time scale for improvement was unreasonable.

Positive findings

1. The OFSTED report was greatly valued where it confirmed that the school was doing well – used as a boost to motivation.
2. It was widely felt that the OFSTED report gave head-teachers a mandate for change with their staff (and with the LEA), one that many had taken.
3. The legislative power of OFSTED generally led to staff commitment to the action plan arising from the report.
4. In cases where problematic leadership was identified in the report, either at the school or department level, OFSTED provided a lever for assertive action.
5. OFSTED was viewed as being more sharp, clear and penetrative (than self-evaluation), particularly in schools which had received strong indications of weaknesses.
6. The fact that the OFSTED inspection and report focused on the whole school meant that all staff were involved.
7. The scale of the OFSTED findings led in many cases to significant structural change.

TVEI: EVALUATION *AS*

Negative findings
In none of the schools visited was the TVEI summative evaluation seen as being a developmental process in itself, and therefore there were no negative findings on this item.

Positive findings
TVEI as a curriculum development project had built into it both formative and summative evaluation. When asked about positive developmental aspects of the TVEI evaluation, the vast majority of schools, whilst not seeing the summative evaluation as a developmental process in its own right, wanted to talk about the powerful impact that the on-going formative evaluation process had had on their schools. As the summative evaluation was viewed by most of the schools as being an evaluation also of their ongoing 'evaluation *as*' processes, it seems appropriate to draw out a few findings from the data collected on this issue.

1. The on-going TVEI formative evaluation process was viewed very positively as having an impact on internal school development processes.
2. The impact of this ongoing evaluation process (evaluation *as*) can be further broken down into aspects of the development process:
   (a) The formative TVEI evaluation was seen as having developed internal capacity for monitoring progress.
   (b) The processes developed within the TVEI formative evalaution were now seen as intrinsic to planning and development.
   (c) Both staff development and the development of teaching and learning were seen to have been positively influenced by the on-going TVEI evaluation process.
3. The on-going evaluation and planning process was seen as having generated the internal capacity for whole-school planning which is now fundamental to school development planning.

4. This ongoing evaluative process was viewed as having a greater capacity to change the school than the OFSTED inspection and report:

OFSTED: EVALUATION *AS*

Negative findings

The OFSTED inspection itself was not perceived by schools as being 'evaluation *as*' and there were therefore no negative findings other than those reported above which relate to attitudes towards the inspection.

Positive findings

1. It was viewed by some schools that the generation of energy associated with the OFSTED inspection was of on-going benefit to the school.
2. Some of the processes introduced within the OFSTED inspection, such as classroom observation and a focus on teaching and learning, were viewed as having an impact on school culture.
3. Schools generally felt that the preparation phase for OFSTED using the OFSTED materials focused energies and provided a combination of pressure and support for school improvement within a common framework that was very positive.

Some conclusions

This chapter is an interim statement from an ongoing action research project. The aim is on the one hand to produce valid data to support the process of improvement through evaluation in schools and educational systems, and on the other to elaborate a model and a theory for evaluation and school improvement. The conclusions we draw at this stage are inevitably speculative and crudely formulated. Despite this we offer the following observations to stimulate debate and to help push our thinking forward.

It is possible to draw a series of fairly straightforward conclusions from the research that is reported in the previous section and elaborated in the appendix. These conclusions relate to the impact of the two evaluation exercises (TVEI and OFSTED) as well as the model of evaluation that has guided the research.

For the TVEI evaluation the conclusions are:

- That external summative evaluations of innovations in schools (such as the TVEI evaluation) have little impact on future school improvement planning.
- That the generalized recommendations contained within summative evaluation reports (designed to be 'evaluation *for*') make little impact on schools.
- That the use made by schools of summative evaluation data is a function of the school's capacity for change and the strength of its internal conditions.

It is clear that use made of the TVEI external evaluation was directly proportional to a school's readiness and receptiveness for development. The lack of statutory significance, its summative nature and its external imposition all contributed to a lack of ownership except where schools had a well developed internal capacity for change. In these cases the TVEI evaluation was perceived as feedback relevant to an overall improvement strategy and schools were able to integrate the evaluation data into their ongoing development processes.

In relation to the OFSTED inspections, we were interested in whether the inspection facilitated school improvement – its expressed intention – either as a direct or immediate response to the action points in the inspection report, or in terms of promoting the 'conditions for school improvement' which, as should now be apparent, we believe to be a necessary condition of sustained development. We therefore conclude on the basis of this evidence that:

- External evaluation of the school in the form of OFSTED inspection has a considerable impact on the school.
- The impact directly results from the action points in the reports and is specifically related to them.
- That the powerful legislative framework surrounding OFSTED is the primary stimulus to change in response to the report.

185

- That the quality of the school's response to the OFSTED recommendations would directly relate to the quality of its internal conditions for school improvement.

The enhanced impact that we have noted as a consequence of OFSTED rather than TVEI is, in our opinion, the direct result of the legislative imperative surrounding the inspection. It has a high profile, and it creates a great deal of anxiety and stress as well as interest. Also some action must occur as a consequence. It is here however that there is the greatest irony and the most similarity with TVEI evaluation. Despite all the statutory force surrounding OFSTED, a school's ability to respond to its findings is once again a function of its internal conditions for school improvement. This is a finding that is confirmed by our recent evaluation of the impact of the New South Wales Quality Assurance Programme on school development.[24] Put simply, high performing schools can and do react positively to OFSTED recommendations. Schools with average to low capacity for development, and by definition those schools who have the more to develop, have the greatest difficulty in responding to the evaluation.

This leads us to a final conclusion:

- External summative evaluation, either in the form of TVEI or OFSTED inspection, has little impact on the conditions for school improvement.

This conclusion resonates with the findings from our ongoing research programme on school improvement.[25] One of the main conclusions for this research is that school improvement works best when a clear and practical focus for development is linked to simultaneous work on the internal conditions within the school. Conditions are the internal features of the school, the 'arrangements' that enable it to get work done. We have found that without an equal focus on conditions, even development priorities that directly affect classroom practice quickly become marginalized.

Within the IQEA project we have begun to associate a number of conditions within the school with its capacity for sustained development. At present, our best estimate of those conditions which underpin improvement efforts, and enable schools to profit from evaluation exercises as described in this paper, can be broadly stated as:

- a commitment to staff development
- practical efforts to involve staff, students and the community in school policies and decisions
- transformational leadership approaches
- effective co-ordination strategies
- proper attention to the potential benefits of enquiry and reflection
- a commitment to collaborative planning

We have described the conditions for school development in detail elsewhere, and are in any case continuing to refine our understanding in light of our continuing work with schools.[26] What is of central importance to the argument here however, is that if we are to take improvement to pupil outcomes seriously, then work on the internal conditions of the school has to complement advice related to classroom practice informed by data from evaluations such as TVEI and OFSTED. When all three elements are pulling in the same direction, then school improvement has much more chance of success. Our research in Essex and New South Wales suggests that in order to utilize the results of external evaluation most effectively, the conditions related to evaluation, planning and staff development appear to be the most important.

Further to this, we are interested in the schools' response to the relative merits of TVEI and OFSTED evaluations as '*of*, *for* and *as*' experiences. Whilst Figure 9.2 suggested overlapping but progressive stages in the relationship between evaluation and school improvement (and that model still represents our view) it is also the case that effective 'evaluation *as*' practices have been shown to have the potential to close the loop once more (Figure 9.1). As we predicted in our first presentation of this analysis, 'By

Figure 9.4 Rethinking evaluation and school improvement

moving through the stages constituted by evaluation *for* and evaluation *as* teachers will be prepared, both in terms of skills and psychologically, to face the rigours of tackling 'evaluation *of* ...'.[27]

Whilst the stages of *of, for* and *as* represent a progression for schools as institutions in the school improvement process, there is a paradoxical inversion for the teacher as evaluator and school improver. Through involvement in evaluation activities, the development of skills and beliefs (evaluation *as*) and the use of evaluation to improve practice (evaluation *for*) there grows a belief in the importance of asking major institutional questions and in the skills to do so with rigour and purpose (evaluation *of*) (Figure 9.4).

In reflecting on this chapter and the research under-pinning it, we draw one major lesson for our own continuing programme of research and action. It is this – that to have any positive impact on development, external evaluations must build in the capacity to impact upon the internal conditions for improvement in a school. We need to focus our future research efforts on the gaps between the evaluation findings and the school's ability to respond to them. It is this concern that informs the title of the chapter. Without the ability to modify in a positive way the internal conditions of the school, or to contribute to cultural change, then external evaluation, despite its legislative authority, will remain at the level of 'giving trinkets to the natives'.

Appendix – the research findings

As outlined in the main paper, we chose to use the analysis of 'Evaluation of, for and as' as the framework for process-ing the data and, below, presenting the findings. In each case the findings are further broken down into those relating to the TVEI evaluation and those relating to OFSTED. These, too, are broken down into positive and negative findings.

TVEI EVALUATION *OF* (NEGATIVE FINDINGS)

1. The external evaluation was frequently perceived as irrelevant, narrowly focused and had received very limited circulation or attention within schools.

   The summative evaluation was a very good paper and it really was a way of taking the school forward, but it has only been seen by senior management.

   I have had a glimpse of the final report, but I can't begin to tell you what was in it.

2. Schools generally felt little ownership of the evaluation. As it was external and common to a number of schools, they viewed it as something belonging to the local authority.

   We saw the TVEI evaluation as Cambridge doing it on behalf of Essex.

   In part we saw it as Essex's evaluation.

3. Schools saw little relevance to the TVEI evaluation and largely ignored it.

   The TVEI report did not have much relevance to the school.

TVEI EVALUATION *OF* (POSITIVE FINDINGS)

1. The TVEI summative report was viewed as a celebration of what had been achieved.

   It helped me clarify what we had done. It tied in with what we were doing.

   The feedback was positive for both the school and Essex in terms of developing teaching and learning.

   It was nice to have someone's outside views reinforcing our perceptions.

2. It was seen as an endorsement of an effective value for money innovation.

   (It showed) effective use of the funding.

3. The TVEI report was seen as having value for the LEA

in its strategic function for planning. In that strategic sense it was seen as evaluation for development.

It was down to Essex to summarize what they felt they had achieved.

OFSTED EVALUATION *OF* (NEGATIVE FINDINGS)

1. It was viewed as a waste of money, demonstrating lack of value for money.

   They are absolutely ridiculous, a total waste of money.

   I could have used the money better.

2. There was some teacher resistance (including resistance by heads and deputies).

   I don't think they (senior management team) appreciate evaluation. They think of evaluation as being something done to someone.

   The hostility towards the OFSTED exercise here ...

3. There was a view that the OFSTED framework narrows the focus of the school's work towards the easily inspectable.

   It causes us to focus too exclusively on specific measurable targets such as 5+ A–C passes.

4. OFSTED was viewed as a 'snapshot', forming judgements at a specific point in time.

   OFSTED is just a snapshot.

   I see it coming in as a snapshot, and a lack of responsibility for progress education.

5. The OFSTED experience was viewed as disruptive, and sapping of staff energies.

   It was too much pressure, and is a totally artificial atmosphere.

   The pieces you pick up in terms of the individual staff at the end of it ... you can only take that sort of pressure for a week. It is immeasurable.

6. One or two schools expressed the view that it was possible to put on a performance for evaluation such as OFSTED.

   We put on a superb performance!

   It was not a true picture, the way we came over.

When the report came through there was a general feeling that we had got away with ... that they had screwed the kids down for a week, everyone had kept shtum.

OFSTED EVALUATION *OF* (POSITIVE FINDINGS)

1. Where OFSTED was viewed positively, it was seen as a boost to morale, and that it re-energized staff.

   It highlighted good practice and gave everyone a boost.

   It gave everyone scope and energy to move forwards.

   It promoted faith in management (because it found the same things).

   It is good to have the positive feedback though it is external.

2. The scope of OFSTED was valued because it was a whole school evaluation.

   TVEI concentrated on what you were developing, whereas OFSTED looked at the whole of the school.

3. Some staff liked the objectivity of having external evaluators – particularly headteachers.

   We knew (Local Authority Advisers) so it was more informal, whereas when the team came in, they descended, it was totally different.

4. Heads in particular found the lever that the information about the school gave them helpful in managerial decisions.

   OFSTED can act as a lever.

   I think of (OFSTED) as something that happened to us, but it was valuable in making them realize how professional the job is.

   OFSTED did give the head the flexibility or lever he wanted to make some changes – we are now minus two senior teachers!

TVEI EVALUATION FOR (NEGATIVE FINDINGS)

1. The TVEI report was viewed as being external to the school's development agenda – on the periphery of things.
   It was rather nebulous.

The evaluation was not very crisp in many cases – not evaluated sharply with outcomes measured.

When was that?!

2. The lack of broad knowledge-base about the evaluation and its findings amongst staff was an insuperable barrier to its effectiveness for school improvement.

I do not believe this has had any impact. I do not think that the teachers could tell you what the 5 main ambitions of TVEI were.

I have had a glimpse of the final report, but I cannot begin to tell you what was in it.

I am not aware of any other issues (rather than gender in IT) taken up as a result of the TVEI evaluation, and I have not seen it.

3. Implementation was at the discretion of the school, and therefore required the advocacy of the head and deputies and a receptive school culture if it was to be undertaken.

The culture of the school was resistant to anything that TVEI was setting out to achieve.

The school has been very slow to adapt to change, so there was little response.

The evaluation at the end was really about how we could affect the management structure of the school so that we could do all the developments that the school might want – but it still has to be taken on board by the senior management, and we were not very good at that, I'm afraid.

TVEI EVALUATION *FOR* (POSITIVE FINDINGS)

1. The TVEI summative evaluation was seen as a useful experience by some schools in preparing for OFSTED!

We would not have coped so well (with OFSTED) if we had not had TVEI.

2. Where the TVEI report harmonized with the school development agenda, it was a useful additional impetus for change.

Aspects of equal opportunities were taken up – the school already recognized this.

3. The recommendations about changes to school structures contained in the report resulted in positive action by some schools.

Working parties were set up to look at particular issues … in some areas policies changed as a result … some groups have a cross section of staff.

Our structures changed as a result of TVEI.

4. Schools which saw TVEI itself as an agent for institutional growth developed long-term relationships with the project and its personnel. This in turn enabled them to deal with summative evaluation more in the light of consultancy – and therefore supportive to their improvement efforts.

TVEI evaluation is seen as something done for us in the way that it was done with positive feedback to staff.

5. TVEI summative evaluation was seen by some as a validation of the regular formative evaluation that was intrinsic to the project.

Although there was a certain logic to the self-assessment in the second half of the project, it is always useful, I think, to have somebody come in from outside and ask you the question, such as 'How do you know that you have achieved this?'

OFSTED EVALUATION *FOR* (NEGATIVE FINDINGS)

1. Many schools (probably a majority of schools) claimed that OFSTED revealed little that was not already known.

There was very little in the actual report that we could not have written before the actual report.

OFSTED did not identify anything that we did not know already … there was nothing there that we did not anticipate. There was not anything we were not already addressing.

OFSTED told us the students could achieve more. Well, fine, I knew that.

No surprises at all.

2. OFSTED was perceived – quite strongly in a number of cases – as identifying weaknesses without providing

strategies, support or resources for improvement.

The OFSTED report did not tell us how to do it.

No support or strategies for improvement – other than informally.

(The Report) is very unhelpful.

If the process is designed to drive the weak down, then they will succeed because they are not going to help me ... they are not helping me at all.

3. The OFSTED action points paid no regard to the internal capacity of the inspected school to respond to their reports recommendations.

The (then) Head went away into a cupboard with an advisor and produced the action plan ... but I do not think he grasped that the key individuals were just drifting.

As a senior management team I guess we have taken action, but have failed to really engage the staff, and I think we are still there.

Sometimes staff do not *know* how to respond to the evaluation outcomes.

There is that problem (the entrenched Area Leader) ... and that is where the action plan falls down. It remains a problem in some areas.

4. The OFSTED report was seen as having missed some key issues, or as being incorrect on some item, which limited its credibility in some schools.

You could see in the report where people with particular hobby horses had nobbled a person.

Some things were not commented upon, which was surprising.

5. Negative attitudes towards OFSTED on the part of the staff were seen as providing an excuse for some to resist taking ownership fo the outcomes.

They stick their head in the sand.... What can I say to them to make them realize just how serious it is, the poor attendance here is because they are boring and unpleasant.

The staff have to become aware themselves.... You have to get them into the situation.

Those who felt threatened by it or thought 'this is my territory' did not get much out of it.

6. Those schools which have been identified as having serious weaknesses saw the lack of support (point 2 above) and continued threat of further inspection on progress as a major barrier to school improvement.

They came in and did this spot check and that paralysed me for a fortnight, to gentle the teachers, to get the evidence together, to prepare the staff for them and to host them – and I don't have that time to waste if I am to turn this school around.

They came in, saw sixteen lessons, they told me that fifteen were not satisfactory and then they went away. They did not tell me who, what subject, why.... They gave me *nothing* that would help me get to grips with the problem. I did not even know where it was. I am extremely cynical about that bit. Without them it might be possible to turn this into an excellent school. I feel that with the OFSTED cosh hanging over my head.... I just feel that they have not got the faintest idea.

I don't think that the kind of fear that the OFSTED process inculcates, in the long term, will benefit a school like this. I do my restructural work and I feel enlightened. I do my OFSTED work and I feel fearful – too very extreme feelings!

7. Schools with serious weaknesses felt that OFSTED's timescale for improvement was unreasonable.

My view is that my re-structure will deliver – (we need to plan for) four or five years' time. Not now. What OFSTED is doing is saying you are responsible NOW – and I don't think it can be done that quickly.

OFSTED EVALUATION *FOR* (POSITIVE FINDINGS)

1. The OFSTED report was greatly valued where it confirmed that the school is doing well – used as a boost to motivation.

It was very useful. If nothing else it confirmed what we felt. It is far better to have that confirmed by an outside body.

We knew things, but it is good to hear them reinforced. We have moved forward again and staff have a lot more pride.

2. It was widely felt that the OFSTED report gave head-teachers a mandate for change with their staff (and with the LEA) – one that many had taken.

It gave strength to the elbow where pockets that were not so good were identified.

Some items provided useful evidence for capital bids. It gives added weight.

As far as the senior management is concerned it lends us weight. It gave the head some muscle to move the school forward.

It gives me a very powerful mandate.

OFSTED gave me muscle to look for resources and support from the Local Authority. I was able to ask them what they were going to do.

Even now we are quoting OFSTED as a way of focusing and establishing priorities.

3. The legislative power of OFSTED generally led to staff commitment to the action plan arising from the report.

We *had* to react (to the outcomes). We had to be seen to react.... All that was going on. There was some outside compulsion. OFSTED has more weight.

4. In cases where problematic leadership was identified in the report, either at the school or department level in the school, OFSTED provided a lever for assertive action.

We had worked hard on the outcomes, sometimes in quite dramatic ways. Staff have left. They made no bones where some things were weakly led, and you want that sort of thing.... So I found it wholly helpful.

OFSTED helped by underlining that we had wastage in senior management.

Eight teachers left in July and five are due to go this year.

5. OFSTED was viewed as being more sharp, clear and penetrative (than self-evaluation), particularly in schools which had received strong indications of weaknesses.

If you isolate the OFSTED process then it is quite a sharp instrument for identifying a school's weaknesses.

The school needed a sharp shock. If we had done self-evaluation, the issues would have been fudged. We did not have the skills to do it.

It was crisp and there were clear indicators for action.

6. The fact that the OFSTED inspection and report focused on the whole school meant that all staff were involved.

The usefulness was that it (the problem identified) isn't necessarily universally known.... It was useful for someone from outside to tell some staff what the senior management team had been trying to tell them.

Everybody felt that this was something to do with them, because everyone was involved.

Everyone was involved and it was such an intense period of time – and everyone had access to the full report.

7. The scale of the OFSTED findings led in many cases to significant structural change.

Structures were changing and OFSTED gave us an excellent opportunity to demonstrate the need for it to everybody.

My new structure, when that's in place this time next year, should be a much more effective management tool in terms of enabling teachers to work in teams to deliver a good curriculum.

Structures have changed in terms of policies and monitoring practices, as well as the *restructuring*.

There has been structural change as a result of OFSTED.

We have used post-OFSTED to say 'let's look at task groups …' (standing groups, task groups, review groups with representation from all 'levels').

TVEI EVALUATION *AS* (NEGATIVE FINDINGS)

In none of the schools visited was the TVEI summative evaluation seen as being a developmental process in itself, and therefore there were no negative findings on this item.

TVEI EVALUATION *AS* (POSITIVE FINDINGS)

INTRODUCTION

TVEI as a curriculum development project had built into it both formative and summative evaluation. When asked about positive developmental aspects of the TVEI evaluation, the vast majority of schools, whilst not seeing the summative evaluation as a developmental process in its own right, wanted to talk about the powerful impact that the on-going formative evaluation process had had on their schools. As the summative evaluation was viewed by most of the schools as being an evaluation also of their ongoing 'evaluation *as*' processes, it seems appropriate to draw out a few findings from the data collected on this issue.

1. The on-going TVEI formative evaluation process was viewed very positively as having an impact on internal school development processes.

   TVEI gave a regularity to targeting and evaluating what is taking place.... As we got into it (staff) respected that process. It helped them to focus. It was a process that they embraced.

   People would perceive that the school moved forward *through* TVEI – rather than the overall evaluation.

   The product was less valuable than the process.

   People got into the habit of looking at what they were doing and evaluating it, and we are now more development orientated.

   The TVEI process, the development principles, have been built into all our work ... identifying needs and planning for them.

2. The impact of ongoing evaluation process (evaluation *as*) can be further broken down into aspects of the development process:

   (a) The formative TVEI evaluation was seen as having developed internal capacity for monitoring progress.

   Objectives and evidence indicators became part of the in-house style – the school development plan is based on those.

TVEI evaluations, both on-going and formal or final – we thought of something for ourselves.

Evaluation is something in general we have taken on as a result of TVEI, and is an on-going process. We are now doing things subconsciously without being aware of them.

As a result of TVEI, evaluation as a metabolic process has grown.

(b) The processes developed within the TVEI formative evaluation became seen as intrinsic to planning and development.

Getting used to the evaluation was good. People are getting used to getting into working groups and developing.... Getting into the ethos of the school that we are about development, which is fundamental to a good school.

It has influenced staff's attitude to planning and made us more businesslike ... but that was a gradual progression, not from the summative.

(c) Both staff development and the development of teaching and learning were seen to have been positively influenced by the ongoing TVEI evaluation process.

The process was useful for staff development.

Constant monitoring every five years eventually has an impact on teaching and learning styles.

3. The on-going evaluation and planning process was seen as having generated the internal capacity for whole-school planning which is now fundamental to school development planning.

We are using a lot of the TVEI processes of evaluation for evaluation of things in school. We are using it for the school development plan, for example.

4. This ongoing evaluative process was viewed as having a greater capacity to change the school than the OFSTED inspection and report:

The method of monitoring and evaluating was more supportive than OFSTED and will probably bring about more change.

The school found the development work that has gone into TVEI ... and the self-evaluation methods as much more progressive.

In many ways TVEI was a mini-OFSTED inspection. It went over the full period of TVEI time, whereas OFSTED, they were in for a week and a couple of days.

I would argue that it is more important, more effective. OFSTED is quite short-term, really.

OFSTED EVALUATION *AS* (NEGATIVE FINDINGS)

The OFSTED inspection itself was not perceived by schools as being 'evaluation *as*' and there were therefore no negative findings other than those reported above which relate to attitudes towards the inspection.

OFSTED EVALUATION *AS* (POSITIVE FINDINGS)

1. It was viewed by some schools that the generation of energy associated with the OFSTED inspection was of on-going benefit to the school.

   We need to have our panic times and OFSTED does that.

   The inspection developed corporate spirit.

2. Some of the processes introduced within the OFSTED inspection, such as classroom observation and a focus on teaching and learning, were viewed as having an impact on school culture.

   Teachers have taken on board that teaching matters and are keen to observe each other's lessons.

   Widespread action plans are part of the process.

   (OFSTED forced us) into a position where we became very analytical, very quickly.

3. Schools generally felt that the preparation phase for OFSTED using the OFSTED materials focused energies and provided a combination of pressure and support for school improvement within a common framework that was very positive.

   ... a brilliant piece of quality management, the OFSTED framework. It has been described by someone from a company who is very much into TQM as really much better than something put in place of TQM because it does actually focus on the core business of the organization, which is pupils' learning – how to achieve that and how to maintain it.

The outcomes were a bit of an anti-climax, but certainly the process was not ... planning for it, checking through all the documentation, looking through with the inspector, very stimulating.

In the past you have departments working in separate boxes, doing their own thing and the quality of what was done depended upon the quality of the staff in that particular part. Now you have got much more of a framework which you can apply to all areas, and that enables departments who are not as confident or experienced to have a system which they could develop.

Notes and references

1. Hopkins, D. *Evaluation for School Development* (Buckingham: Open University Press, 1989).
2. Barth, R. *Improving Schools from Within* (San Francisco: Jossey-Bass, 1990).
3. Hopkins, D. *Improving the Quality of Schooling* (Lewes: Falmer).
4. Hopkins, D., Ainscow, M. and West, M. *School Improvement in an Era of Change* (London: Cassell, 1994).
5. Stenhouse, L. *Curriculum Research and Development in Action* (London: Heinemann Educational, 1980), 122.
6. Hopkins op. cit. p. 17.
7. Louis, K. S. and Miles, M. B. *Improving the Urban High School: What Works and Why* (New York: Teachers College Press, 1990).
8. Fullan, M. *The Meaning of Educational Change* (Toronto: OISE Press, 1982).
9. Fullan, M. and Park, P. *Curriculum Implementation* (Toronto: Ministry of Education, 1981).
10. Cousins, J. B. and Leithwood, K. A. Current empirical research on evaluation utilization *Review of Educational Research*, 56(3), 1986, 331–64.
11. e.g. Cousins and Leithwood op. cit., Hopkins, D. 1989 op. cit.
12. Hopkins, D. *Doing School Based Review* (Leuven, Belgium: ACCO, 1988).
13 See Hargreaves, D., Hopkins, D., Leask, M., Connolly, J. and Robinson, P. *Planning for School Development* (London: DES, 1989).

Hargreaves, D. H. and Hopkins, D. *The Empowered School* (London: Cassell, 1991).

14. See OFSTED *Handbook for the Inspection of Schools* (London: OFSTED, 1993, revised 1994).
15. OFSTED *Improving Schools* (London: OFSTED, 1994), 5.
16. Hopkins, D., West, M. and Skinner, J. Improvement through inspection?: a critique of the OFSTED inspection system: school evaluation in England and Wales. *Zeitschrift für Sozialisations: forschung unhd Erziehungssozologie*, 15, 1995, 335–348.
17. Hopkins, D., Ainscow, M. and West, M. op. cit.
18. Ainscow, M. and Hopkins, D. Aboard the moving school *Educational Leadership*, 50 (3) 1992, 79–81.
    Hopkins, D. and West, M. The yellow brick road *Managing Schools Today*, 3 (6) 1994, 14–17.
    Hopkins, D. and West, M. Teacher development and school improvement. In D. Walling (ed.) *Teachers as Learners* (Bloomington: PDK, 1994).
19. Terrell, I. and Hopkins, D. *The Impact of TVEI and Student Learning* (A Summative Evaluation Report Prepared for Essex TVEI) Cambridge: University of Cambridge Institute of Education, 1995.
20. See OFSTED *Handbook for the Inspection of Schools* (London: OFSTED, 1993, revised 1994 p.1).
21. OFSTED *Improving Schools* (London: OFSTED, 1994).
22. OFSTED *Annual Report of Her Majesty's Chief Inspector of Schools* Part 1 (London: HMSO, 1995 p. 2).
23. OFSTED *Annual Report of Her Majesty's Chief Inspector of Schools* Part 2 (London: HMSO, 1995 p. 14).
24. Hopkins, D. The impact of the quality assurance review process on school development: a preliminary analysis (Mimeo from NSW Department of School Education, Quality Assurance Directorate. Restricted Circulation), 1995.
25. See for example, West, M. and Hopkins, D. Reconceptualising school effectiveness and improvement BERA/ECER Conference Discussion Paper, Bath, 15 September 1995.
26. Ainscow, M., Hopkins, D., Southworth, G. and West, M. *Creating the Conditions for School Improvement* (London: David Fulton, 1994).
27. Holly, P. and Hopkins, D. Evaluation and school improvement *Cambridge Journal of Education*, 18 (2), 1988, 221–45.

CHAPTER 10

Profiling and Self-assessment: an Evaluation of Their Contribution to the Learning Process

ANN-MARIE LATHAM

Introduction

In this chapter the process of profiling is explored in a variety of educational contexts, with a particular focus on the relationship between the purpose and the processes involved. This will entail consideration of various aspects of profiling from both theoretical and practical perspectives. The chapter will consider profiling as a means of assessment, before discussing in more detail the relationship between purpose and implementation in a range of teaching, learning and training situations including schools and further and higher education.

The use of profiles and the process of profiling have appeared in a variety of guises, from records of achievement to professional development and appraisal. Records of achievement schemes which began to develop in the 1970s were one of the earliest structures to utilize profiling within a school and later a vocational context. The early historical development of records of achievement and the profiling movement was set against the backcloth of public examinations and was regarded as an alternative method of assessment which focuses on recording various facets of achievement.[1] Records of achievement were seen to bring together a range of pupil achievement and progress both within and outside the classroom, including experiences and achievements not tested by examinations.[2] The Government recognized the growing interest in Records of Achievement and issued both a draft (1983) and a policy statement (1984) on records of achievement for all school leavers.[3] Eventually ten years later in January (1993) the National Record of Achievement was officially introduced. As pupils left school with their records of achievement, interest within colleges of further and higher education, including universities, began to emerge. These institutions began to experiment with alternative assessment structures based on various aspects of profiling. This work was supported by projects funded by the CNAA which subsequently produced guidelines on introducing and using profiling systems.[4] Within these educational contexts, profiling systems have played a variety of important assessment roles from the formal collection of evidence of achievement to the more informal self-assessments with a focus on personal development.

It is important to make a clear distinction between a profile and profiling. The term profile represents a product, a document which records a range of assessment information from a variety of contexts. Profiling is the process by which the profile is produced and therefore is more concerned with teaching, learning and the whole assessment process. The process of profiling 'enables an individual to chart his/her development and achievements against a set of learning objectives.[5] This description highlights the more formal role of profiling within the assessment process. This role tends to rely on individual reflection, self-assessment and a review discussion with a person in authority in relation to pre-planned or negotiated learning outcomes. The individual evaluates his or her ability, acknowledges success or failure, and discusses personal performance in relation to the learning outcomes. This structure encourages the individual to have an active role which impacts upon the formal assessment process. A key element is the review discussion which provides the individual with the chance to articulate achievements, recognize difficulties and present logical arguments to justify underachievement. However, even though the individual can have some influence on the assessment process the final mark or verification of achievement is usually dependent upon the person in authority. The underlying philosophy within this profiling assessment process is to encourage individuals to be actively involved, motivated and more responsible for their own learning.

In contrast to this formal assessment process, the main emphasis of the profiling scheme may be informal self-assessment which promotes personal development. The system is built around individual reflection, self-assessment and the recognition of achievements in relation to personally set or negotiated action plans which may or may not be related to learning outcomes. Some of the action plans could be regarded as long-term goals and their successful achievement will be dependent upon a combination of setting more immediate short-term targets and self-assessment. A profiling system which focuses on personal development must involve self-reflection, self-assessment and the setting of realistic, relevant and obtainable goals which provide a clear structure for future learning and achievements. The process usually involves a review discussion, which provides the individual with the opportunity to articulate personal thoughts and judgements about progress, in relation to previously set action plans. During this discussion the individual needs to provide evidence to support and validate his or her achievements. This profiling framework of self-assessment, review discussion and the setting of action plans enables individuals to develop greater understanding of themselves and their achievements which should have an impact on self esteem, motivation and future learning. This could either be positive or negative depending on the outcome in relation to previously set action plans.

In summary, profiling provides a framework for two aspects of assessment. One is formally based on specific learning outcomes, by which achievements are measured and acknowledged. The second is focused on self-assessment and personal development. These aspects can be integrated to provide a range of organizational structures which will fulfil a variety of assessment purposes. For example, the formal assessment process could involve short-term goal setting, self-assessment and a review discussion which not only focuses on progress towards the achievement of specific learning outcomes but allows the individuals to identify underlying principles which have influenced their behaviour. It is the recognition of the factors involved in achieving the learning outcome which could have a significant effect on future behaviour and subsequent learning. For example, the recognition that a seminar presentation was successful due to a clear, confident, and well-rehearsed delivery, based on sound subject knowledge which was developed from extensive reading, should ensure that the individual knows how to prepare for and present future seminars. It is therefore not just the successful completion of the task, but the self-analysis process which enables students to understand what they did to achieve success. It creates a feeling of control over their learning which is going to have a significant impact on motivation and personal development. Self-analysis should provide the personal knowledge on which future learning decisions can be planned. The opportunity to integrate both the formal and informal assessment aspects of profiling enables a range of different objectives to be achieved. The implementation structure of self-assessment, review discussion and target-setting tends to remain constant, but the actual emphasis and focus of the individual processes may vary and it is these subtle differences which allow profiling to fulfil a variety of roles.

However, before considering the 'purpose–process' issue in greater detail, the terms self-reflection and self-assessment which are used to describe profiling process activities need to be clarified. These terms are closely related and are often used interchangeably, causing confusion. Self-assessment is dependent upon self-reflection but this relationship is not reciprocated. In this chapter self-reflection involves the cognitive activity in which the individual recalls/reconstructs actions, events and/or thoughts which are personal. When the individual starts to make evaluative judgements about those personal reconstructions then the reflection moves into self-assessment. This description suggests that self-assessment tends to occur in conjunction with self-reflection. However, an individual can be involved in pure self-reflection where neutral statements which relate to personal images and thoughts are expressed free from judgement.

The 'purpose–process' debate

Records of achievement will provide the initial context for the purpose–process debate. The Government's original policy statement in 1984 defined the following four purposes for records of achievement, which indicate both a formal and informal assessment function:

Recognition of achievement
Motivation and personal development
Curriculum organisation
A document of record.

These four purposes were seen as a combined package which should have a significant effect on the overall quality of pupils' learning. This would appear to be the main underlying purpose of Records of Achievement within school.

Originally, individual schools devised the organizational framework for Records of Achievement which involved the pupils in self-assessment and the setting of educational and personal goals. This provided the opportunity for each individual to recognize success, achievements and acknowledge personal progress. Fundamental to the records of achievement philosophy was 'planned pupil/teacher discussion and self appraisal about objective, performance and progress'.[6] With the publishing of the *National Records of Achievement* schools were provided with clear guidelines about what information must be presented in the summative profile but the collection of the data and the processes involved were still open for individual organization. Within the various implementation structures used to produce the summative Record of Achievement, profiling processes were used extensively and often referred to as the 'formative process'. It was this formative process which was seen to be at the heart of records of achievement. '... formative process as the real focus of the records of achievement initiative since it is in this area that the most fundamental opportunities for actually influencing the quality of pupils learning are located.'[7]

The main questions to be addressed are what does the

formative process involve and how can it fulfil all four main purposes of Records of Achievement, and ultimately influence the quality of pupils' learning?

Within the school context the formative process was regarded as an ongoing collection of information and experiences of a pupil which continuously gives direction to future learning.[8] This collection of data could involve teacher, peer and self-assessment information and consequently should raise the pupils' awareness of personal performance and allow them to recognize achievement. Using this knowledge, pupils are involved in setting future learning targets. This target-setting process could be completed during a review discussion with the teacher guiding the pupil to set appropriate and realistic goals. The formative process structure of self-assessment, review discussion and target-setting encourages the pupils to be actively involved in the learning process. This process has been recognized as a powerful structure to aid learning because it provides pupils 'with regular detailed, positive and individual feedback on their progress and development'. It would appear that when profiling in the form of the formative process has the potential to influence the quality of learning, the extent to which this is achieved depends on the implementation structure. The active involvement of the pupils in the formative process could also provide some additional outcomes, such as personal knowledge and the development of self-appraisal, self-organization/management and goal-setting skills. Through self-assessment tasks within the formative process pupils could be introduced to and experience a variety of assessment processes and contexts including ipsative and criterion-referenced, based on pupil and/or teacher set criteria or personal targets. These assessment experiences not only provide a knowledge base from which future learning can be planned but can be regarded as learning experiences in themselves as pupils develop an understanding of assessment processes. Regardless of the assessment context the pupils not only have to individually acknowledge and recognize their strengths and weaknesses but also be prepared to share this information on paper or orally during the review discussion. This communication between the pupil and teacher provides the opportunity for setting realistic future learning goals based on relevant assessment information.

Within the school context the review discussion was recognized as 'an essential part of assessment and recording if records of achievement are to fulfil their diagnostic, developmental and motivating purposes.[10] The results from pilot studies indicate that the actual focus of the discussion could vary from learning/target-setting to personal qualities/motivational aspects. This aspect of the formative process therefore has the potential to fulfil various purposes depending on the emphasis within the discussion. However, within the school context the implementation of the review discussion has proved difficult. Time and a conducive environment have been identified as important factors for the successful implementation of an effective review discussion. Within school it is difficult to structure the teaching and learning environment to provide both the time and a private atmosphere for individual discussion with each pupil; consequently this aspect of the formative process does not always occur. Without this key element of the formative process the effectiveness of profiling in terms of the quality of pupils learning must be questioned.

A secondary outcome of the formative process is the pupils' development of personal knowledge, their recognition of strengths and weaknesses through self-evaluation and the setting of relevant learning targets. This structure would appear to have a significant impact on personal development and motivation in that the process provides them with personal knowledge and the opportunity to experience control over learning and progress. However, this feeling of control is dependent on the successful achievement of relevant and realistic goals. The individual's perception of the goal is a key factor. Unless it is viewed as important by the individual the outcome in terms of achievement will have very little impact on self-esteem, motivation and future learning. It is important to remember that perception can be different from reality, and this will not only influence the relevance of the goal but also the individual's interpretation of his/her performance in terms of success or failure. The review discussion process has the potential to encourage pupils' personal development, a point that is discussed more fully later, in the context of futher and higher education.

The assessment information which is generated during the formative process and the target-setting activities has the power to influence curriculum organization. The teacher can utilize the information to evaluate the material, teaching strategies and assessment processes in order to improve the quality of the pupils' learning experience. Consequently, the formative process can have an indirect but significant impact on the quality of teaching and learning. However, this impact is influenced by the teacher's willingness to evaluate and analyse the teaching/learning relationship in relation to pupil progress and act upon the evidence produced.

The final purpose of Records of Achievement is the production of a summative document of record. This appears to be a little more difficult to fulfil from a formative collection of data and the setting of goals for future learning. An ongoing list of previous achievements is not directly relevant to the final summative Record of Achievement. The process of collecting the data, self-assessment and target-setting is more important and should provide the basis on which the individual pupil can articulate his/her achievements. The quality of the profile is dependent on the formative experiences which should provide the pupil with knowledge and confidence about his/her ability. Overall, the formative process, if implemented correctly, appears to be able to fulfil the four main purposes of Records of Achievement and influence the quality of pupils' learning. However, actual success for the pupils will depend on an appropriate organizational structure, committed teachers, adequate resources and time.

At this stage it is important to recognize that Records of Achievement provide the first initial experience of the profiling processes.

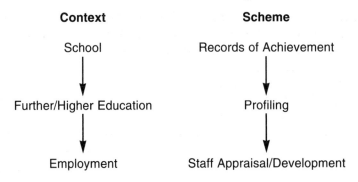

Figure 10.1 Continuum of profiling experiences and context

If profiling is going to have a significant impact and be utilized effectively throughout the learning continuum then this experience must be regarded as positive and worthwhile by the individual. The overall teaching environment and the Records of Achievement scheme should encourage the development of a range of profiling skills, including self-assessment, communication, self-management and goal-setting which can be utilized effectively within subsequent learning situations.

In colleges of further and higher education three basic types of profiles have been utilized as recognized by the CNAA.[11] These relate closely to the formal and informal assessment profiling structures described in the introduction. The prescribed learning outcome profile and the negotiated outcome profile are designed to fulfil a more formal assessment role, with the main purpose to improve student learning, compared to the informal assessment structure of the personal development profile. The profiling processes utilized in higher and further education are recognized by Fenwick, Assiter and Nixon as similar to the formative processes used by pupils in school: processes of empowering students to be involved in the assessment, recording and reviewing of their own personal development, and learning. The essential components of profiling are identified as reflection, self-assessment, discussion with a tutor on progress and the setting of targets for future learning/development.

Within higher and further education the review discussion has been acknowledged as a key aspect of the profiling framework. Assiter and Shaw describe the dialogue between student and tutor as central to any characterisation or recording and reviewing.[12] The dialogue situation provides an opportunity for various further processes to occur; it should encourage the student 'to reflect on experiences, to give and receive feedback, diagnose strengths and weaknesses and agree future learning targets/action plans.[13] This interchange can generate a range of useful information for both student and tutor. If the tutor utilizes probing questions which force the student into reflective self-assessment with a focus on factors which have influenced performance and achievement, then relevant personal knowledge can be developed alongside the recognition and the recording of more formal achievements. There appears to be a reciprocal relationship between formal learning and personal development within the context of the profiling framework. Profiling actively involves the individual in a learning cycle: setting individual goals, self-assessment, recording of achievements and the setting of future learning goals. The actual completion of the profiling tasks provides the opportunity for a variety of personal facets to be fostered. For example individuals could develop:

- a greater insight into themselves as learners.
- a feeling of control over their learning.
- increased motivation to inspire future learning.
- improved communication skills.
- increased confidence in articulating personal ideas/ achievements.

This relationship between learning and personal development was recognized by Assiter and Shaw who suggest that the process itself can have a significant impact on the individual which should influence their future learning performance. This in turn will empower them to become more confident, self-aware and capable people.

The potential outcomes of the profiling process can be divided into personal knowledge/positive attitudes towards learning and personal skills.

Personal knowledge/Positive attitudes

greater insight into themselves as learners
a feeling of greater control over learning
increased motivation to inspire future learning

Personal Skills

improved communication skills
increased confidence in articulating personal ideas and
    achievements

The development of personal knowledge and positive
attitudes towards learning has the potential to increase independence within the learning situation. It enables the
individual to take a more responsible role, leading towards
being an effective learner. Ultimately, the individual should
be totally self-aware and independent so that effective learning decisions will be made, which provide the maximum
opportunity for the fulfilment of his/her potential as a learner.

Personal skill development was recognized by the CNAA
who suggested that profiling has a significant role to play in
helping students develop core skills which are transferable
across a range of contexts, skills such as communication and
critical thinking. Not only did profiles provide a framework
for the development of these core skills but also allowed
'formative assessment of such skills to occur'.[14] However,
the document does not indicate specifically how profiling
would develop personal skills such as communication and
critical thinking. The review discussion would appear to
hold the greatest potential for the development of personal
skills, in that the individual through discussion with the
tutor could be forced to think, make decisions, and utilize
communication skills to express themselves. Through the
use of probing questions the individual can be encouraged
to practise a range of personal skills whilst becoming more
self-aware, recognizing achievements and difficulties.

Within further and higher education the processes of

profiling are combined and implemented in a similar structure to those in schools. However, the review discussion element appears to play a more significant role, providing the older student with the necessary forum to acknowledge factors which influence performance, the opportunity to develop personal skills and take control of future progress through target-setting. These outcomes which are initiated through the review discussion are not just specific to post-school education, but as previously discussed the school context is not conducive to the implementation of this profiling process. The review discussion process should be more successful in colleges and universities because the clientele are older, the timetable organization provides time for individual tutorials and private room space is more readily available. However, the effectiveness of the review discussion is dependent on students' prior preparation and tutor listening/questioning skills. The processes of self-assessment and target-setting could be carried out entirely within the review discussion, but this is not the most effective structure. Time for reflection and self-assessment is important. Preparation for the tutorial not only involves self-analysis but the collection of evidence to support achievement claims and verify assessment information. The verification of self-assessment information is a key issue of any profiling system. The data the student presents must be questioned, as to what extent it represents a correct and true picture of his/her capabilities. Presenting formal evidence of achievement is an effective method of substantiating personal statements and increasing the validity of the results. This is obviously crucial if the profiling system is being used predominantly as part of a formal assessment scheme. If the focus is mainly on personal development then the profiling process itself is more important than the actual product.

Practical implementation of a personal development profile

The chapter so far has presented a theoretical discussion of various aspects of profiling with a particular focus on process and purpose. To develop this further, a practical working example of a profiling system follows, with discussion relating to its implementation. The issues raised within the discussion are based on both student and tutor responses to questionnaires, collated during the first and second year of implementation.

The Faculty of Education, Sport and Leisure, University of Brighton is presently in its third year of implementing a faculty-wide profiling system for all undergraduate students, these include Primary and Secondary BA with QTS students in various subjects, BSc Sport Science students and BA Leisure Policy and Administration students. The profiling scheme was implemented in conjunction with the change to a modular course system. Within the new modular scheme, profiling was regarded as a central feature providing the students with the opportunity to reflect upon and evaluate their various experiences, achievements and areas of knowledge so that a coherent course was perceived as leading to a specific award.

The scheme could be classified as a personal development profile, with an underlying aim to encourage students to be effective independent learners. Self-assessment, review discussion and target-setting were utilized to foster personal knowledge and development. The main objectives of the student profiling scheme are listed below (Tutor guidelines for profiling system, University of Brighton 1993):

1. To involve actively, and raise student awareness of the overall learning process.
2. To provide a support structure which encourages the student to utilize and develop the skills of self-appraisal/assessment and reflection.
3. To raise student awareness of their potential and limitations.
4. To provide the opportunity for personal development, through working towards individual targets/action plans.
5. To provide a tutorial structure, which will ensure some individual identity is maintained within the modular

    degree system. Students will have a very important contact point with University staff.

6. To provide the opportunity for tutors to gain an understanding of their students' development and progress through the course. This information will be useful in the writing of final transcripts.

7. To develop student awareness of the relationship and coherence between various experiences, subject knowledge and modules leading to a specific award.

The combination of self-assessment, review discussion, and target-setting for further development were similar to those previously discussed. However, the structure of the scheme revolved around the students completing various self-assessment sheets prior to a tutorial discussion with an allocated member of the academic staff. The timing and frequency of these tutorials are dependent on year and degree course (Appendix 1: Organisational Structure). The focus of the discussion is based around the student's self-assessment with the tutor asking questions to help the students to reflect, analyse and recognize the underlying issues which influence his/her performance. Without this focus on behaviours which influence performance, the students' understanding of the learning processes is minimal, with little opportunity to take control and make progress. This dialogue leads into the setting of future action plans which the students formalize on the profiling documentation. During subsequent tutorials the action plans are revised and updated if necessary. Evidence is an important feature of the scheme and students are required to bring information to substantiate self-assessment reports such as formal module assessment papers, additional work or certification of relevant qualifications.

The profile consists of four main components which are completed at various times during the year and are dependent on the individual degree course structure. These are relevant experiences, academic, professional/vocational and coherence.

1. **Relevant experiences** This section focuses on personal qualities/experiences. The students have to reflect and

identify strengths, areas for further development and opportunities available.

2. **Academic** This section requires the students to identify strengths and areas for further development within various aspects of academic work including presentation skills, written and verbal (Appendix 2: Academic Profile).

3. **Professional/vocational** Here the student is required to assess his/her performance either during work placement or teaching practice and identify strengths and areas for further development.

4. **Coherence** The student is required to identify relationships between various modules in terms of experiences, subject content and how they relate to the final degree classification (Appendix 3: Coherence Section).

The profile also consists of an additional section for the collection of relevant *curriculum vitae* information. As the course draws to a close this collection of data is useful for both the tutor and student, providing information for the writing of personal transcripts and job applications. Each student receives a ring file in which to keep the profiling documentation plus any evidence accumulated to support self-assessments and/or the achievement of action plans. The profiling system is explained to the new students during induction week and information is included in the student handbook, reinforcing the importance of the scheme.

The implementation structure, the proposed focus of the tutorial discussion on underlying issues and the paper work documentation should provide the opportunity for all the objectives of the scheme to be achieved. However, the key to success and the student experiencing positive benefits from the system are dependent on the following factors.

1. Students realizing the inherent value within the system and being prepared to be fully involved.

2. Committed tutors who can guide the tutorial discussion towards fostering students' personal development, including an understanding of the learning process

and assisting in the planning of future learning targets. To achieve this level of expertise some tutors may need training which must be provided.

3. The availability of a 'private space' and uninterrupted time for the tutorial discussion.
4. The setting of relevant and realistic action plans which can be achieved within the time frame, structure and opportunities readily available.

If both tutors and students are committed to the scheme there will be benefits for both parties, the student gaining control and moving towards being an effective independent learner and the tutor gaining knowledge of the student as well as a feeling of satisfaction from assisting the individual's development. In addition, the student evaluation of the scheme highlighted the importance of a point of contact with a tutor, recognizing the need for someone who was prepared to listen, give advice and was interested in their development. However, difficulties arise when either party regards the process as futile and in this situation very little is gained. The student's attitude to profiling may have been coloured by previous negative experiences of records of achievement which could prove difficult to change.

A second key factor influencing their involvement is the lack of a formal assessment structure within the profiling process. Consequently, the students do not perceive that the scheme has any direct benefit in terms of their degree qualification. The outcomes of the profiling process are not tangible and difficult for the individual to recognize and/or measure. The students tend to be driven by the assessment forces, working for marks that will contribute to their final degree classification. The attitude of the students towards the profile scheme appears to fluctuate depending on the year and the degree course. Overall, the students involved in initial teaching training (BA with QTS) tend to be more interested in and take an active role in the profiling process. This commitment appears to be fostered by the professional aspect of the profile, with the students recognizing the importance of setting future action plans to guide professional development during teaching practice. The professional profile is related to a list of teacher competences which is used for the assessment of teaching practice. Even though the profiling structure does not involve the students in making a formal assessment, they are aware of the list of assessment competences and see the relevance of self-assessment and goal-setting to improve professional capability. The BAQTS students also appear to be more comfortable with the overall self-assessment process. This could be due to their active involvement in both written and verbal lesson evaluations and self-analysis throughout the school experience. Teaching practice involves numerous profiling processes, including self-assessment, discussion and target-setting. This additional involvement in profiling through professional work could have a significant impact on the students' personal and professional development.

The Sport Science students lack this professional element and consequently interest tends to wane during the second year. However, interest in the third/final year returns, driven by the need for a written reference for employment purposes. To foster this interest a testimonial profile for final year students was created. This section allows the student to have an indirect input into the tutor written transcript, by providing information for discussion about strengths and areas for further development in relation to his/her future career. To further encourage student involvement and commitment to the profiling scheme, the testimonial section could be re-structured allowing the students to be more directly involved in preparing his/her personal references.

The tutors' attitude to the system is based on their underpinning educational philosophy, knowledge and understanding of profiling, and the time available to implement the scheme. The successful implementation of the scheme is influenced by the tutors' knowledge of the structure, interest and skill level. Consequently students' experiences vary considerably, which can cause tension not only between students but also between tutors. Student entitlement is an important consideration which should reflect the need for consistency within the scheme. Staff development is crucial for raising standards of implementation and addressing the issue of inconsistency. Time has been regarded as a critical factor which has seriously influenced the successful implementation of this profiling scheme. The time aspect is closely related to the number of students each tutor is allocated. With the increase in student numbers and a decrease in staffing the tutorial group size makes the scheme difficult to implement and the benefits of the scheme are significantly reduced.

Within this scheme a major problem, which is integral to the profiling process, is the setting of future action plans. The self-assessment process and identification of areas for further development caused no problems. However, the setting of relevant and achievable targets based on the resources and time available proved difficult. The students could not clearly identify how they would achieve the action plans, what strategy or organization was required. The tutor is critical at this stage not only in providing knowledge of the opportunities or support mechanisms available within and outside the university, but through asking appropriate questions which guide the student to devise strategies to achieve success. This target-setting process is important; it provides the opportunity for the individual to take control and plan future learning developments. Its success is dependent on setting realistic targets, identifying appropriate strategies to achieve each target and a commitment to carrying out the various tasks leading to success.

The initial theoretical discussion suggests that, if the combination of profiling processes are correct and the focus of the review discussion is appropriate, a successful match can be achieved between purpose and process. However, when the theory is put to the test, the success of any profiling scheme is not entirely dependent on a positive relationship between structure, processes and purpose but on individual commitment, interest and skills of all parties involved. The structure and the personnel who implement the scheme all have an important role to play in creating a valid and beneficial profiling experience for all participants.

An understanding of and commitment to profiling are essential as well as the interpersonal skills to develop a safe environment for reflection and honest self-assessment to occur. The main problems which surround the successful implementation of any profiling scheme are based on the validity of the self-assessment information and the lack of direct tangible outcomes. To increase validity the profiling system needs to be linked to a formal assessment structure which incorporates evidence from an external source. However, if the process is seen as the main focus then validity of the assessment information is not as important. In this context the real value of profiling lies within each individual who takes part in the process, not the paper documentation which outlines personal achievements. In theory, the process has the potential to be effective in encouraging personal development and autonomy as an independent learner, but in practice, one cannot underestimate the power of the individuals involved.

Appendix 1

ORGANISATIONAL FRAMEWORK UNIVERSITY OF BRIGHTON: PROFILING SCHEME 1995/96

BA with QTS PE

	FIRST YEARS		SECOND YEARS		THIRD YEARS
	SEMESTER 1		SEMESTER 3		SEMESTER 5
Week 1	Group Tutorial	Week 1	Group Tutorial	Weeks 1–8	Individual
Weeks 2–4	Individual	Weeks 12–17	Individual		
	SEMESTER 2		SEMESTER 4		SEMESTER 6
Week 1/2	Group Tutorial		Professional Semester	Weeks 8–17	Individual
Weeks 3–5	Individual				
Weeks 11–17	Individual				

BSc

	FIRST YEARS		SECOND YEARS		THIRD YEARS
	SEMESTER 1		SEMESTER 3		SEMESTER 5
Week 1	Group Tutorial	Weeks 6–12	Individual	Weeks 1–8	Individual
Weeks 2–4	Individual				
	SEMESTER 2		SEMESTER 4		SEMESTER 6
Week 1/2	Group Tutorial	Weeks 6–12	Individual	Weeks 8–17	Individual
Weeks 3–5	Individual				
Weeks 11–17	Individual				

BA LEISURE

	FIRST YEARS		SECOND YEARS		THIRD YEARS
	SEMESTER 1		SEMESTER 3		SEMESTER 5
Week 1	Group Tutorial	Week 1	Group Tutorial	Weeks 1–5	Individual

FIRST YEARS	SECOND YEARS	THIRD YEARS
Weeks 2–4 Individual	Weeks 12–17 Individual	Individual
SEMESTER 2	SEMESTER 4	SEMESTER 6
Week 1/2 Group Tutorial	Vocational Semester	Weeks 8–17 Individual
Weeks 3–5 Individual		
Weeks 11–17 Individual		

BA QTS PRIMARY

FIRST YEARS	SECOND YEARS	THIRD YEARS
SEMESTER 1	SEMESTER 3	SEMESTER 5
Week 1 Group Tutorial	Week 1 Group Tutorial	Weeks 1–5 Individual
Weeks 2–4 Individual	SEMESTER 4	SEMESTER 6
SEMESTER 2	Weeks 1–5 Individual	Weeks 8–17 Individual
Week 1/2 Group Tutorial		
Weeks 3–5 Individual		
Weeks 11–17 Individual		

BA Two Year

FIRST YEARS	SECOND YEARS
SEMESTER 1	SEMESTER 3
Week 1 Group Tutorial	No Tutorial
Weeks 2–4 Individual	SEMESTER 4
SEMESTER 2	Week 1 Whole Group Tutorial
Week 1/2 Group Tutorial	Weeks 2–6 Individual
Weeks 3–5 Individual	
Weeks 11–17 Individual	

Appendix 2
Academic profile

This part of the profile is concerned with identifying academic strengths and weaknesses through self evaluation and reflection.

Consider carefully the feedback you have received in relation to your academic work in each module. (verbal feedback, module report, assignment comments)

On the following page write a personal end of semester report which highlights the strengths and weaknesses in your academic work. Specific evidence from your module assignments must be included to support your statement.

Try to identify the underlying factors which influence your academic performance and results. e.g. consider why a seminar was successful, or an essay mark disappointing?

The following statements may be used as a guide to evaluate and reflect on your academic work; in addition to the assignment marking guide criteria used to grade your work.

WRITTEN ASSIGNMENTS
1. Answered the question 'set'?
2. Logical and coherent presentation?
3. Relevant use of literature?
4. Relative information to support argument?
5. Critical analysis and synthesis of evidence?
6. Accurate and detailed references?

SEMINAR PRESENTATION
1. Lively, confident presentation?
2. Clear, accurate information?
3. Promote and control appropriate discussion?
4. Utilise effectively supportive materials?
5. Summarise, draw logical conclusions?

DISCUSSION SKILLS
1. Confident and involved?
2. Clear, logical contribution?
3. Listen, make relevant response to issues raised?
4. Appropriate use of questions?

ADDITIONAL FACTORS
1. Appropriate time management?
2. Effective use of appropriate available resources?
3. Displayed safe and effective laboratory/equipment skills?
4. Appropriate numerical and statistical analysis?
5. Recording relevant verbal information?
6. Additional reading to consolidate/extend knowledge?

Academic Profile
(*Write an end of semester report, which includes specific evidence to illustrate your academic strengths and weaknesses*)

Tutor Comment
Make reference to the realism of the report and any significant omissions.

The academic report will be discussed with your personal tutor and a future action plan devised.
Action Plan
(*prioritise the action plans and indicate the time scale*)

Update *Any of the action plans if necessary.*

Appendix 3
Course Coherence

This part of the profile is concerned with identifying the relationships between modules, and their application to professional/vocational work and the final degree qualification. Reflect upon the various modules taken in semester 1 and 2, select what you consider to be the six most valuable modules for you, in relation to your chosen route/expected degree. Write the module number and title in the boxes below.

Module Number _____	Module Number _____
Title _____	Title _____

| Module Number _____ |
| Title _____ |
| |
| |

| Module Number _____ |
| Title _____ |
| |
| |

| Module Number _____ |
| Title _____ |
| |
| |

| Module Number _____ |
| Title _____ |
| |
| |

Are there any relationships between the modules you have selected? Use arrows to indicate any modules that appear to be related.

a) Explain why these selected modules are valuable/important to you.

Explain the connections you have identified between your selected modules. Do the modules relate in relation to subject knowledge professional/vocational outcomes or final degree qualification? Try to explain these relationships.

b) Module Connections (experiences, subject knowledge, professional/vocational)

Are there any modules which have been especially valuable to you? What were the outcomes for you in relation to personal development, academic/practical knowledge and understanding, professional/vocational knowledge and experience?

c) Module Outcomes (personal, academic, professional/vocational)

Notes and references

1. Broadfoot, P. (ed.) *Profiles and Records of Achievement: A Review of Issues and Practice* (London: Holt, Rinehart and Winston, 1986).
2. DES *Records of Achievement: Report of the Records of Achievement National Steering Committee* (London: HMSO, 1989).
3. DES Records of Achievement for School Leavers: A Draft Policy Statement (London: HMSO, 1989).
   DES *Records of Achievement: A Statement of Policy* (London: HMSO, 1984).

4. Fenwick, A., Assiter, A. and Nixon, N. *Profiling in Higher Education: Guidelines for the Development and Use of Profiling Schemes* (London: Department of Employment, 1992).
5. Ibid. p. 4.
6. National Steering Committee, op. cit. p. 5.
7. Ibid. p. 15.
8. Latham, A. M. 'Recording achievement in physical education', in BAALPE *Report of the 70th Annual Congress and Course: Physical Education 1990: A Foundation for the Future* Nafferton Books, 1990, 62–69.
9. National Steering Committee, op. cit. p. 158.
10. Ibid. p. 9.
11. Fenwick, *et al.* op. cit.
12. Assiter, A. and Shaw, E. (Eds) *Using Records of Achievement in Higher Education* (London: Kogan Page, 1993).
13. Ibid. p. 20.
14. Fenwick, *et al.* op. cit. p. 5.

CHAPTER 11
Is Self-assessment a Valid Concept?
RALPH TUCK

Some people consider that self-assessment is a contradiction.[1] How can any individual be trusted to be perfectly objective when judging the quality of his/her own performance? In private life this may not matter but in academic life or at work the success or safety of others may ultimately be at risk. 'People are just not as reliable and as honest in their own cause as ...' As what? Machine testing? Multiple choice?[2] Continuous assessment (SATs)? Externally marked exams? Externally moderated and verified performance achievements? Performance in the workplace on the job?[3] Oral examination? Tests set and marked internally by qualified and experienced academics? Possibly! But none of these alternatives is perfectly valid and reliable either.[4] Each of these methods involves an element of subjectivity and unreliability at some moment in its drawing up, its execution or its marking and checking. Nobody involved in the assessing procedures really knows the limits of the understanding of those being tested nor their mind set when faced with the testing.[5] Assessment of others can only be, at best, an approximation of quality of performance made at any time under particular circumstances. On the other hand, self-assessment can be continuous through a whole range of circumstances and repeated tests. However, between these occasions, consciousness of previous performances is retained together with failures and successes.

But the sceptics may then insist, 'Even if we accept that no assessment method is perfectly objective, valid and reliable, self-assessment is the least effective of them all, surely? After all, it is not acceptable that both the *object* of assessment and the *agent* carrying out the assessment are the same person, is it?'[1, 4]

This is the frequent spontaneous interpretation of the self-assessment process. However, to isolate self-assessment in this aspect is to disregard the limited potential and delicacy of any method of assessment; also the vulnerability of all methods to mis-use or mis-application.[6] It is a truism to say that all assessment should take place with maximum possible scrupulousness, fairness and objectivity. Also that every test should be successful in testing what it is intended to assess (validity) and consistently do so (reliability).[4] Test designers work within the acknowledged limitations of their chosen method of assessment and then put them to trials accordingly. Users ought not to require insights from tests beyond their designers' limited intended purpose. This may result in users appreciating just how little a good valid and reliable test can actually produce in meaningful and authentic results. Such a realization can be very frustrating. Too much weight can be placed on tests, e.g. the 11-plus: its intended predictive capability has been recognized by many LEAs as being flawed, partial and disruptive. Many other factors (emotional, physical, temperamental, attitudinal and social) played significant roles during the taking of the 11-plus and in later variable scholastic careers. These factors were strong enough for many to invalidate the overt claims of the 11-plus compilers to any predictive validity for the exam. But despite this, not all LEAs have discontinued using the 11-plus to segregate secondary age pupils. Some continue using it today, e.g. Kent and North Yorkshire. This touches on the possible covert political nature and purposes for administering examinations. For each examination involves an element of self-revelation by the per former. On the basis of the self-revelation, questions are asked, judgements made and roles-prospects determined![6,7] Such important actions are often made by outsiders, people unknown to the examinees, whose cultural, educational and social characteristics and assumptions may be very different, even alien, to those of the examinees. But such features/drawbacks are not unique to the 11-plus exam. Similar accusations have been made against Advanced Level GCE, degree qualifications and NVQs.[7]

Too much can be read into the results and the examinees have no means of explaining their performances.[8] It is almost as though there is something inherently *unsatisfactory* about being compelled to expose yourself to a public test of knowledge, or performance. (This is especially true if the considered result is uncomplimentary and below your expectation.) You may end up by being resentful because you are aware that you *knew* the right answer but were influenced by other factors (see above) into giving a wrong answer! Only you, the examinee, can know what was going through your head during the course of the test and why you performed as you did![6] You know your own motives and what exactly you were trying to articulate during that assessed performance. Nobody else can ever enter into your head, as you yourself can, and know what really happens.

Any three-way collaboration between tutor, assessor and student/examinee is in line with progressive practice today, for example TRADEC/Youth Training/NVQ/Project 2000 for Nurse Trainees/Accreditation of Prior Experience.[9] This more 'open' style of learning/assessment is more easily done in the workplace than in colleges or schools.[10] National Vocational Qualifications require just such collaboration between trainee, work-based supervisor/assessor and internal verifier. The trainee decides when he or she is ready for assessment and has the chance to discuss problems.[4] The trainee knows the competences which are required. The publicly available competence requirements should leave the trainee with no surprises when it comes to knowing the assessment requirements.[11] This is a positive approach because it is intended to confirm just what skills/competences the trainee has mastered successfully and can use reliably. Validity and reliability are not forgotten. The intentions of the National Vocational Qualification Council is affirmative. This contrasts with the normative apparently adversarial traditional approach to assessment procedures in schools and colleges. Students may still be surprised (on the actual day of the written examination) at the probing, unanticipated questions presented for their attention and interpretation. But educationists do not yet fully know how people learn. So assessment of foundation learning at schools and colleges cannot yet be carried out with that clinical accuracy all would like. The NVQ competence-based model of work-based performance competences, is more open and collaborative.[12, 13]

Indeed, a more collaborative approach to assessment may enable a rather more realistic understanding of the individual's process of learning.[14] It is an admission that replicative[15] learning alone is not sufficient today but, equally, that applicative learning[16] involves a more complex process with imaginable and unimaginable difficulties on the part of the learner.[16,17] How can a 50-year-old academic from higher education suspect all the patterns of significance a teenager is trying to impose on limits of knowledge today? This applies especially to those from another very different culture, those with learning difficulties, adult returners, and those from very different social circumstances and class.[18] These form a considerable proportion of the learning population and can include individuals with several of these learning disadvantages. Collaboration and sharing the realities and intricacies of learning are especially important for this latter group, some would say vital.[19, 20] Equally, the working assumptions of the examiners and assessors need to be articulated and identified as unique personal constructs which may intrude into and distort the examining and assessment processes.[21] They may create unique mismatches between the intended performance of the examinee and the powerful judgements of the examiners. This dilemma touches on the question of standards today. Are standards authentic, realistic and justifiable or are they constructs devised by a particular social class? Are they intended to exclude some citizens from success while favouring others?[22]

Meaningful learning

Learning cannot be imposed completely. For one of the profounder definitions of learning is 'learning is the discovery of meaning.[23] Stanton goes on:

The problem of learning, modern psychologists tell us, always involves two aspects: one is the acquisition of new knowledge or experience; the other has to do with the individual's personal discovery of the information for him/her.[23]

So far this definition suggests that there is an active cognitive role for the learner to undertake and that this is an idiosyncratic personal process.

Kolb reinforces this by proposing a Learning Cycle based on personal experience.

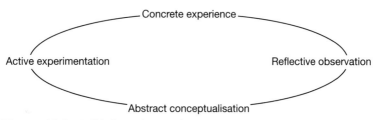

Figure 11.1. Kolb's learning cycle.

This discovery of meaningful learning through activity and reflection is personal but not exclusively so. It is set within the context of people and institutions. Ideally, the individual is being required to lay claim to what is meaningful to him or her in terms of learning and growing. Experiences cannot be ignored but the individual is a key participant in the sequence of rational action, thinking, defining and re-ordered experimentation. This is a central feature of self-assessment.[24]

Kolb: how he draws on theories of learning and development

Kolb's experiential learning cycle is not in itself original. It is clearly related to Piaget's model of learning and cognitive development. The action research model of Lewin[25] clearly has much in common with it. Dewey[26] was aware of the possibilities for learning from experience and his model too is related to Kolb's cycle. Indeed Kolb emphasizes these links: he summarizes the process of learning as:

a didactic process integrating experience and concepts, observations and action ... experience gives ideals their moving force and ideas give direction to impulse. Postponement of immediate action is essential for observation and judgement to intervene, and action is essential for achievement of purpose ... through the integration of these opposing but symbiotically related processes ... sophisticated, mautre purpose develops from blind impulse.[24]

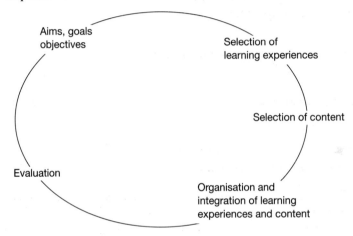

Figure 11.2. Wheeler cycle for curriculum planning[27]

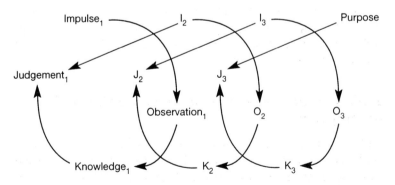

Figure 11.3. Dewey's model of experiential learning[24]

A four-stage cycle is not unique either.

None of these cycles is closed. They are processes. Whenever they are entered, they can be worked through and repeated with appropriate variations until a satisfactory conclusion is reached: learning becomes an alternation of thought and action. This is not the same as 'learning by doing' because Kolb's[24] approach is a cognitive reflective experience in which the learner imposes meaning and order onto his/her experiences and sensory data. In experiential learning, neither theory nor practice is adequate by itself. They need to be integrated. It is thinking and doing, then reflecting and doing, and so on. This will be recognized as the method of science. This is how any researcher sets about his/her work: an authentic learner will be observing, thinking, planning and doing repeatedly. This process generates new knowledge within the appropriate bands of the learner's context.

Various techniques are available in the experiential learning cycle, e.g. action plans, setting objectives, designing experiments, observation checklists, devising criteria, learning contracts, action research, diaries, logbooks, structured discussions, reflection checklists and questionnaires, case studies, structured debriefing, and self-assessment.[28] Many of these are relevant to supervised work experience (SWE) and work placements, as well as student-centred learning in pre-16 settings (GCSE/GNVQ (F) and A Level GCE and Home Learning).

The critical transformation occurs as the receiver of the information or experience is enabled to interpret the flow of information on the basis of his/her own culture, character, ambitions and learning style continues. [24] 'The discovery of MEANING, however, can only take place in people and cannot occur without the involvement of people'. This suggests that time and opportunity need to be made available to the learner to examine, contextualize and evaluate experience and/or information.[29] If the learning is to become an active dynamic part of the resources of the learner then he or she can deepen its significance. On the other hand, if passive knowledge is being offered then the outsider's view would suffice because the outsider is likely to have determined and made evident in what context the learning would have meaning. Reflecting, challenging, questioning, applying, rejecting and re-contextualizing of information or new experience are, therefore, of the greatest importance to active use of learning.[30, 31, 32, 33] It may be that the intention of the provider of the new knowledge/experience may only wish to give the increments of limited independence of action or application.[33] This raises an important learning issue. Without a clear agreement of the purpose for the learning experience it is possible for a learner to be working to a different set of expectations and criteria to the tutor.[34] Without agreement on the validity and relevance of the tutor's purposes by the learner there is scope for misunderstanding and frustration.[35] Even ultimately, inability to process the new knowledge or even to receive it![36]

Once a satisfactory mutually supportive relationship has been established, there are many questions which can be asked of the tutor and much continuing learning obtained.[38]

Experiential learning: the role of tutors

How is any gap between participants, tutors or work supervisors to be bridged so that the learning process is to be shared, self-sustaining and effective. Stanton and Potts[40] conclude that it is the tutor who must make efforts to bridge these gaps. Does the learner need acceptance, access and freedom in order to be able to discover the meaning for him/herself of information or experience? In his classes at the Department of History at the University of Melbourne, Dr Potts gives the learners a measure of autonomy. They can thus initiate explorations into meaningfulness from their experience of academic didactic instruction.

So that he is not misunderstood Potts[40] offers caveats: [These are important in order to reassure the sceptics identified at the start of this chapter.]

1. Student autonomy is not total.

2. A measure of freedom is extended into effective student-to-student learning and the development of personal skills.
3. Total autonomy is not wanted by the students.
4. Freedom 'spilling over' into political action is not desirable either.
5. The teacher can lose authority in such a process and, consequently, needs training in experiential learning techniques. Only thereby can his/her commitment to this innovative style of learning be successfully maintained.

Underlying such moves towards taking experiential learning seriously by tutors are 'hidden agendas'. Heron is convinced that the development of inter-personal skills is part of effective learning.[36] In it tutor and learner may come to an authentic realization of each other's distinctiveness and also similarities at appropriate levels. In so doing each becomes aware of the limitations of the other, each can interpret the other's interventions accordingly and share mutual understanding. He defines these levels as:

1. *The role-relevant level*: technical competence in roles.
2. *The level of personal distress*: experiences of angers, griefs and fears.
3. *The level of the human condition*: the tensions here are those that relate to basic conditions of human existence; for example transient phenomena, fallibilities of human endeavour, social living and relationships, the unknown and the unseen; the uncertainties and probabilities of the future; the potentialities and the possibilities of free choice. This is acknowledgement of the common human condition between learners and tutors, an insight usually afforded by tutors to a privileged few.

These universal characteristics affect everybody at profound levels of the psyche at different times to different extents. They represent the likelihood of distortions in tutors' (and learners') behaviour which are personal yet not beyond

236

empathy if not yet understanding.[41] The individual may not be aware of them nor identify them nor know how or why they operate. This appears to support the need for Rogers's 'unconditional positive regard'[38] especially at moments of change, challenge and unpredictability. This implies logically that tutors, too, will need to come to terms with themselves (level 2 above) before they can help a learner to make sense of his/her experiences.[36] This is after tutors have been convinced of their technical suitability for the role of facilitator/mentor (level 1 above). At level 3 (above), self-questioning comes as different generations meet at review sessions.[42] Heron insists on the indispensability of recognizing these spiritual psycho-social responses as dynamic integral shapes of individuals' understanding and experience. This is, therefore, likely to be true for all individuals involved in learning through experience whatever their role especially for the tutor who has become facilitator/mentor. Careful preparation of facilitators/mentors is essential as a consequence. Since personal 'deep' features of individuals can interfere and distort learning especially if the object of learning experiences is personal development and not exclusively the mastery of an objective technique or basic understandings. In learning from experience the initially subjective is transformed into objective learning, hence the need to respect the tensions created by this personal achievement.

EXAMPLE: ASSESSMENT OF LEARNING FROM EXPERIENCES AT THE WORKPLACE

Ashworth and Saxton[43] suggest that assessment is part and parcel of the whole work placement package. It is not just a one off nor simply limited in time. For Ashworth[43] assessment is a central value and is also a means towards several ends. These include the more pragmatic and realistic use of the opportunities for learning offered by the work placement. Whereas Cowans[42], as a tutor, is still very much in control of activities, Ashworth acknowledges the need for a close partnership between employer, tutor and student.

This proposal confirms a growing trend to maximize learning from a unique experience, for example work placement. Such a degree of partnership, co-operation and planning between the three main partners has been tried for 18- to 19-year olds in formal academic education in some higher education institutions too.[44, 45]

> The principal value in profiled assessments is that it encourages regular review and planning discussions between the teacher and individual students; it provides a means of managing learning. If this is to be effective, however, it is important that the learning identified in assessment, whether for diagnosis, monitoring, planning or reporting, is identified as precisely as possible. General descriptive statements are not likely to do this; instead particular, specific pieces of work need to be identified as exemplifying the type of learning under discussion.[46]

Learning through doing and working are important features of pre-vocational education. Can this provide a valuable interface between academia and the company's workplace? How do the learners themselves relate to both now that they are recognized as dynamic and no longer passive? Is there a new role available for the learners? Can patrons learn from the following examples?

1. Youth Training (YT) is pre-vocational. Its distinctive feature is that it is based in the workplace rather than in full-time education. There is emphasis on the broader skills and knowledge and on the vocational qualification.
2. The Technical Vocational and Educational Initiative (TVEI) is not a qualification but a curriculum framework, a set of principles about how education should be designed and delivered. It is intended to inform the curriculum and so to prepare young people for working life in a rapidly changing technologically geared society (students in full-time education between 14 and 18).
3. In further education (a much expanded section with the inclusion of the former sixth form colleges) numerous NVQs are offered. Learning from the workplace is a problem though in this section.

Each of these initiatives provides some new helpful

processes, principles, tools and mechanisms. These help to orient the learners towards developing themselves for their vocational and life success. The learner is more at the centre. He/she in theory is given more status, is allowed to negotiate initiatives and is meant to enjoy being a partner in a learning process.

All industrialists have developed their own expectations of city technology colleges, comprehensive high schools, colleges, 'opted out' schools, private schools and HE institutions with regard to supervised work experience and work-based learning schemes in general. Employers are articulating their requirements more and more precisely because they need the best equipped employees to make their companies profitable and indeed to guarantee their survival. These requirements change and grow as seen in 'Project Trident', the Nationwide Scheme for allocating 15-year old *students* in work placements.

The challenge facing industry, too, should not be forgotten.

> We [industrialists] also need to change our culture. In the old model of management, the aim was to get the ideas of managers implemented by employees, for employees to act as managers' lackeys. Today, the core of management should be the art of drawing on the brainpower of all the employees in the business … it carries a number of implications. Employees need to have commitment for their work so we need to empower them, giving them more responsibility and greater recognition (not just financial) for what they do. We also need to develop teamwork, and there should be common ownership of problems.[47]

There are major shifts here too: respect for the employees' imagination and intelligence; ability to work co-operatively without needing to be told all the time what to do; being given power; being praised for achievements; advised when things go wrong.

So, are the dependants (employees) now coming much nearer 'centre stage' in good practice in industry?[48] If they are in certain areas don't they still need to be prepared to make appropriate judgements and to contribute in different groups and plan for the unknown?

Examples of student-empowered education

Pre-vocational education seeks to enable students to develop their unique all round abilities within a vocational context, e.g. former CPVE/Certificate in Pre-Vocational Education and General National Vocational Qualifications at all levels. This has the effect of increasing the expectations of the tutors and vice versa. Relevance and integration count for a great deal. Traditionally the synthesizing of concepts and practice is left to take place within the learners' own heads. This is certainly true in universities where so much is left to the individual aptitude of students. Sometimes this approach works perfectly well, but we can no longer take it for granted.[49, 50, 51]

Given the explosion of specialist knowledge and the fragmenting and alienating effect of the modern market society, it is not safe to assume that cerebral processing of information can be left to the learners alone.[36, 52, 53] (cf. Government Academic League Tables at Key Stages 2, 3, 4).

For example, students on the General National Vocational Qualification (GNVQ) programmes negotiate, discuss and agree their own learning programmes with their tutors. This requires much flexibility. The learners are taking more responsibility for the successful ultimate outcomes of their work. They are having to make judgements, rarely easy in any situation.

> Negotiation is important in any case because it gives students some sense of control and ownership of their activities. The learning activities and the assessment to the learning should also be negotiated.

> Effective learning is, in part, a matter of consistent interest and guidance from the teacher. What is required is regular, planned and detailed personal guidance for each student on an individual basis.

> To keep the students' motivation, learning must be interesting. Students should learn by being able to carry out tasks for themselves rather than by passively listening to the teacher and writing notes. They should also be provided with experiences through which they learn: work experience, residentials, visits, simulated work situations, role play, projects and similar activities.[46]

In pre-vocational education, these students are aged between 14 and 18 (post-compulsory). They, and adults as well, can take GNVQs. They are often staying in education for their own reasons, not necessarily because the law insists on it. Often their motivation is instrumental and vocational. They want and need a job. They are also free to leave the (modular) courses whenever they wish. Their freedoms and rights as quoted above are compatible with an 'adult client or customer relationship' within the educational institution; it should be more like that of a client with a trusted professional adviser. This is a very different relationship to that of pupils and teachers in schools in general.

Does this relationship maximize the opportunities for learning from experience through a student-centred negotiated curriculum? Does it provide a basis for learners' self-assessment, too? Do tutors need to remember this and learn to adopt it as far as possible? There is a much longer, more powerful tradition of higher education in England than of organized state-provided comprehensive education for all. The status of HE and the power of the Vice Chancellor is impressive.

Can tutors in HE institutions remain insulated indefinitely from the changes occurring in pre- and post-16 education? It is an open question. But appropriate adaptation may not be easy. It will require changes in the process of learning and of the organizing of learning in HE. Can this be done more analytically and consciously? The modes of teaching/learning can usefully be opened up to more public debate and scrutiny. But this runs counter to the expected status and authority of University lecturers.

> Higher education is used to pre-determine what is done and then assessing it. By its very nature, work-based learning challenges that model. It makes the case for thinking afresh about learner-centred education and related assessment procedures. There are clear arguments in favour of student involvement, fostering transparency and ownership on the part of learners. But this threatens the current orthodoxy.[29]

LEARNING STYLES

Postman[22] provides a list of deficiencies of schooling identified by psychologists. They range from 'irrelevant' to 'punishes creativity and independence'. Why is there no countervailing lists of the perceived achievements of schools? Advocates of autonomous learning suggest that clashes between the individual learner's preferred learning style and the teaching approach of the school could account for some or all of the deficiencies. Given the cultural changes in society these could at times be levelled against HE institutions to some extent. Learners in Higher Education are autonomous adults and are able to engage in two way communication. Whether this is encouraged is a separate matter.[36]

Boud[54] wrote that

> the teacher needs to retain in mind that within the same class there will probably be students with radically different outlooks on what is taking place who will be reacting in very different ways.

There are nine positions identified as describing the main line of development of his American undergraduate students at Harvard:

Position 1: Knowledge and goodness are perceived as quantitative accretion of discrete rightnesses to be collected by hard work and obedience. [paradigm: a spelling test]

Position 9: The student experiences the affirmation of identity among multiple responsibilities and realises commitment as a constant unfolding activity through which he expresses his lifestyle.

The first would represent complete dependence on the tutorial staff. The latter integrates the learning into his/her lifestyle and makes appropriate judgements depending on other events in his/her life. This is a position of adjusting for integration, synthesizing and greater autonomy. It is likely, surely, that such a learner could manage to co-operate with tutors in negotiating his/her programme.

Perhaps Kolb's four basic learning styles can clarify what

is needed[24]. They are 'convergent', 'divergent'. 'assimilative' and 'accommodative'. These describe very different learning styles rather than simply generalized developmental stages. Notwithstanding, Kolb highlights the need of the education system to recognize variations in learning styles and to devise strategies to accommodate them. In order to ground them in the realities of the world (rather than exclusively in terms of academia) Kolb identifies the professional areas which can make best use of the learning styles, e.g. convergent learners relying on learning abilities of abstract conceptualization and active experimentation tend towards science-based professions and technology. Divergent learners emphasize concrete experience and reflective observation. They are interested in people, tend to be imaginative and find employment in service to people, arts and entertainment. They tend to study arts and humanities in higher education. This is of direct relevance to institutions of higher education as they continue to develop stronger links with industry. Kolb's learning style inventory provides access to individual learning styles.[42] They are pointers, perhaps, towards a method of 'learning to learn'

Are these authentic pointers to the contents of learning programmes which can encourage and complement the learner's own inclinations (as opposed to the requirements of the national economy)? The process of deciding a career orientation is not necessarily that simple. Many factors can contribute. As mentioned above, it is all too easy to criticize current education provision and to discount whatever it does well. As well as those learners who have very definite conscious preferences for particular learning styles, there are others who may prefer a mixture. So, if learners can be encouraged and enabled to identify their own learning preferences, could they achieve a greater degree of self-directed learning from them? This is especially relevant for the placement on work experience where self-knowledge helps the student face the new challenges of the business processes.

Evans warns about the influence of the learners' 'cognitive

repertoire' acquired from the actions of former teachers/parents/employers.[55] This may compete with any principles, concepts or strategies learned in college. No academic or company supervisor can afford to think that the learner comes with a 'virgin clean' mind or with only certain predictable attitudes. One only needs to receive the 'truth', as the academic perceives it, in order for any previous influences to be diminished or disappear. Can an academic objectively claim to know the 'architecture' of any student's mind easily? Is this possible only when the latter is enabled to tell what is in his/her mind without feeling inadequate and incompetent?[36] How else can there be deep authentic engagement of two intellects? The validity of the student's (and the tutor's) personal constructs need to be examined with mutual respect. Yet are there opportunities for this to happen as frequently as necessary? Could more be done to align learning style with tutorial method? Very possibly.

> [Too often you] find students not clear about what is going on, or they don't really understand what the criteria mean, or they didn't have enough discussion with their tutors before their placements.[56]

This statement suggests that what was straightforward for the tutor (information) was not so for some students. Perhaps time, awareness or commitment are lacking. This confusion of the students can be compounded by the misinterpretation of reactions. Expecting and providing for interaction between different student learning styles from the outset make it possible for tutors and learners to come together in rich information exchange, discussion and learning.

It is arguable that successful application of one's 'personal learning style' is the key to equipping learners to learn anywhere, especially in the workplace. But any learning style can be made ineffective if conditions do not cater for it, especially in industry (the culture of the firm, for example). Evans confirms that much careful preparation needs to be done before learning can be effective.[55] This applies especially to any senior form of self-assessment by learners or by tutors (Figure 11. 1).

The new paradigm (empowerment of the learner)

Heron insists that research activity undertaken without the knowing co-operation of the persons being interviewed is not truly authentic.[57] It does not reveal the real state of affairs, motives, causes and interpretations. Habermas identifies a sometimes inchoate array of feelings, conditioning, indoctrination ideologies and procedures (personal and social).[53] These limit the freedom of individuals to take on new roles and responsibilities or to be harmonious personalities. Therefore, even if learners are invited to become partners in assessment of supervised work experience (SWE) they would probably find that they had reservations, queries, worries and even perhaps constraints stemming from their past conditioning.[54] Since according to Heron each learner is a unique individual, albeit with shared characteristics, his/her individual reservations would need to be heard and accommodated in order to achieve a greater degree of authentic disposition and power to learn.

Freire uses the term 'conscientisation' to describe the process by which a person's false consciousness of his/her own position becomes transcended through education.[57] Freire has worked closely with the marginalized and oppressed peoples of Brazil enabling them as individuals to become aware of the structures of oppression, the constructs imposed on them and their own capacity to emancipate themselves from these constraints of society. Such examination can give them understanding and power to act and obtain justice for themselves. Freire uses adult literacy classes as a forum for individual and communal reflection on language and on how political control is used/abused.

It is not being suggested here that learners on SWE should be 'conscientised for revolution' in England by challenging the political culture. However, for generations learners have been conditioned to accept other people's assessment of their own performances in schools without being given the opportunity to give an 'authentic' personal contribution themselves. The power in the school classroom and, to a somewhat lesser extent in higher education, lies with the tutors. Their judgements affect the pupils' futures. Giving the learners the power to contribute to their own self-assessment and self-evaluation is a step forwards. Asking the learners to assess themselves within given structures which enable reflection (albeit mostly 'technical reflection') to take place is a cultural and political change of some significance. This characteristic should not be underestimated in significance. As with the oppressed in Brazil, some learners may not initially be able to understand this concept. They may be suspicious of motives, and the range of freedom being offered. They will need to have opportunities to reflect critically on their involvement and what it will mean for them. Also they will need to know how to do it authentically with validity. The self-assessment model of University of Huddersfield[28] (Figure 11.4) provides ample opportunity for this over the two years preceding the work placement.[28] The learners explore the limits of the new freedom and how their power to take responsibility for negotiating their own programme and assessing themselves can be exercised authentically. Schemes which are giving some power to the students can be seen as part of this transition from the traditional paradigm to a new dynamic paradigm, an opportunity for self-assessment or learning through working. This is a feature of the Huddersfield University Model for Self-assessment of Work-Based learning. It may be asked why radical changes have not been introduced since the 1880s when the first sandwich course was introduced at the Royal Technical College in Glasgow. Some reasons have already been discussed. However, the dynamics of the culture of learning are better understood today. Some of the barriers which prevent students from maximizing their potential during SWE have been revealed. These are especially relevant and important if we want to shift power to the student as a partial solution to problems confronting SWE today, the nation and the economy and individuals.[58,59,60] These authorities do not deny that creating a new paradigm is fraught with difficulties, but it is no less necessary. Given all the changes in technology and society since the 1880s, does the traditional paradigm not need to change? Indeed, education institutions are offering more 'open' opportunities for learning to students: CATS, Open University, and distance learning. New initiatives do raise epistemological questions. Questions arise about cultural and cognitive conditioning, subjectivism, freedom, political power, status, personal style and identity. Recognizing such features is important. It can help innovators to respect the diffidence and anxiety, expressed in different ways. Sensitivity is called for and a willingness to proceed co-operatively and innovatively.

It is significant that pre-vocational education schemes emphasize the all-round development of the learner with only that amount of vocational focus as is appropriate for the individual, e.g. generic and transferable personal skills in GNVQ. The developmental process of interaction of experience, reflection, re-assessment and then new experience opens up possibilities for the learner to make sense of all kinds of data and come to his/her own conclusions. For some this may raise the unwanted spectre of individualism run rampant, the intellectual version of 1960s experience.

For example, nursing education has externally prescribed curricula which indicate uncompromisingly what skills and qualities should be acquired and to what level of competence. This is vocational education. This does not, however, exclude some measure of learner empowerment although much less than for the General National Vocational Qualification (GNVQ). For example, on one psychiatric nurse programme, the learners (all qualified State Registered Nurses) draw up their own learning contract. On arrival for the course they are 'very depowered' according to their director of studies. In fact empowering them to become proactive takes six months. They each receive a list of competences together with a Contract of Learning. Each one negotiates the learning opportunities which he/she feels are right personally. They negotiate the how, who, where, and when. This is more difficult than it looks. They are being asked to anticipate the nature of their educational experience before experiencing it. If, as Glasborow[64] states 'all learning experience is a meaningful organisation of life's experiences', how can these

247

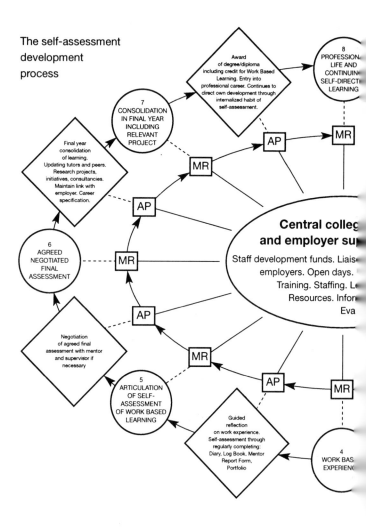

Figure 11.4 The self-assessment development process

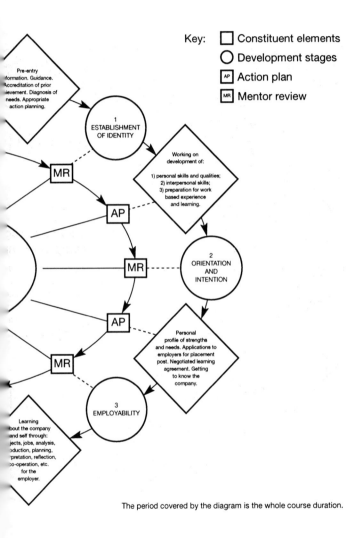

Key:
☐ Constituent elements
◯ Development stages
AP Action plan
MR Mentor review

Pre-entry
information. Guidance.
Accreditation of prior
achievement. Diagnosis of
needs. Appropriate
action planning.

1
ESTABLISHMENT
OF IDENTITY

MR

AP

Working on
development of:

1) personal skills and qualities;
2) interpersonal skills;
3) preparation for work
based experience
and learning.

MR

2
ORIENTATION
AND
INTENTION

AP

Personal
profile of strengths
and needs. Applications to
employers for placement
post. Negotiated learning
agreement. Getting
to know the
company.

MR

3
EMPLOYABILITY

Learning
about the company
and self through:
projects, jobs, analysis,
production, planning,
interpretation, reflection,
co-operation, etc.
for the
employer.

The period covered by the diagram is the whole course duration.

learners anticipate their learning needs *prior* to clinical practice?[61] Is it that these learner psychiatric nurses are only disempowered? Or do they find the requirement to look into the future from the limited standpoint of their present too nebulous? Is the transition from the busy, highly skilled, technical setting of the general ward to a new counselling role very delicate and not to be taken for granted? Probably.

Their 'contract' serves as a tool for critical feedback. There are two supervision sessions per week. Any initiative must have a rationale. The learners must be accountable to their mentors. In contracting, it is claimed, the learners 'set their own goals' at different levels. In theory, they should become more self-aware. Summative assessments are made on the basis of the contract. The visiting tutor has a checking role. According to Kiernan 'we must enable students to challenge politely. It is immoral [sic] not to do so! Challenging skills are needed'.[62] The contract *can* form the basis for an authentic discussion and mutual sharing of understanding and perception. In such a vocational contract scheme there is a limited place for student initiative. But the need for empowerment of the learner is acknowledged. It is facilitated by other informal means and relationships which are indispensable within the group, e.g. with the facilitator and by means of reflection. The nurse's responsibilities are considerable. It is therefore essential that each nurse understands and masters the knowledge and skills satisfactorily for him/herself. The same applies to all other jobs today.

Emancipation

Since the introduction of SWE in Glasgow in 1888 learners have not usually been in a position to determine the content, assessment and structuring of the work placement: they have been in a dependent relationship with the college tutor and the company supervisor. This was for many decades seen as right and proper. They were not yet graduates nor fully integrated permanent company employees. Also they may not yet have decided on their first professional post or career start. Today this insecurity is compounded by a possible relocation   to   the   company workplace. These insecurities were tolerated for a long time because the combined efforts of all those involved in SWE guaranteed a job at graduate level. This relative passivity of the learners may have reflected relatively simple predictable relationships between learning, placement and job.

However, the growing complexity of each of the roles mentioned above and the varied personal qualities expected by employers of new graduates means that the traditional passive receptive role by the learners on placement can put strains on supervisors and tutors. A pro-active role for the learners is now needed. Self-assessment can release the potential which a rapidly changing society and economy need from each and every worker and individual.

How the model works

The learner begins to develop the skills of self-assessment from the very start of the course. He/she is allocated to a tutor at the university who is responsible for encouraging and enabling the learner to develop the skills of self-assessment. In this particular role the tutor will be called a mentor. Regular reviewing sessions of one hour each (MR in diagram) between mentor and learner need to be timetabled. Each review will lead to the development of a Personal Action Plan (AP in diagram) aimed at the means of progressing towards the next step (large circles numbered 1–8 in Figure 11.4). The next Review Session checks on progress made from the previous Action Plan. Thus the learner is enabled to develop understanding and awareness, and the skills associated with self-assessment, self-direction and employability.

The learner will be enabled to diagnose his/her own strengths and weaknesses in the light of the personal and technical qualities which characterize employability at graduate level. This process will result in a Personal Profile which can be sent to any employer who best appears to satisfy the requirements for work experience of the specific learner. Once an employer has shown interest, a Learning Agreement for the work-based experience will be negotiated.

This Learning Agreement will specify a number of

Learning Categories within which the learner will identify his/her own growth and development whilst performing jobs of value to the firm. This agreement will include those categories of personal understanding, performances, skills, personal management and interpersonal skills which the college course team (in conjunction with employers) considered relevant. This agreement will be made as early as conveniently possible in the three-year course. Learners will therefore have time to learn more about the firm and industry, put right personal deficiencies, work on their needs and establish an informal relationship with the placement firm.

Once on placement the learner will be required to follow definite self-assessment procedures which will enable reflection on his/her work experience. The identified learning will be defined, articulated, and ultimately accredited to the learner. The personal Diary, the Weekly Report to the mentor at the university and the definition of the specific learning in the official College Log Book should be completed regularly.

The supervisor at the workplace will authenticate the claims to learning by regularly checking and signing them. The learner will be required to satisfy the supervisor that she or he has acquired the appropriate range of adequate knowledge and skills. This will be done through the accreditation of a minimum number of learning claims based on the formal Learning Outcomes. It is hoped that this prescribed process of reflection and identifying learning from work experiences will become internalized by the learners and be useful as a means of continuing self-directed learning in full professional life after the course.

Notes and references

1. DFEE Fourth annual DFEE table of GCSE, A level and VQ examination performance for England including data on all year 11 pupils + 15 year olds (+ *Guardian added* information on A–G grades because GCSE was devised as an exam for all). *Guardian, Education Supplement*, 21 November 1995.
2. Copey, A. Review of GNVQs NCVQ (1995).
3. Beaumont, G. Clear criticisms and benefits Recommendations from his Independent Report on the Review of the Top 100 NVQs and SVQs SCOTVEC Review issue 3 January 1996 1 + 8–11.

4. Benett, Y. The validity and reliability of assessments and self-assessments at work based learning. *Assessment and Evaluation in Higher Education*, 18 (2), 1993, 83–94.

5. Fennell, E. Implementing NVQs: the individual's perspective in Department of Education and Employment, *Competence and Assessment*, 30 1995, 2–5.

6. Otter, S. What can graduates do? UDACE, 1992.

7. Slipman, S. We make futures not widgets [NVQs for Advice, Guidance, Counselling and Psychotherapy (AGCP)] *Guardian, Career Section*: 18 November 1995.

8. Roberts, K. and Horton, P., Lifelong Learning Project. Good practice on breaking down the barriers to lifelong learning. Information sheet (1995).

9. Anglia Centre for Cooperative Education Ford ASSET Project. Conference Papers Executive Summary, 1993.

10. Hodges, P. An employer's perspective education advisor, Parcel Force In FERA Conference Papers (1995) Reviewing NVQs: the way forward, 29–33. *FERA Bulletin* 60. (Filed in B6).

11. Jessop, G. Review of top 100 NVQs/SVQs: Context and issues paper, 1995.

12. Hodkinson, P. A critical overview of NVQ issues *in* FERA (1995) Conference papers: Reviewing NVQs: The way forward, 12–25. *FERA* Bulletin 60. (Files in B6).

13. Stepping, T. A Training and Enterprise Council perspective *in* FERA Conference papers (1995) Reviewing NVQs: the way forward, 36–37. FERA Bulletin 60. (Filed in B6).

14. Anglia Polytechnic University, Ford and Employment Department *Ford Assett Project* (1994).

15. Broudy, H. S., Smith, R. O. and Barnett, J. *Democracy and Excellence in American Secondary Education* Chicago: Rand McNally, 1984).

16. Eraut, M. *Developing Professional Knowledge and Competence.* (London: Falmer , 1994).

17. Further Education Unit Implementing CPVE: practical advice on designing, operating, and evaluating CPVE, 1989.

18. ALBSU *Basic Skills Support in Colleges: Assessing the Need* (1993).

19. Freire, P. *Cultural Action for Freedom* (London: Penguin, 1972).

20. Heron, J. Philosophical basis for a new paradigm. In Reacon, P. (ed.) *et al. Harman Inquiry: A Sourcebook of Paradigm Research* (New York: Wiley, 1981).

21. Harri-Augstein, S. and Thomas, L. *Learning Conversations* (London, Routledge, 1991)

22. Postman, N. and Weingartener, C. *Teaching as a Subversive Activity.* (London: Penguin, 1971)

23. Stanton, H. Independent study: a matter of confidence. In Bond,

D. (ed.) *Developing Student Autonomy in Learning*, 119–131.

24. Kolb, D. A. *Experiential Learning: Experience as the Source of Learning and Development.* (Englewood Cliffs: Prentice Hall, 1984)

25. Lewin, K. *Field Theory in Social Science* (London: Tavistock, 1952).

26. Dewey, J. *Democracy and Education.* (New York: Free Press, 1916).

27. Wheeler, D. *Curriculum Process,* (London: University of London Press, 1967).

28. Tuck, R., Lee, B., Benett, Y. (1992). A self-assessment model for the integration of work-based learning with academic assessment. Department of Employment and the University of Huddersfield Project report and implementation annexes. Department of Employment.

29. Duckenfield, M. and Stirner, P. *Learning Through Work* (Sheffield: Department of Employment, 1992).

30. Wolf, A. (1993) Assessment issues and problems in a criterion-based system. FEU.

31. Weil, S. Creating capability for change in higher education: the RSA Initiative *in* Barnett, R. (ed.) (1992) *Learning to Effect.* (London: Society for Research into Higher Education and Open University Press, 1992) 186–203.

32. Edwards, P. and Wilson, P. Two urban stories: the development of APL in Newham Community College and Sheffield LEA. Learning from Experience Trust, 1991.

33. Heron, J. Assessment re-visited. In Bond, D. *Developing Student Autonomy Into Learning* (London: Kogan Page, 1988).

34. Orbach, S. *Fat is a Feminist Issue.* London: Hamlyn, 1978).

35. Bond, D. *Developing Student Autonomy into Learning* (London: Kogan Page, 1988).

36. Heron, J. Experiential training techniques. Human Potential Research Project. University of Surrey, 1973.

37. Rajan, A. *1992: A Zero Sum Game* (London: Industrial Society Press, 1990).

38. Rogers, C. *On Becoming a Person.* (London: Constable, 1967).

39. Shackleton, J. Converting workers into learning, FEU. (L). 1985.

40. Potts, D. Student autonomy. In Bond, D. (ed). *Developing Student Autonomy in Learning*, 132–149, 1988.

41. Drever, J. and Wallerstein, H. *A Dictionary of Psychology* (Rev. edn) (Harmondsworth: Penguin, 1964).

42. Cowans, J. and Garry, A. Learning from experience. Further Education Unit/Professional Industrial Commercial Knowledge Update (PICKUP), 1986.

43. Ashworth, P. and Saxton, J. Experiential learning during sandwich degree placements and the question of assessment. Centre for Educational Management & Administration. Sheffield

Polytechnic, 1988.

44. Davies, L. Experience based learning within the curriculum. Association for Sandwich Education and Training. CNAA, 1990.

45. Department of Employment Development of assessable standards for National Certification. Guidance Note 7. Project management standards and NVQ/SVQ development, Sheffield, 1991.

46. Further Education Unit. *Implementing CPVE.*(London: HMSO, 1989).

47. Usherwood, T. and Joesburg, H. Assessing specified competences in medical undergraduate training In Employment Department (1993) Competence and Assessment Issue No. 22, 6–9.

48. Marchington, M., Goodman, J., Wilkinson, A. and Ackers, P. New developments in employee involvement. Manchester School of Management UMIST. Research Series No. 2. Employment Department, 1992.

49. Confederation of British Industry (1990). 17- and 18-year-olds going on to higher education: survey of students' attitudes.

50. Department of Employment *Skillsnet* Sheffield, 1992.

51. Doran, C., Preece, R. and Hills, J. Entrepreneurial Skills, FEU. (L). 1987.

52. MacFarlane, K. (1993) Towards best assessment practice. In Employment Department's Methods Strategy Unit (1993) Competence and Assessment. Issue 22.

53. Habermas, J. *Knowledge and Human Interests* (London: Heinemann Education, 1972).

54. Reny, W. *Motivation in Students in Higher Education* (London: MacMillan, 1979).

55. Evans, H. Learning from experience: the case of field experience *Journal of Further and Higher Education*, 11 (2) 1987, 58–70.

56. Heron, J. Philosophical basis for a new paradigm. In Reason, P. (ed.) *et al. Human Inquiry: A Sourcebook of Paradigm Research.* (New York: Wiley, 1981).

57. Freire, P. *Pedagogy of the Oppressed* (London: Latimer Trend, 1972).

58. Benett, Y. Development of placement and assessment procedures in supervised work experience. Project report and annexes A–F. CNAA/Polytechnic of Huddersfield, Huddersfield, 1989.

59. Chatterton, D., Huston, F. and Roberts, C. The assessment of supervised work experience: a review of test practice in higher education. Ealing College of Higher Education: 1988.

60. Bond, D. *A Sense of Freedom* (London: Pan Books, 1973).

61. Glasborow, A. N. C. An evaluation of the industrial training period of a sandwich course for undergraduate engineers. PhD thesis, Brunel University, 1980.

62. Kiernan, B. Discussion at the School of Nursing (Halifax), 1990.

CHAPTER 12
Pierre Bourdieu and the Sociology of Assessment and Evaluation

LEWIS OWEN

By our informal day-to-day judgements, as well as by systematic evaluation processes in education, and by the ever present process of assessment, we are to a considerable extent determining the future. We need to treat that process seriously.

A crucial principle of contemporary sociology is that the reality we experience is socially constructed, no matter how objective it may seem. What appear to be 'real' and solid structures, such as the administration of schools or examination standards, are in fact social realities that have been developed by the agency of human beings and are kept in place by the exercise of that human agency in the day-to-day practices of everyone concerned. The 'practical sense' of those agents is however profoundly affected by the deep structures of power and ideology in which they practise and of which they may not be conscious. The discourses we use, our perceptual frameworks, our habitual behaviour (which are all rooted in those deep structures) tend to reduce the quality of our agency, and this can only be counteracted by the conscious formulation of different practices based on insight into the deep structures, and also into the modes in which they are reproduced on a day-to-day basis.

We are presently in a phase of great social change. The end of the Cold War has reinstated the onward march of international capitalism, now dramatically accelerated by the advent of modern technology. The world appears to be re-arranging what had formerly seemed to be immutable social relations both within and between countries. The speed and unpredictability of change in economic relations means that every country in the world is involved in some form of socio-economic structural adjustment, in a continuous attempt to cope with the ups and downs of the global market. A key element in these attempts is the continuous adjustment and readjustment of the world's educational systems.

The question of what we mean by education has become more and more problematic as different interest groups struggle to define their countries' educational needs in the light of their own perceptions derived from their own spheres of action. As educationists we should not be worried by that, since it is the main engine of change and development in capitalist systems, and since it is evident that, for example in Britain, the education system has gradually become more and more dysfunctional in the post-war period, not merely in terms of the structural adjustment process but also in terms of the equitable distribution of resources.

What we should be concerned about is whether or not we are equipped intellectually to grasp the complexities of the issues involved in structural adjustment, and skilled enough to initiate those practices which are appropriate and practically feasible. The chapters in this book are about the ways in which various groups of agents are approaching that task. The importance of Bourdieu's statement stems from the fact that not only is he one of the world's best sociologists, who has written extensively on education, and whose grasp of the underlying issues is particularly acute, but that the main body of his work is focused on the question of how we can theorize and investigate the modes of transmission of the forces at work in the deep structures of society, in order that we can optimize our agency.

What Bourdieu's short essay does is to stress the importance of the untheorized, taken for granted surface definitions of the problems that we face, and to locate these definitions, which seem to epitomize contemporary liberal systems, as sources of tyranny. This tyranny entails the control of both individuals and large social groups, under the slogan of 'market choice', or 'public opinion'. In the educational sphere this tyranny increasingly hangs on the question of the short-term exigencies of the world's capital and consumer markets, as to whether or not we can persuade the world's investors that we have a labour force skilled enough, flexible enough and cheap enough to guarantee that investing the limited supply of world capital in Britain will be more profitable than investing it in China or India. Of course this is a very real issue, and making the right decisions on which way to proceed in order to attract investment is crucial. But market signals are almost always short-term, and the educational system is by its nature long-term in its effects.

We have therefore both to deal with the very real and pressing problems of structural adjustment through the education system, and also to anticipate what may be a startlingly different world by the turn of the century. Merely acceding to the blandishments of any group, no matter how powerful, is mortgaging our future by giving control of it to the strongest market player. Bourdieu's vision is one of a choice between tyranny and enabling men and women to become the masters and owners of their own individual and collective history.[1] The only way to achieve the latter is through a scientific practice, through bringing to bear all the tools in the human armoury of natural and social science on our problems. That scientific practice is crucial for the processes of evaluation and assessment which are such significant forms of control and development in educational systems.

In assessment processes we are presented with the continuously shifting surfaces of speech, writing, other sign systems, human actions and so on. The essential task is to interpret from these the qualities of mind and character of the person being assessed, not only in terms of subject knowledge, though that is difficult enough since subjects are socially constructed and carry a lot of social assumptions with them, but also in terms of the intellectual, social and psychological requirements of the contemporary and future social formations. Our modes of judgement are steeped in our mental perspectives and social relationships, and these tend to be formed by the past rather than the future. To assess in a way which liberates people so that they can realistically take charge of their individual and collective lives, requires an enormous effort of sustained intellectual sensitivity and rigour. Some of the tools are there to begin to do that, in social analysis: linguistics, cognitive psychology, political economy, and social theory. The process of evaluation is even more embedded in the broader social context and requires these tools even more than the processes of assessment, as well as considerable insight into the way socio-technical systems work.[2] In the light of this, careful as it is, the OFSTED system of inspection is little more than an untheorized set of surface observations constructed on the basis of very mechanical models of school systems. Nevertheless it can be improved and made much more sophisticated, providing the process of evaluation becomes reflexive and the whole process more intellectually serious.

The last twenty years have been very exciting for anyone frustrated with the blatant inequity in British education. A system that was rarely evaluated in a theoretically objective way at any point, and appeared to be controlled by a particular historical and ideological bloc had suddenly, by the early 1970s, been shown to be massively in contradiction with the social and economic system it was supposed to serve.[3] The assessment systems were largely run by teachers from the higher education and secondary systems, with some small employer influence in further education. Inevitably these groups, conscientiously pursuing what they perceived to be high standards, driven by the particular subject traditions and tensions in which they were working, were insensitive to the broader sociological and psychological significance of their practices. As a former chief examiner, the writer became increasingly aware of the importance of the social construction of learners' identities via the assessment process. The normal evaluation processes – by HMI, local authority inspectors and agencies such as the Schools' Council – were also largely within this broad paradigm. The effect of all this on the educational system has clearly been to generate far too little change too slowly, and to freeze the system in a most inequitable way in the name of 'equality'.[4]

The structural adjustment process that took off in the 1970s has now gathered pace and many new voices have been added to the discourses around evaluation and assessment. All that is of course potentially creative, but insofar as those new voices are merely alternative interest groups to the previous bloc, then there is great danger of another ideological bloc forming, this time driven by market concepts. The only way out of this would seem to be the instating of a scientific rigour so far lacking. Bourdieu argues for a 'reflexive science' so that the practitioners of the processes of judgement are made continuously aware of the way in which they are constructing a view of reality, and therefore that they must not reify these processes but can actually continually reconstruct them, as new possibilities of human agency emerge within the constraints of the social context.[5]

The alternative that seems to have developed in some of the NVQ courses is relatively mechanical box-ticking based on what are very subjective observations. If those observations were theorized in a sophisticated way, they could be made significant, but that depends on the whole learning context. My own experience of that process suggests that any category of judgement can be justified on almost any behaviour pattern. Given the global market, we have no choice but to accept that the whole workforce, at every level, must be cheap and flexible, but if it is also made unthinking by the short-term perspectives and unscientific practices of the teachers, trainers, assessors and evaluators, then we will create a large reserve army of workers competing for employment and wages with the reserve armies of the South, rather than a society whose members have taken control of their individual and collective destinies.

Notes and references

1. Bourdieu, P. *Sociology in Question*, Sage, (London: Sage, 1993).
2. Bourdieu, P. *Outline of a Theory of Practice* Translated by Richard Nice (Cambridge: Cambridge University Press, 1977).
3. Gramsci, A. (1971), *Selections from the Prison Notebooks of Antonio Gramsci* Edited and translated by Quintin Hoare and Geoffrey Nowell Smith (London: Lawrence and Wishart, 1971), 60–61.
4. Heath, A. Class in the classroom *New Society*, 17 July, 1987.
5. Bourdieu, P. and Wacquant, L. *An Invitation to Reflexive Sociology*, (London: Polity Press, 1992).

CHAPTER 13
Social Sciences and Democracy
PIERRE BOURDIEU (TRANSLATED BY LEWIS OWEN)

Many absurd things have been said about the social
sciences: that they serve no useful purpose; that they are
deterministic therefore ideally suited to discourage and de-
activate people; that they favour relativism and therefore
disillusionment, indeed irrationality or even nihilism; that
they provide weapons for all the enemies of liberal thought,
of critical discussion, of democracy: for propagandists,
admen and demagogues. The arguments, used by both
budding and recognized intellectuals to acknowledge each
other, are innumerable, mostly as old as the social sciences
themselves, often contradicting one another; they are tire-
lessly invoked, under the misused banner of philosophy,
and under the pretext of defending the sacred rights
belonging to the liberty and uniqueness of the 'creative'
individual.

By an extraordinary inversion, science is held to be
responsible for a psychological or social principle that it
merely exposes: that, in providing the means of acquiring
knowledge, it also creates the opportunity to liberate itself
from that knowledge. And some people, thanks to a reac-
tionary political climate, today push the terrorism of
anti-terrorism to the point of confusing the concern for
coherence and verification with dogmatism and authoritari-
anism.

As a matter of fact, far from pushing us towards a
sceptical sense of disillusion, and generating indifference
and opportunism, science, and especially social science,
provides the best methods for the day-to-day practice of
the critique of social illusion, which is the necessary
condition for making democratic choices. At the same
time it enables us to build the foundations of a realistic
utopianism, as far from irresponsible voluntarism as

from the pseudo-scientific acceptance of the established order.

In so far as it does not try to get away from the process of objectification, using the highest quality of logic, in the effort to bring to light the hidden forces behind the production and reproduction of the structured relationships constitutive of the social order, it exercises a critical function that is quite decisive, without even needing to be explicit about it. This function is becoming more and more indispensable at a moment when those in economic and political power rely on the improper uses of science to support their practices. Through the growing influence that the verdict of the ratings has on television, and by the agency of this on the whole field of journalism, through the dominating influence of the opinion-testing processes, which increasingly relegate the political field to a short-sighted demagoguery, it is the laws of the market that tend to impose themselves more and more completely on the relatively autonomous social microcosms of the worlds of art, of literature or of science and even of the political world. How can we avoid the fear that the electors or the audiences will be reduced to the state of mere consumers enslaved to a production system capable of modifying its products in anticipation of the most slavish needs, or of creating and imposing the need for its particular products, when all the bogus measuring tools of this social construction we call public opinion are being used cynically as demagogic or marketing tools?

As a source of critical countervailing power, with the ability to bring to light the practices of those who specialize in the process of individual and collective control, social science can also provide us with realistic methods for unsettling the immanent tendencies in the social order and facilitating the discovery, through precise evaluation, of the chances of success or failure for strategies that attempt to use knowledge of social laws to thwart their effects, in the manner of the engineer who focuses on the law of gravity in order to construct flying machines which defy it.

With regard to explanation of the relative nature of traditions and customs, far from condemning people to a disillusioned relativism, as the pseudo-clever claim, it liberates us from the conservative pessimism which depends on the belief in an immutable nature, the conviction that there is nothing new under the sun, and therefore that it is pointless trying to change whatever is in force in the established order. Teaching us that those things which are claimed to be 'natural', particularly the concepts of 'masculine' and 'feminine', are the products of history, and that what history has made, history can unmake, opens up immense possibilities of action, focused on turning men and women, whoever they are, into the masters and owners of their own individual and collective history.

There remains the issue of the encouragement that social science might give to relativism, even cynicism and nihilism. As for those who maintain that the membership of the historian within the historical process and of the sociologist within society are insurmountable obstacles to the credibility of both as sciences, how can they ignore the fact that the social sciences are privileged in being able to take their own origins and their own social functions as subjects? And that they are therefore in a position to expose the constraints which bear on scientific practice, and to utilize the consciousness and knowledge they have of the history and structure of the social fields in which they are produced to try to remove some of the social obstacles to their progress? Far from destroying its own foundations, as so many people have said, such a reflexive science can, on the contrary, provide the principles of a *realpolitik* aimed at establishing the social conditions for the progress of scientific rationality, that is to say, for a type of justice, or democracy, in the scientific microcosm. The main principle of this *realpolitik* is the defence of autonomy against all intrusions from non-scientific (therefore tyrannical) sources of power, capable of distorting the relations within which scientific constructions are produced, communicated, debated, criticized, evaluated. This is one of the most fundamental contributions to democracy, even if it sometimes happens that, because it appears to be élitist, it seems contradictory to the usual way that democracy is depicted. It is in effect the *sine qua non* condition for the exercise of this fourth area of power, purely critical, which social science alone is in a position to exercise fully today, and without which there is no longer any true democracy.

CHAPTER 14

Conclusion: The Personal Effects of Assessment

CEDRIC CULLINGFORD

As the chapters in this book amply demonstrate there are tensions and contradictions surrounding the concepts of assessment or evaluation. There are many issues at stake. When we first look at the service industry that assessment has become it is easy to assume that it is necessary. Assessment becomes an academic way of life. We constantly make judgements and build theories against which to make them. We can be forgiven if we sometimes lose sight of the consequences.

The chapters in the book explore both the positive and the negative aspects of assessment. One of the negative effects is that very assumption that testing is all that matters, for its own sake. Testing, or making judgements and comparisons, might seem inevitable but it is not therefore necessary. There are some things that we do without thinking, but that does not make them good. We perhaps inevitably form opinions of other people and their work, but we can as easily hurt them, as help them in these opinions.

The potential to help through diagnosis, as a doctor helps a patient, is clear. If it is inevitable that judgements are made, how can this be turned to advantage, become constructive criticism? There is a moral and an ethical dimension to assessment: the moral dimension concerns the responsibility to help others, the ethical concerns the avoidance of damage.

Each one of us has been assessed, formally and informally, countless times. There cannot be anyone who has not suffered as a consequence. From the earliest days of the sense of shame and humiliation, of disappointment or embarrassment, to the sense of failure at work or in domestic life, exposure to other people's judgements has left scars, however different the circumstances. All assessment has the potential to be damaging. Some 'failures' may hurt more than others, from marriage to an exam, but the word 'failure' brands the experience. In the public machinery of assessment it is easy to forget that there are also victims. The assessor no doubt is secure in his or her own judgement, but, for good or ill, that judgement has a consequence for others.

There are three groups of people who feel the effects of the present emphasis on accountability, on assessment, on competition, and the labelling of the better and the worse. The first group are the teachers. Stress is the shadow that grows as fast as the assessment. The literature that describes it almost matches that on assessment itself. This is because the assessment delineated in this book is not just a mechanical operation, something to be administered. It is also, some would suggest primarily, directed against teachers. Teacher appraisal can be individually constructive, but league tables show up failure. OFSTED inspections might reveal as yet hidden strengths, but they are feared for their destructive criticism. So much depends on tone, and the climate of the time goes against all the conclusions of research on effective teaching and effective schools; the headlines are all negative.

The evidence for the general disillusionment in the teaching profession does not need elaborating here, but it does need defining. When teachers feel they are successful they feel that it is despite undermining opposition, they feel they triumph despite obstacles, as more than one chapter makes clear. But the sense of being undermined comes about because they feel that their voice is ignored. The curriculum and its assessment is thrust upon them from outside. The sense of personal involvement and freedom to be inspired are constrained.

One precise and typical example of teacher helplessness is the debate surrounding class size. There is no teacher who has actually faced a class of pupils for any length of time who does not acknowledge that the size of the class makes a significant difference, firstly to the teacher's own sense of purpose and secondly to the performance of the pupils. But this wealth of experience is dismissed against what is cited as

266

evidence from a few 'tests'. Marginal reductions of numbers from 32 to 31 might not make a measurable difference, and the quality of the teacher, whatever the size of the class, might be more significant. But to have the whole case so publicly dismissed is to diminish teachers' personal and professional lives. The fact that the most significant factor in parents' choice of private education is class size, is just an added irony.

The issue of class size is significant because teachers are being assessed in difficult conditions, and being assessed without being listened to. As several chapters in the book have made clear, useful assessment includes and convinces everyone involved. Teachers may feel that they have been replaced by batteries of tests. But they also realize that the real subject of the tests are not the pupils but themselves.

Parents are also aware of the effects of assessment on teachers.[1] Many of them, as the research demonstrates, do not know how they cope.

> To be honest I don't know how some of the teachers cope with it … they don't need that extra pressure … the teachers have their hands full. (father)

The image of the teacher, in parents' eyes, is of someone struggling hard in the face of inexorable odds, without room for manoeuvre.

> I mean the hours that teachers have to put in must be very stressful to them, no wonder they get fed up with it. (mother)

Parents are witnesses to the changing circumstances of teaching. They detect high standards of professionalism but they also see it being undermined.

> They all seem to be running around and doing a lot … whether it's better I don't know 'cos I think it's possible to achieve a lot without leaping around and appearing to be dashing around. (father)

They recognize the approachability of teachers, but miss that freedom that could lead to inspiration like someone

> who was not dashing around like a National Curriculum fiddler abouter. (father)

Parents look on, with a certain bewilderment, to all the changes that are imposed on schools, and their sympathy, if not that of the Government, lies with the teachers.

> My awareness is that teachers are under tremendous pressure ... teachers are under great stress, they've got the National Curriculum, they've got ... pupil numbers are up, pupils are more difficult than they used to be ... that doesn't mean that they aren't doing a tremendously good job but the pressures are now on. (mother)

One of the most significant of external pressures is the many SATs – standard assessment tasks, or tests. It seems a little known fact that parents find these meaningless. Whilst a small minority think they might be necessary in order to make judgements on teachers and schools, all view them as giving information that they already know.

> I think it makes far too much for teachers work; time which could be spent on teaching as opposed to non-stop scribbling on bits of paper. I don't think they're a good thing at all. (mother)

The disbelief in the information which is derived from SATs is demonstrated by the dismissive way that parents talk about the new style of reporting. The reports deal with the way in which pupils have met (or failed to meet) targets, and are considered meaningless. Parents continue to rely on the professional judgements made by teachers and presented (since written reports are no longer useful) verbally. But parents do not worry solely about the stress on teachers. They see the stress of the SATs on their own children.

> Stress starts to build up and I think it's unnecessary, unnecessary stress and I don't think we should be doing it to our children. (father)

> I think there seems to be a lot of pressure put on testing and assessment ... I think it could make them against school and learning. I think there's too much of it. (mother)

Parents are naturally concerned for their own children. They wish them to be happy. They also wish them to do well. They would not be against the principles of assessment if they were seen to make improvements. But what they see are tests which seem to them at best unhelpful in terms of communicating something not previously known and at worst harmful.

> They're too young. They're not developed sufficiently, again, it can make children feel insecure and end up with psychological problems. I don't agree with it. (father)

SATs are therefore seen by parents as failing to contribute anything positive – unless the government is learning something about schools and teachers. Those being tested, and those in whose name they are being tested, are marginal.

But what of those who are the subjects of all these assessments and tests and examinations? How do they view their preparation for life as a series of competitions? Parents are aware of the experience of SATs.

> I mean my ten-year-old took his end of Key Stage 1 SATs. He was absolutely mortified by the amount of time it wasted. He thought it was a waste of time. They were easy to do and partly he felt he was going over and over things he had done before. (mother)

This is a view that derives from exasperation. The children might exhibit stress to their parents but they do not draw that much attention to the anxieties that they might experience at Key Stages 1 and 2. Why?

One reason is that pupils accept school as a *fait accompli*, designed for the teachers by the teachers. At primary school they do not feel that they ought to question it. It might seem a difficult environment and they might not be happy, but the results of this are not seen until later. They accept school as a mixture of events orchestrated by teachers. If tests fill the day, then that is simply how it is. Another reason is that pupils perceive virtually everything that takes place in the classroom as a form of testing. Teachers ask questions to find out how much is known. The number of 'open' questions without just one right answer is very few. If lessons feel like constant tests, attempts to please the teacher, then formal assessment will not seem so different.[2,3]

Perhaps the least obvious but deepest reason that children do not cite tests as traumatic is that they live in their own competitive worlds.[4] Just as parents wish to know if their children are doing better or worse than other children, so the children place themselves in comparison with their peers. They are quick to label themselves and others. By the time they are eight they realize that there are clear distinctions to be made between application and success. To some, good work seems to come easily. Others, however hard they try, cannot keep up.[4]

Children are constantly monitoring their performance against that of others. Their greatest fear is to hold up the general progress of the class. What SATs and other tests provide is a strong indication that this aspect of school work is more and more important. Tasks are not carried out for their own sake, or for the sake of learning, but for the acquisition of knowledge that can be measured. The experiences that children are aware of are the daily mechanics of comparison; but they realize that there are other agendas beyond their own. The everyday experience is like this:

> Some people in my class read a lot better than me. Because I can't read really long words and most people can. Some people have problems. I'd like to be able to read really long books because some of them sound quite exciting and I can't read all the words and it bothers people a lot if I keep asking them what that says and things. (girl, 8)

> I like maths but I don't like really hard like times tables maths. I like normal ones like takeaway and add. It doesn't really make me feel bad because they might be older than me and I might not have been here the day before. I don't really mind if I'm not first but I don't really mind if I'm last but I hope I'm nearer the first one. My best friend, he might have done it before me and I think I'm going to be really embarrassed. (boy, 8)

The important prerogative is not so much to do a piece of work well but to do it fast, to 'keep up'.[5] The personal sense of failure, of negative comparisons, is something which besets many children in the conditions of the classroom.

> I don't like myself because I'm not very good at maths ... it's

just like they're on another thing and l
they've got it all right and they're on to ti.
feel like I want to know it all. (girl, 8)

I do feel terrible when I'm not the best at somᴇ
always go last. Terrible, because I would never ᵤ
done. It would take me probably all week. (boy, 6)

The sense of failure expressed by so many childreɴ ⸴es
from their comparisons of themselves to others anɑ from
their failure to keep up with norms and standards. The
more tests there are, set against standard criteria, the more
opportunities there are for some to fail. Because of the
social aspects of competition and because of the fear of not
pleasing the teacher, school is never an easy environment.[3]
Never before have so many weapons been handed to the
school to bring out these aspects of fear and embarrassment.

Nevertheless children in their pragmatism, or helplessness, accept these things as a central experience in school.
They do not necessarily notice the growing proliferation of
tests as a new phenomenon, but this does not mean that the
tests do not have emotional effects. It is just that the results
of this aspect of assessment are not a series of marks, but are
long term. Whilst primary children are aware of the competition and the need to fulfil expectations, secondary pupils
apply that kind of self-awareness to the definition of success
or failure in terms of exams, leading to success or failure in
their futures. The following brief examples of pupil attitudes derive from about 200 interviews with pupils in Years
10 and 11, who are preparing for or taking GCSEs and
contemplating their future.[6] Many of the attitudes and ideas
reveal the long-term effects of years of assessment.

It is important to understand the consistently held beliefs
that all the pupils share. As they are about to leave school, to
go on to college or further training, to employment or
unemployment, they reflect on their years in school. All take
with them regrets. The greatest of these is that they did not
work harder, that they did not make use of the opportunities. The second is that teachers never explained to them
the purpose of what they were doing. It was assumed that
the only real and obvious purpose was the passing of exam-

ns. But the pupils wanted more, they wanted a far greater dialogue with the teachers rather than being, as they saw it, hounded by assessable subjects. The lack of purpose, the lack of explanation about relevance meant that their liking or disliking of a subject depended almost wholly on their attitude towards the teacher. That glimpse of the human in the midst of a fog of knowledge had a great influence on them.

Schools are social centres and whilst this is of the greatest importance to the pupils, the way that schools are run does not seem to make use of this fact. It is as if the demands of the curriculum and assessment were so significant that the social aspects of school consist mainly in organizing groups into classrooms to imbibe knowledge. Pupils' reflections on school are dominated by the social, the pleasure in friends, the fear of being bullied, the excitement of doing drama as opposed to memorizing facts, and again, the slow realization as they near the end of their schooling that they can have relationships even with teachers. This recognition that teachers are also human, and that they are more than deliverers of the curriculum is an important one. It deepens their regret that because of the demands of assessment, and the competition to do well, to hit set targets, they have not been able to share a deeper sense of purpose.

That examinations dominate schools is no surprise. Indeed it is usually taken for granted. But the consequences are rarely explored. Assessment is not only an attempt to judge but is a powerful influence on the way people think. What follows are some examples of the way that school pupils think as a result of exams. They not only have a realistic and pragmatic recognition of the importance of doing well, of passing so that they can have better chances in life, but have a way of 'placing' themselves in terms of their chances that reflects the way that primary children label themselves and their abilities against others. The underlying theme is that the hope of doing well, the striving to be better, is taken away in the face of reality, in the acceptance of comparative failure.

There is always a tension between a future career and the

examinations needed to make it possible. At least three-quarters of the pupils make a distinction between the career they would like to have and the career that they think they will have. Most of the rest have forgotten even what an aspiration was like. Their success or failure in exams matches their adaptability to their own chances. It is hard to say which comes first, an interest, say in child care, and a realization that it is a realistic hope given exam results.

> In some subjects, like in French, we hardly do anything, and in physics it's just all copying down, it's certain subjects that are challenging, others are just copying and not understanding. My science is the main one I don't think I'll do well in. I hope to be getting As in Child Care, Bs in Maths and English, but Cs in stuff like French and D's probably in science ... I've been enquiring about tech NEB ... I just love looking after little children. I think qualifications give you more of a chance of getting a job, but I still think it will be fairly hard. (female, Year 10)

> Well I did want to be an accountant ... And you've got to be quite good at maths, then I wanted to be something to do with sports, like sports teachers, or, I think someone told me you have to learn two subjects to be a teacher, so if I do good at both of them and a few others ... like French and science because they're saying we don't get enough lessons a week, they'll like put something on the board and we'll write that down and they talk to you about what they've put on. So you've got to listen and write down and that ... Anything above a C that's all, if I get Cs I'll be happy with that, because they keep saying that C's all right. (male, Year 10)

The connection between qualifications and careers becomes obvious towards the end of schooling but it affects pupils far earlier.[7] Primary children also see the main *raison d'être* of schools as fitting them for jobs. As they make progress all the assessments they undergo become more and more significant, with tensions between subjects they do well in and subjects they enjoy. It is no wonder they learn to be pragmatic, to adapt.

Adaptability includes a realistic sense of their own chances. It means being able to contemplate failure and deal with it. The possibility of not doing well enough is an added

:: to give up. But the sense of failure also affects
/ho are in general terms successful like the pupils
ewed here.

> Maths and science. Teachers just say they'll be the most useful to
> you, so I'd better do good in them. I find maths difficult. The
> science can be all right except for physics. I never used to be
> able to spell ... When I've finished I might not learn stuff about
> what I should have learned in high school, I might fail my
> GCSEs, I might have to re-take them. Some have easy and some
> have quite hard. (Male, Year 10)

> English sometimes is [hard], physics and chemistry I just find
> hard. I can't do them. Not do well. I don't think so; no. I
> haven't done that much revising. I thought I did really well in
> my mock but I didn't ... I'll be able to go out and earn money.
> Get a job. Not having to come back [to school] again. (female,
> Year 11)

Failure at exams, like any failure, is a painful experience,
but by the time they leave school most pupils have had so
much of it that they have had to learn to be pragmatic, to
accept. Doing well or badly at exams is personal and social;
it is like a judgement made public. For some it is not just a
short shock or pleasure, but dominates their view of work.

> I can't concentrate on it and I always have to break off which I
> think that's going to be a problem when I leave. I don't really
> work hard for a long time, like, say I have to take breaks every
> ... often I can't get started at all ... trying to get as many good
> grades as I could ... to please my mum and dad ... My mum
> said about a week ago that if I get good grades she'll give me a
> tenner for every good grade so I said I don't like stuff like that
> so she's eased off a bit. Don't like having pressures and stuff like
> that. (male, Year 11)

Parents' hopes are just one of the many pressures on pupils;
there are many more. These include the stress that examinations place on memory and the sense of the arbitrary.

> I don't like home economics because we were gonna be doing
> the syllabus all about food and we've not done that at all, we've
> just been doing about other stuff. Because on our exam paper,
> on our mocks, we got a few pages on all about plugs and we've

not done anything about plugs. That's why we all got low marks in it. And she said it was our fault, but it wasn't, because we hadn't done anything about plugs. (female, Year 11)

Whilst the pupils have a realistic assessment of their own abilities and chances they also acknowledge the element of chance. One result of this is to try to mitigate their own expectations, not to aim too high. All the SATs from key Stage 1 through to the formal public examinations are designed to divide individuals into comparative success or failure, and this has a negative impact even on those (amongst the minority) who hope to continue their education. Some might say that this is a realistic lesson to be learned, that this is the way that schools prepare their pupils for the 'real' world. Perhaps, the same people might continue, being depressed is a necessary preparation. It is quite clear that the demands that schools make are difficult for some, involving constant targets.

I don't like things ... like chemistry. I find these subjects pretty hard and the teachers don't get it across so much and it just seems so difficult ... It's like I'm not really bothered about what I'm doing. It's just different teachers I have ... In the long run I would prefer a hard teacher because she gets you, it gets you working. In the end she's giving you detention and then you do the work ... If you're totally stuck and the teachers can't help it's just so depressing. Just can't do it. Can't do any of it then. (male, Year 11)

These quotations are all small illuminations of a huge theme. The pupils towards the end of their school career all demonstrate important shared experiences. They reveal the mixture of the private and the public, private difficulties and understandings in the midst of public organizations and public accountability. They reveal the number of different agencies that affect them: parents, peers, teachers and anonymous examiners. There are constant tensions between the formal and the informal, the need to fulfil certain tasks and the temptation to give up. They demonstrate how many influences are brought to bear on the most crucial of choices and decisions, from the short-term to the long-term from a longing they all share not to have to get up early in the morning when they leave school, to the fear of unemployment. The pupils also show how they are struggling to find personal meanings in the face of what seems like a vast and anonymous public system. There is a tension between their sense of their own worth and their desire for personal meaning and the acceptance of public approval or disapproval, the competition for places, the assessment of who will win and who will not. The whole system might be unquestioned by those who are part of it, but for some it means a public arena for private pain, and for others something to be avoided.

When one examines the life chances of those who have failed in this system, and the desire to avoid pain, one is tempted to wonder whether the surprising fact is that so many people continue to struggle rather than give up. The pupils in this research are all relatively successful. And yet they all share moments of psychological exclusion, when they feel that the system, with all the people in it, goes on and they are not part of it. It is like that moment in a public examination when one looks up at all the others in the same hall facing the same way, all busy working and concentrating as if one were the only person there to be at a loss. The question is how deep that sense of exclusion goes, to what extent there is a juxtaposition between the private feelings and the public examinations. The question is how their subsequent view of society depends on such experiences.

The term 'alienation' has a clear meaning in theological terms: being excluded from heaven. The term is philosophically less precise in its more usual sociological sense, for how can one be 'excluded' or an 'alien' from a society of which one is part? And yet the term has its uses in that it suggests the very illogicality, the feelings of being excluded from a system or society of which one is part. Everyone is caught up in a system of examinations, formal or informal. There are successes and failures as a result of that system. At the same time everyone has had some moments of disorientation, the desire to ignore the diurnal necessity of attendance, concentration, demands and failure. These quotes come from the successful, but what do we find in their discourse? 'It's just so depressing.' 'It just seems so difficult.' 'I'm not really bothered.' 'She said it was our fault.' 'I don't like stuff like this.' 'I can't do that.' 'What I should have learned?' 'I might fail.'

This short account of the effects of assessment merely offers a glimpse into unexplored territory. At least the issue deserves raising. There are many private as well as public consequences to the whole machinery of assessment, and these need evaluating. They represent a point of view that should be taken into account.

Contemplating the effects of assessment should lead us to spend more time on evaluating the whole process. All the assessments of pupils and teachers, of schools and other institutions seem to generate an energy of their own. We tend to take for granted that the whole industry attached to it is inevitable and necessary. This attitude is itself an interesting symptom of our time. Can one, therefore, with a still small voice, ask the question: It might seem inevitable, but is it necessary?

Notes and references

1. For a fuller elaboration of the research evidence from which this derives see Cullingford, C. *Parents, Education and the State* (Aldershot: Arena, 1996).

2. See for example Bennett, N., Desforges, C., Cockburn, A. and Wilkinson, B. *The Quality of Pupil Learning Experiences* (London: Erlbaum, 1984).

3. Cullingford, C. *The Inner World of the School* (London: Cassell, 1991).

4. See Cullingford, C. *The Politics of Primary Education* (Buckingham: Open University Press, forthcoming).

5. See also the work on children's sense of achievement (or lack of it), e.g. Eshel, J. and Kurman, J. Academic self-concept: accuracy of perceived ability and academic attainments *British Journal of Educational Psychology* 61 (2), 1991, 187–96.

6. From research carried out for Industry in Education, see *Towards Employability: Addressing the Gap Between Young People's Qualities and Employers' Recruitment Needs.* (London, 1996).

7. See Cullingford, C. (1991), Chapter 10.

Name Index

Subject Index